A TENDERFOOT IN
MONTANA

I shall take great pleasure in complying with your request for my photograph, as I am very proud of being numbered with the pioneers of Montana.

Yours
Francis M. Thompson

A TENDERFOOT IN
MONTANA

REMINISCENCES OF THE GOLD RUSH, THE VIGILANTES,
AND THE BIRTH OF MONTANA TERRITORY

by Francis M. Thompson

edited by
Kenneth N. Owens

MONTANA HISTORICAL SOCIETY PRESS
Helena, Montana

BOOK & COVER DESIGN BY Arrow Graphics
TYPESET IN Sabon and Roman Shaded

PRINTED IN Canada

Generous support from the Charles Redd Center
for Western Studies helped to fund publication of this book.

Distributed by the Globe Pequot Press, 246 Goose Lane,
Guilford, Connecticut 06437, (800) 243-0495

04 05 06 07 08 09 10 11   10 9 8 7 6 5 4 3 2 1

ISBN 0-9721522-2-9

LIBRARY OF CONGRESS CATALOGING-IN-PUBLICATION DATA

Thompson, Francis M. (Francis McGee), 1833–1916.
    A tenderfoot in Montana : reminiscences of the Gold Rush, the vigilantes,
and the birth of Montana Territory / by Francis M. Thompson ; edited with
an introduction by Kenneth N. Owens.— 1st ed.
        p. cm.
    Includes bibliographical references and index.
    ISBN 0-9721522-2-9 (pbk. : alk. paper)
        1. Thompson, Francis M. (Francis McGee), 1833–1916.   2. Pioneers—
Montana—Biography.   3. Gold miners—Montana—Biography.
4. Frontier and pioneer life—Montana.   5. Montana—History—19th
century.   6. Montana—Gold discoveries.   7. Gold mines and mining—
Montana—History—19th century.   8. Vigilantes—Montana—History—
19th century.   9. Montana—Biography.   I. Owens, Kenneth N.   II. Title.

F731.T53 2004
978.6'031'092—dc22   2004000788

To Aderyn, Seth, and Noah

A Wild New Generation of Westerners

CONTENTS

ILLUSTRATIONS

ACKNOWLEDGMENTS

FRANK THOMPSON'S PUBLISHED recollections first came to my attention while I was doing dissertation research on government and politics in Montana and other federal territories of the Northwest. I was charmed and impressed with Thompson's narrative, and so made a mental note to edit the work for republication whenever time and circumstances allowed. That was many years ago, and at last I have found it possible to return to this project. In the interim the editorial task has been made infinitely easier by the fine scholarship of other historians and by the encouragement of friends who have come to share my enthusiasm for Judge Thompson's remembrances of his tenderfoot adventures in the gold country at the headwaters of the Missouri River.

First in promoting this publication was Chuck Rankin, then editor of *Montana The Magazine of Western History*, who agreed that today's westerners would welcome the opportunity to see frontier Montana through Frank Thompson's eyes. Chuck's successor at the Montana Historical Society, Clark Whitehorn, happily agreed to see the project through. My thanks go to Clark; his excellent staff—Tammy Ryan, Molly Holz, Amy Baird, Glenda Bradshaw, and Annie Hanshew; and their faithful volunteer Mary Alice Chester, who have joined their talents to help bring Thompson's reminiscences once more into print. Glenda's initiative in finding illustrations and her mapping skills have combined with Annie's painstaking efforts as a copy editor to vastly improve this volume.

Completing this work at a distance from Montana has been possible only with the assistance of talented professionals at many research institutions. Particularly important contributions came from Jason Stratman of the Missouri Historical Society, who helped my efforts to document Frank Thompson's upriver journey aboard the *Emilie* in 1862. Staff members at the library of California State University, Sacramento, and the California State Library have come to my aid again and again. I am especially indebted to Charlene Porsild, director of the Montana Historical Society Library and Archives, who not only expedited my search for obscure records but also made my visits to Helena more pleasant with her gracious hospitality.

Over the years I have enjoyed discussing Montana's territorial history with many valued friends and associates. Among those early coming to my aid were Mike Malone and Rich Roeder, always generous in sharing their knowledge and interpretive views with an enthusiastic outsider. During the preparation of the manuscript, Clark Spence offered helpful suggestions for improving my editorial embellishments. Frederick Allen assisted me by a vigorous exchange of opinion about the legal situation at Bannack when Chief Justice Sidney Edgerton arrived there. In a broader way, a generation of western history colleagues and students have contributed to my thinking about frontier crime and vigilantism. Let me single out for special thanks Richard M. Brown, Al Hurtado, Gordon Bakken, and Martin Ridge.

For this project, as for all my research and writing efforts, my greatest thanks go to Sally Owens. She has willingly traveled to distant places and volunteered her services as a researcher and scribe, working with efficiency and an intuitive sense of what was necessary. Back home, she has brought to this project her practiced editorial skills and a relentless insistence that my writing should make sense, which is a good thing. Our partnership is much more than history, but doing history together has certainly added to our enjoyment of life as an adventure in common.

KEN OWENS
Sacramento, California
March 2004

EDITOR'S INTRODUCTION

IN 1861, AT THE BEGINNING of the American Civil War, Francis McGee Thompson was ready to join the Union Army with an officer's commission. He lacked military experience, but because of personal connections he expected to become a major either in the Massachusetts volunteers or in a company of Wisconsin volunteers. Before he actually joined one of these units, however, Thompson agreed to carry out a personal errand for the family of a young woman he intended to marry. This errand took him down the Ohio River by steamboat to the town of Cairo, where federal gunboats and troops were blockading the Mississippi to halt Confederate incursions. From his safe vantage aboard ship, Thompson got a brief, close look at the war. "After spending almost a day viewing the incompetency of the officers commanding the several bodies of troops," he later declared, "I lost all faith in the success of such men, and made up my mind that I would not join the army in any position that I was likely to be awarded."

No Union enthusiasm was strong enough to overcome this gut reaction against military life as Thompson had observed it. "Little youngsters," he related, "were commanding good, sensible-looking men, who appeared as though they knew a good deal more than their commanders. I must say that I was thoroughly disappointed and disgusted."[1]

Done with martial ambition, Thompson paused at Chicago to reconsider his career alternatives. A New Englander by birth, he was twenty-eight years old and experienced with banking and financial affairs in St. Louis, Chicago, and the new states of the upper Midwest. Moreover, he had funds to invest—the profits from his successful prewar business. He also had a taste for frontier adventure that had begun, he candidly admitted, with a youthful reading of a tale of romance and heroic derring-do set along the Oregon Trail and in the upper Missouri country.

At this point Thompson's older brother Hugh, a mineralogist in St. Louis, wrote him about newly reported gold discoveries in the northern Rockies. He told Frank that a group of St. Louis businessmen were organizing a company to go by steamship to rich mining regions near the headwaters of the Missouri and Clearwater rivers. Fully financed by private subscription, the promoters expected to send upriver a well-equipped, generously supplied cadre of a dozen able-bodied men to prospect for moneymaking opportunities. They anticipated that the members of their field party would make good returns for the investors and for themselves by digging gold, by trading, and perhaps by staking out a townsite that could be developed into a mining country commercial center.

Thompson liked the plan. He went to St. Louis to volunteer for the expedition and in short order became the field secretary, treasurer, and official journal keeper for the group. Grandly named the American Exploring and Mineral Company, this enterprise was the largest and best-organized speculative effort to focus on the upper Missouri goldfields in 1862, at the very start of the Montana gold rush. But, as Frank Thompson later ruefully reflected, a prepossessing name and airy plans on paper did not guarantee success.

IN THESE MEMOIRS Francis M. Thompson relates the story of his trip to the upper Missouri mining region and the rapid disintegration of the St. Louis company. He describes his efforts to rescue his investment by mining and then by opening a general store in Bannack, the first gold rush boomtown in what would become Montana Territory in 1864. Partly for adventure and partly to order fresh supplies for his store, he next made a remarkable late-season trip to the Pacific Coast with a few of his mining country companions. He spent an active winter in wartime San Francisco, where the new telegraphic connection enabled Thompson to exchange business messages with his brother Hugh. He then returned to Bannack by way of Portland, Walla Walla, and Fort Benton. Unsuspectingly, Thompson made the last part of the journey with a small party of men who subsequently figured in the outbreak of lawlessness that soon caused great alarm throughout the upper Missouri gold region.

While looking after his business ventures at Bannack, Thompson took a brief but enterprising part in Montana's early political, social, and cultural growth. He writes about the social scene and provides interesting details concerning his part in lobbying Congress to create Montana Territory in 1864. Following the organization of the territory by Thompson's friend, territorial governor Sidney Edgerton, Thompson gained a seat as one of the two Beaverhead County representatives in the Council, the upper house of the territory's legislative assembly. He had achieved a place of prominence in Bannack at the beginning of the territory's development.

Two and a half years after his arrival, however, Thompson returned east. During a brief visit to his hometown, Greenfield, Massachusetts, he at last married his long-term fiancée. With his bride, Thompson moved to New York City, where he opened an office to market Montana mining properties for himself and a few partners, including Governor Edgerton. In New York he also served as an official commissioner for Montana Territory, promoting western emigration and investment. Successful in the sale of mining claims, he soon closed out the business and retired to Greenfield, where he settled into a career as town clerk, lawyer, and probate judge. He and his wife, with one daughter, lived quietly in Greenfield for the rest of their days.

Fortunately for the historical record, Thompson's memories of his Montana gold rush experiences remained fresh, and he kept in touch with western friends. Encouraged by the two most history-conscious of these friends, Nathaniel Pitt Langford and Wilbur Fisk Sanders, he committed his memories to paper. Beginning in 1912, Thompson published his "Reminiscences of Four-Score Years" in successive issues of a local journal of history and literature, *Massachusetts Magazine*.

This volume reprints Thompson's original text as it appeared in *Massachusetts Magazine*, omitting material concerning his youth and early employment in the western banking business and adding explanatory notes and source citations. Thompson designed his reminiscences to present the account of his time in the mountains separately, setting apart this section under the title "A Tenderfoot in Montana." It required no great stretch of the editor's imagination to use his title for this volume.

FRANK THOMPSON'S REMINISCENCES are historically valuable in at least three respects. First, he provides a rare description of travel between St. Louis, Montana, and the Pacific Coast in the early 1860s. Second, he vividly recounts the beginning of Montana's mining era and the lawlessness in the mining country, as well as its sequel: the abrupt, brutally effective extralegal reform movement carried out by secret vigilante committees in Virginia City and Bannack. Thompson knew very well Henry Plummer, the popularly elected sheriff of Bannack and nearby mining camps, along with a good many of Plummer's purported associates in crime. He was close by when Plummer became the most prominent casualty of vigilante action. Thompson was also on good personal terms with many of the men who hanged Plummer and the others in January 1864. An eyewitness, he offers evidence concerning these events that is more reliable and more judicious in its telling than any other single firsthand source we have. Third, Thompson contributes an anecdote-laden narrative of the formation of Montana Territory and the first session of the territorial legislature, providing a rare insider's description of the somewhat-haphazard, liquor-fueled legislative process that started Montana's governmental history.

Beyond his description of these events, Frank Thompson gives us a well-informed, highly literate participant's view of the gold rush excitement as it began to make a permanent psychic impress on the society of Montana's mining region. A self-styled tenderfoot, he saw a great deal and recorded it not only with accuracy but with a perceptive appreciation for the uniqueness of his time in this place.

JUDGING FROM HIS PERSONAL HISTORY, Frank Thompson came well prepared for western adventure when he set out for the upper Missouri region in 1862. A native of northern Massachusetts, he had been born in 1833 on his grandfather's farm near Colrain, a rural village close to Greenfield and just a few miles south of the Vermont border. On his father's side, he was a fourth-generation descendant of Protestant Scotch-Irish immigrants who had come from the town of Colrain in Northern Ireland in 1749. His mother, Elvira Adams, was a distant relative of John and John Quincy Adams. She could trace her New England ancestry back eight generations to the first Henry Adams, who in 1632 had settled in what became Quincy, Massachusetts. During his childhood, Thompson's parents and their eight children worked on the farm of his maternal grandfather, Captain Edward Adams, one of the wealthiest men in the district. In 1843, when Frank was ten years old, Captain Adams purchased a larger property in Greenfield that included a sawmill and related businesses. Frank's parents became the managers of this establishment, with all the children included as a part of the family work force.

The seventh in line, with three older brothers, three older sisters, and one younger sister, Frank learned early that he would have to work hard to make his way in the world. He and his brother John were able to attend school only during winter terms. Both became competent mechanics, to use the early-nineteenth-century term for machinists, by working in the sawmill and carpentry shop. By 1854 his grandparents, father, and oldest brother had died, leaving the Greenfield property jointly to the three surviving brothers. Frank and Hugh agreed to convey their separate interests to John, with the proviso that John would remain in charge of the farm and provide a home for their mother. At age twenty-two, Frank now faced the need to strike out on his own.

Because he had pursued his schooling part time through the upper grades, then briefly attended Williston Seminary, Frank felt himself equipped to teach common school—a reasonable professional beginning for a young New England man in the 1850s. He secured a teaching license and a one-year position at Deerfield, close to Greenfield. Truly, his teaching experience proved educational. By the time the school year ended, he was pleased to dismiss his classes early, despite the offer of more pay to prolong the term; and as he wrote in the first chapter of his reminiscences, "I have never since had any desire to teach school."[2]

His brother Hugh offered him the opportunity to try another career path, hiring him to help build a foundry and machine shop in Connecticut. When he finished the job a year later, Hugh and Levi Jones, husband of the oldest Thompson sister, made Frank the book-keeper and cashier in their newly purchased gristmill and machine shop business in Greenfield, with responsibility also for running the firm's stove and tin shop. "All went well until the hard times of 1856-7 began," Thompson remembered, "when it was sometimes pretty hard work to meet the maturing indebtedness."[3]

With the Jones and Thompson partnership facing bankruptcy, the young man fortuitously received a letter from Cincinnati banker George Wright offering him a clerical position in Wright's banking and exchange office. This unexpected invitation was based on the recommendation of another Thompson relative who was already a trusted employee in Wright's firm. Horace Greeley's advice, "Go west, young man, go west," was ringing in his ears day and night, Thompson recalled, and so he gladly accepted Wright's proposition. Like many of his peers who had joined the California gold rush in 1849, Frank was adventurous and infected with a desire to sample life beyond the circumscribed boundaries of his upbringing. Early in 1856, not yet quite twenty-three years old, he moved to Cincinnati and began a life of travel and high-risk financial dealings, with assignments that took him to Indiana, Illinois, Kentucky, Tennessee, Minnesota, east to Pittsburgh and New York City, and finally to St. Louis.

The Wright firm's principal business was money exchange. The company purchased from merchants and other bankers, at discount, the non-current paper money issued by small private banks throughout the western states. The firm's representative then presented these bills on short notice to the issuing banks for redemption in gold coin at face value. A business with many intricacies, it could be quite profitable. Thompson soon became the main field representative for Wright's banking house, developing a keen knowledge of commercial practices while often proving his nerve and shrewd instincts in dealing with uncooperative, ill-tempered country bankers. Frequently he found himself traveling by stagecoach and riverboat with large sums in gold—ten thousand dollars or more. He learned to keep a tight hold on his heavy valise, with his revolver tucked securely in the mouth of the bag atop the coins.

Trustworthy, capable, and clever, Frank Thompson rapidly rose to higher positions in the money business. He remained with the Wright bank for three years, becoming a bookkeeper and briefly comanager of a branch house on Wall Street in New York City. He then left the firm to pursue other opportunities, relocating to St. Louis. Hugh had moved there following the bankruptcy of Thompson and Jones in Greenfield, and now was prospering in his own business. With his brother's encouragement, Frank opened an exchange office on Broadway, in the commercial center of the city, his main resource being his expert knowledge of the western region's banks of issue and the actual net value of their non-current bank notes. The business quickly began to bring generous returns, but the threat of political disunion and civil war had so badly unsettled the bond and money markets by the late fall of 1860 that Thompson permanently closed his office doors and returned to Greenfield, as he phrased it, "to await events."[4]

During the 1860 presidential campaign, Frank's first choice for the presidency was Edward Bates of Missouri, a Whig moderate who had become popular among border-state leaders enlisted in the Republican cause. After joining a Bates club in St. Louis, Thompson traveled with hundreds of others to the Republican Party's national convention in Chicago on behalf of his candidate. Though Bates's supporters were unable to advance his candidacy, Frank thoroughly enjoyed the political spectacle. The nomination of Abraham Lincoln at the Chicago convention was a dramatic moment for Thompson, not the least because he had already formed a slight personal acquaintance with the candidate. Two years earlier, while Lincoln was engaged in the Illinois senatorial campaign against Stephen A. Douglas, Frank had gone to meet him in Springfield regarding a legal case that involved Thompson's then employer, George Wright. Frank's diary and memo book contained crucial evidence in the case, making him a key witness. He found Lincoln at his law office, "a man of homely, but attractive face, beneath a shock of unkempt hair, [sitting] tipped back in a chair, with book in hand and feet upon the office stove, who awkwardly arose and bade me welcome."[5] After Thompson showed his memo book to Lincoln, the two men chatted genially for some time, with Lincoln telling stories about his experiences while traveling the Illinois court circuit and Frank responding with tales about his own travel adventures. It was this brief personal contact two years earlier, rather than his political convictions, that made Lincoln's nomination especially meaningful for Frank in 1860.

After the Chicago convention, Thompson again met Lincoln in Springfield for a brief discussion of the court case. Despite all his other concerns, Thompson was surprised to learn, the Republican presidential nominee still intended to argue the case if it ever went to trial. As it happened, principally because of Thompson's evidence, the case was dropped. But based on these two meetings Frank was so impressed with Lincoln that he traveled from Massachusetts to the national capital to attend Lincoln's inauguration in March 1861. What he recalled half a century later was James Buchanan holding Lincoln's tall silk hat while the new president took the oath of office, then an inaugural address that began with Lincoln's voice barely audible, "but as he reached the part where he declared it to be his duty and intent to see the constitution and laws maintained and enforced in all parts of the nation, he spoke with such power that he could be easily heard."[6]

Back in Greenfield at the time of the siege and surrender of Fort Sumter, Frank Thompson prepared to join the Union Army. With the backing of prominent Greenfield citizens, he offered to raise a company for the Massachusetts state volunteers. After waiting patiently through the summer of 1861 and hearing nothing, he accepted the offer of a major's commission from a friend who was raising a company of Wisconsin volunteers. But just at this point he agreed to make the trip on the Ohio and Mississippi rivers that resulted in his decision to avoid service in the Union Army. No true conscientious objector when he joined the American Exploring and Mineral Company, Thompson nonetheless found it congenial to leave behind the scenes of political strife and armed conflict in Missouri for what he expected would be thrilling adventures in a distant, romantic frontier region.

Clearly, Frank Thompson's reminiscences of his time as "a tenderfoot in Montana" are not the work of a political zealot. Although he identified himself as a Republican when he won a position in Montana's first territorial council, he was temperamentally disinclined to wave any partisan banner with enthusiasm. Experienced and cautious in judgment, though daring and brave enough to venture boldly into risky situations, he got along well with men and women from many different backgrounds.

Frank was a teetotaler, a churchgoer when opportunity allowed, and a choir leader in Bannack, certainly striking traits by the standards of early day Montana; yet he fit himself easily into the boisterous social life of the gold camps. He greatly enjoyed hunting. His eagerness to kill any and every wild creature that crossed his path during his western travels apparently was undiminished when he set down his reminiscences a half century later. He did not, however, customarily carry a handgun or other weapon as he went about his business and personal pursuits in Bannack. Thompson freely associated with men of rough character; yet he earnestly cautioned young Miss Electa Bryan against her intended marriage to one such man, Henry Plummer. In summary, life in the Rocky Mountain mining country suited Frank Thompson for a brief period, but clearly he retained his New England principles and middle class social standards throughout his western sojourn.

THE ENTERPRISE THAT TOOK Frank Thompson to the upper Missouri gold country did not prosper. Like dozens of similar joint ventures launched during the California gold rush, the American Exploring and Mineral Company was founded with high expectations quickly dashed by the realities of mining life and the frailties of human nature. Though its twelve-member field force was well funded and more than adequately equipped, the company relied on a cooperative style of management that failed to survive its first months of operation. When Thompson and a few others left their mining claims at Gold Creek in search of a better paying site, remaining company members gave away on scant security the larger part of the group's stock of supplies and tools to strangers newly arrived from Colorado. The details are vague in Thompson's telling, yet his sense of outrage remained clear enough when he recorded these events after a lapse of fifty years. Following a short, generally unsuccessful experiment digging for gold, most of Thompson's comrades in the enterprise decided to return to St. Louis. Of the twelve who had headed upriver together in May 1862, only Thompson remained in the Montana region through the following two seasons.

After making a reasonable effort to strike it rich by placer mining during the summer of 1862, Thompson turned to less physically demanding work. Calling on his business experience and entrepreneurial talents, he opened a general store in Bannack. He probably arranged to sell the remaining property of the American Exploring and Mineral Company as his chief stock in trade. Once established, he relied on his brother to ship goods from St. Louis that would find a ready market in the gold camps, while he also bought bargain-priced merchandise from others as opportunity allowed. Thompson describes few details of these business matters. We may, however, reasonably infer from his activities in the months before he started upriver and during his first year in the mining country that he had quit his prewar banking venture with significant profits, and that his Bannack store supported him quite decently. In 1864 he also made good money with a sawmill that he put into operation near Virginia City, an enterprise he subsequently sold to Wilbur Sanders. But it was his later success selling Montana quartz mining properties in New York City that allowed Thompson to retire in comfort from his adventure-filled life and take up a calmer existence back in Greenfield.

Like many among the New Englanders who headed for California in 1849, the financial rewards from his western gold country experience enabled him to return home as a man of property and substance. He then claimed in the community a place that had been far beyond reach during his youth. Although he never returned to Montana, Frank Thompson had ample reason to be grateful for his brief time in what later would be called the Treasure State.

Because he was a keen observer, sensitive to the historical nature of his western experiences, Thompson's tenderfoot reminiscences fit well into the body of pioneer accounts about Montana and adjacent territories. It was his good fortune to meet many old-timers who had come to the region during the fur trade era, before the gold rush began. Thompson kept a journal record of these encounters and his other activities, and after returning to Massachusetts, he carefully read other relevant accounts that came into print. As will be seen in this volume's editorial notes, his writing was aided by reference to these earlier publications. His scholarship allowed Thompson to prepare a fuller, more accurate historical memoir by setting his personal adventures within a broader framework of fact.

OUR FASCINATION WITH STORIES of crime and punishment inclines us to give priority to Thompson's description of the Montana vigilante movement during the winter of 1863–1864. In truth his version of this oft-told tale deserves close study, for Frank Thompson offers one of the most authoritative firsthand narrations known to the historical record. From the time he let himself be enlisted reluctantly as a member of Henry Plummer's wedding party at Sun River until he heard the vigilante squad marching the sheriff and two other prisoners to the Bannack gallows under cover of darkness, Thompson closely observed Plummer's career. He ate at the same table as Plummer and knew the man well. Plummer asked Thompson to serve as his personal banker, apparently entrusting him with a substantial deposit. Subsequently, Frank took responsibility for burying Plummer and administering his estate: the holdings of the Montana Historical Society Archives include a receipt from George French to F. M. Thompson, for "Making Coffin and burying late H. Plummer."[7] Then, as he tells us, Thompson conscientiously sent the balance of Plummer's funds to his young widow in Iowa.

He was also on terms of close friendship with Sidney Edgerton, the designated chief justice of Idaho Territory who subsequently served as Montana's first territorial governor. He was particularly close to Edgerton's nephew Wilbur Fisk Sanders, forming with Sanders a lifelong friendship. Thompson does not hesitate to name Sanders as "the acknowledged leader" in the vigilante movement, writing that "in constant peril of his life he led the way to the establishment of law and order." He fills in details about events leading to the vigilantes' first meeting that no other author provides, while his description of the impact these proceedings had on his young friend Joseph Swift Jr., on Plummer's sister-in-law, and on the women in the Edgerton household offers fresh insight concerning the emotional turmoil surrounding this episode in the small community on the banks of Grasshopper Creek.

CRITICAL HISTORICAL PRACTICE recognizes that every statement of fact rests ultimately on one or more primary sources—sources derived from firsthand, eyewitness observation of the event or series of events in question. Accurate knowledge of the past depends entirely on primary source data, whether that data is derived from written documents or verbal accounts, whether it is recorded in published or unpublished materials, whether it is the testimony of a trained observer or the most naive, befuddled spectator. Just as with a court of law, the court of history does not countenance hearsay evidence. Intrinsically, what we can know with certainty about the past is limited by the primary, firsthand sources we have at our command. Of course, every primary source must be tested and evaluated for authenticity and bias according to fixed principles and accepted practices of investigation often termed the historical method.[8] Although historical writers may indulge in speculation about issues of interpretation, ultimately good history can only rest on a foundation of good sources.

Frank Thompson's reminiscences can rightfully take a privileged position among other sources that document the early days of the upper Missouri gold rush and the history of the mining camp vigilantes. Since the time of its publication in 1866, the best-known account of the vigilante episode at Virginia City and Bannack has been Thomas J. Dimsdale's *The Vigilantes of Montana*, long regarded as the standard work.[9] This little book originally appeared in 1865 as a series of articles in the *Montana Post*, the newspaper that Dimsdale edited and published at Virginia City. It presents the case for the 1864 Montana vigilante proceedings in the strongest terms, admitting no doubts about the substantive justice of the secret actions carried out by self-appointed committees of Virginia City and Bannack residents. In highly colored Victorian-era prose, Dimsdale indicts and convicts Sheriff Plummer and his alleged associates in crime without the slightest hesitation or doubt. His judgment rests in large part on testimony supposedly volunteered by purported members of the sheriff's gang of robbers and murderers when faced with death. This was testimony heard only by a few of the vigilante band in their closed proceedings. In some cases it came, according to Dimsdale, from men standing with the hangman's noose already around their neck.

Dimsdale's work, aside from its quite evident authorial bias, has always presented to critically minded historians the problem that it contains no verifiable documentation for its narrative. Much of the volume may be described as the stuff of public knowledge, the street corner and barroom talk that any newspaperman would be likely to gather in a small community. Yet Dimsdale also reports in detail the deliberations and activities of the Montana vigilantes from the perspective of an insider, frequently quoting the supposed actual dialogue between vigilante leaders and men they had taken prisoner. Since Dimsdale himself was not one of the vigilantes, substantial portions of his work must rest on hearsay, which would make this testimony inadmissible in a well-run court of law. Evaluated according to the canons of historical methodology, *The Vigilantes of Montana* is neither a primary source that can withstand critical scrutiny nor a wholly trustworthy secondary source.

Second on the list of Montana vigilante narratives is Nathaniel P. Langford's *Vigilante Days and Ways*. This book, published in 1890, contains Langford's recollections of his own Montana gold rush experiences and a comprehensive recounting of crime and vigilante episodes in early Montana and the adjacent territories and states.[10] Because he was prominently involved in public affairs, even serving as chairman of a jury in a miners' court proceeding for murder in Virginia City during the summer of 1863, Langford's account has an apparent higher credibility as a source than Dimsdale's. Yet on the topic of the hanging of Henry Plummer and his alleged companions in crime by the vigilantes, it too is grievously marred. Langford spent the winter of 1863–1864 in St. Louis, far from the violent scenes in the mountains that he recounts. Like Dimsdale—and apparently using Dimsdale's work as a major source—Langford provides critical bits of the supposed dialogue from the vigilante interrogations. And like Dimsdale he strives to justify the actions of the vigilantes by painting the character of the vigilantes' victims, Henry Plummer and his supposed crime ring, in the darkest colors.

Neither Dimsdale nor Langford provides a verifiable documentary record of the vigilante episode. For details of the story, they each relied on the word of others who were present and who remain unidentified by the authors. Based on the internal evidence and the circumstances of the case, we can conclude that Wilbur Fisk Sanders was a main informant for both writers. From him and perhaps from others, they apparently gained information known firsthand only to members of the secret Bannack and Virginia City vigilance committees. In the process of relating his history of the vigilante movement, Sanders naturally put his own spin on the narrative, presenting to Dimsdale and Langford what amounted to a lawyer's brief on behalf of his clients—himself and his vigilante associates. Clearly, neither Dimsdale in 1865 nor Langford in 1890 was inclined to criticize Sanders' pro-vigilante interpretation.

We should not doubt the dangers of the situation in December 1863 and January 1864. Nor can we rightly impugn the sincerity of Sanders and his vigilante associates in attempting to end the outbreak of robberies and murders by road agents that had overtaken the upper Missouri gold camps. While sifting the evidence, we should also observe that Sanders had self-interested motives for seeking a leading role among the vigilantes and subsequently for polishing to high luster his reputation as a vigilante chief.

Sanders had arrived in Bannack in mid-September 1863 with his uncle, Sidney Edgerton, who was an antislavery Ohio lawyer and politician and an early recruit to the Free-Soil Party. In 1856 Edgerton became an organizer of the Republican Party in his home state. Elected as a Republican, he served in Congress from 1859 to 1863, where he was identified with the radical antislavery, anti-Southern faction of the new party. When Edgerton's second term expired in March 1863, President Lincoln responded to the recommendations of Ohio's leading Republicans by naming him the first chief justice of Idaho Territory. This was a newly created jurisdiction that extended from the eastern boundary of modern Washington and Oregon to the western boundary of modern North and South Dakota and south to Colorado and Utah. In other words, Idaho then encompassed not only modern Idaho but also all the vast expanse of mountains and high plains subsequently set off as Montana and Wyoming territories.[11]

Like most fresh territorial appointees, Judge Edgerton had higher political ambitions. So did Sanders, then twenty-eight years old and also a lawyer, who resigned a lieutenant's commission in the Union Army to accompany his uncle to the northern Rockies. Apparently Edgerton and Sanders intended to start their political and legal careers anew in the West, for both men brought along their families to risk the tedious, dangerous journey from Missouri to an unknown western destination. They traveled by ox-drawn wagon from Independence overland on the Oregon–California Trail route to Salt Lake City, then headed northward to the upper Missouri country by way of Fort Hall and Monida Pass, a route more suitable for freight wagon bullwhackers than a family steeped in middle-class gentility.[12]

For Edgerton and Sanders, Bannack must have appeared a place with promise. In this newborn mining camp, where fresh gold discoveries held out the prospect of quick riches for everyone, they could hope to improve their financial condition while establishing themselves as leaders in the region's legal profession. At the same time, the two men, closely allied in their professional and business interests, obviously anticipated they would dominate the local Republican organization. Their rule would be reinforced, so they could believe, by astute partisan control over all local territorial appointments. They would be the chief advisers for the Lincoln administration at a time when every federal office was filled according to well-practiced methods of political favoritism under the patronage system.[13]

Edgerton and Sanders found their political ambitions shaded, however, by the lack of broad-based support in the upper Missouri mining districts for the Republican Party and its Northern sectional ideology—antislavery, anti-immigrant, and pro-Union. The machinery of party politics was not yet developed in Bannack and the surrounding area when the two men arrived, but partisan sentiments were fully in evidence. Excited public displays spontaneously burst forth in each mining camp with the arrival of any fresh news from Civil War battlefields. Many miners had come up the Missouri River from the slave-owning states, bringing Democratic party loyalties and anti-Union, anti-Republican sympathies as part of their ideological baggage. Some also brought a proud record of military service in the Confederate cause. A few very vocal "secesh" sympathizers delighted in demonstrating their rebel affiliation. They ran up the Confederate stars and bars on improvised flag poles, cheered lustily, and exuberantly shot off revolvers, rifles, and small cannons to celebrate Southern victories.

Montana's early mining camp society held other challenges for ambitious Republican politicians. Alongside the Southerners, the immigrant Irish were a second major element in the population. Traditionally the American Irish aligned themselves with the Democratic Party, but they were separated from the Southerners by cultural background and their firm affiliation with the Roman Catholic Church. Many Irish newcomers in the mining regions had kinship ties with the large Irish communities in New York, Philadelphia, and Boston. Among other distinctions, they differed from the Southerners in their tendency to support the Union cause, even as they too distrusted many Republican Party leaders' nativist views, anti-Catholic attitudes, and inclination to sympathize with England in international affairs.

A third distinct element in the Montana mines were the "Pike's Peakers." These men had rushed to the Colorado gold camps in 1861 and 1862 only to be disappointed in the richness of the placers. Frequently with origins in the middle border states, these veteran miners came to the upper Missouri mining region with an urgent need to make a living and, with few exceptions, little in the way of a political agenda. Among them, however, were a few experienced Democratic campaigners as eager as Edgerton and Sanders to claim a leadership role in the emerging political life of the upper Missouri mining camps.

In addition, according to some observers, Montana's pioneer

miners in 1862 and 1863 included a fair number of Northern
men anxious simply to avoid the federal wartime draft and all
scenes of military conflict. They sought to ignore the most divisive partisan issues and keep out of harm's way. Frank Thompson, friend to both Republicans and Democrats, fit securely into
this classification.

The nation's strong Union men, the bedrock of Republican strength
throughout the Northern states, had other priorities in mid-1862 than
gold hunting far off in the upper Missouri country. A year later the
fall of Vicksburg and the simultaneous Union victory at Gettysburg
raised Union spirits high while dampening the ardor of Southern
nationalists. When the news of these two decisive defeats for the
Confederacy reached the upper Missouri country, Alexander Toponce
recalled years later, "the Union men took heart and from that time on
the Secession sentiment was not so strong."[14] Back in Ohio, Wilbur
Sanders, with his health impaired by military life, then decided to
leave the Union Army and head westward with his uncle and their
two families.

For other reasons, the remote upper Missouri area also attracted
men who felt it circumspect for one reason or another to get away
from scenes of wartime partisanship. Samuel T. Hauser, for example,
was one of Frank Thompson's shipmates on the 1862 upriver voyage from St. Louis. A lifelong Democrat, Hauser had become a
marked man in Missouri because of his protest against the judicial
lynching of a young Kentuckian by Northern sympathizers. He found
it expedient to leave and seek his fortune in the mining regions,
safely distant from the political passions and violent threats of
the moment.[15]

After his arrival at Bannack, Judge Edgerton made no effort
to organize a court under Idaho jurisdiction. There was no proper
officer on hand, he later explained, to swear him into office.
Moreover, he also stated, he could not be certain that the Union

men would be strong enough in numbers or sufficiently determined to uphold federal authority.[16] But at least equally important, Edgerton was really in an untenable situation for the administration of justice under territorial authority. Just created in the spring of 1863, Idaho Territory was still essentially unorganized. The legislature needed to meet and adopt codes of civil and criminal law. The territorial governor, William H. Wallace, was preoccupied by his own campaign for election as territorial delegate. Theoretically, the laws of Washington Territory continued to apply within Idaho, all the way eastward to the Dakota border, while Idaho's government remained in an inchoate condition. But neither Judge Edgerton nor any of the lawyers who had arrived in the upper Missouri mining camps had expertise in territorial precedents. If Judge Edgerton had attempted to establish a court under federal authority at Bannack, absent either an Idaho territorial legal code or a properly authorized assignment to the Bannack District, any decisions he might hand down would have likely been overturned immediately on appeal to the Attorney General's office in Washington, D.C. Even the least skilled lawyer in the upper Missouri mining camps in 1863 possessed the mother wit to point out that Chief Justice Edgerton was essentially powerless, an unsworn officer without a legitimate office.

The administration of mining camp justice remained in the hands of self-constituted popular tribunals, the so-called miners' courts. This institution for do-it-yourself justice was based on California gold rush precedents, where the miners' courts had usually served well for adjudicating mining claims and other property issues. In fact, the California state legislature made the decisions of miners' courts the recognized legal basis for mining property rights.

Just as they had in California, however, the miners' courts were proving imperfect mechanisms for the administration of criminal justice in the upper Missouri mining camps.[17] As Thompson relates, by fall 1863 it had become obvious at Bannack and Virginia City that property and life were at constant, extreme risk for anyone traveling through the countryside, particularly if the traveler was known to be carrying significant amounts of gold. But was there for Edgerton and Sanders a link between this perilous condition and the political situation as they saw it?

Early in the history of every new western territory, before party structures and the lines of party interest became fixed, local affairs were characterized by a politics of personality. Loyalties were fickle; alliances shifted rapidly. Small, narrowly defined voting blocs fought hard for the economic spoils of office and advancement of their petty chieftains. A condition that has been termed "chaotic factionalism," this embryonic form of frontier politics challenged anyone who, like Sanders and Edgerton, hoped to create a strong and stable political organization as a way to realize personal ambitions for high office.[18] The obvious path to success, every politician knew then as now, was to take up a popular, polarizing issue—a wedge issue—that cut across traditional party lines and factional interests.

In Bannack and Virginia City during the final months of 1863, that issue was crime. Voters of all description would welcome efforts to end the danger from road agents, establish public security, and ensure a reign of law. As it developed, the fact that the central figure among the road agents was evidently Sheriff Henry Plummer, who identified himself as a Democrat, might have seemed an unexpected political boon to Sanders and Edgerton. The vigilante movement provided an expedient solution to the crime problem, and indirectly it called into question the character of the gold camp Democrats, who were led in 1863 by Plummer's political patron, the portly and voluble hail-fellow-well-met Colonel Samuel McLean.[19]

Very soon after the events of January 1864, the story of the secret gold camp vigilante movement and its substantial list of victims, sent to their death without due process or public trial, became known in the eastern states. In May Judge Edgerton's apparent role in condoning these executions was the reason for an unsuccessful objection to his nomination as chief executive of Montana Territory posed by a U.S. senator.[20] Edgerton's identification as a friend of the vigilance committees did little to ease his brief and stormy tenure in the governor's office. But it was President Lincoln's assassination and the change in regime in the national capital, leaving Republican Radicals cut off from federal patronage, that had the greatest influence in convincing Edgerton to return to Ohio and resign his Montana position.

Wilbur Sanders and his family remained in the territory. He encouraged Thomas Dimsdale to extol the vigilantes in print and insist on the justice of their actions. He thus became identified even more solidly with the cause of law and order, while indirectly he promoted his reputation as a man of probity, courage, and decisive character. Sanders and his Republican friends hoped these qualities would elevate him in his profession and assist him in winning political preferment from Montana voters. He suffered repeated setbacks, but kept alive his political hopes for a quarter century until the migration boom of the 1880s made statehood possible. The new voters tipped Montana's political balance toward the Republicans, and in 1889 Sanders finally gained a seat in the U.S. Senate. And so, later rather than sooner, his identification with the vigilante movement in Virginia City and Bannack helped him achieve the lofty political station and prestige that in 1863 he had traveled west to find.

In its telling and retelling by Dimsdale, Langford, and countless others in later years, the story of the vigilante movement
during the winter of 1863–1864 came to have a certain quasi-
mythic resonance in Montana. It has been fixed as a founding
legend for law enforcement in the state, signified by the 3-7-77
symbol. Erroneously associated with the 1864 vigilantes, this
symbol is now incorporated in the official heraldry of the Montana Highway Patrol—despite the fact that, as historian Frederick
Allen states, its meaning "is a complete and utter mystery" to
everyone living in Montana.[21] The same mythic effect is reinforced by a heroic bronze statue of Wilbur Sanders that long
graced the rotunda of the Montana state capitol building, posed
in a stern gesture above the legend "Men, do your duty."[22] That
duty, everyone conversant with vigilante lore clearly understands,
was to execute those who posed a danger to the lives and property of good citizens. The Montana vigilante myth, then, has
stood for an unswerving standard of righteousness administered
by incorruptible, hard-hearted men, presumably with no petti-
fogging quibbles or too-delicate qualms about legal due process
and the rights of the accused.

Frank Thompson's reminiscences contribute a body of firsthand evidence that can help us reappraise the historical ground-
ing for Montana's vigilante myth. His account is almost entirely
devoid of the rhetorical excesses and special pleadings that mark
the works by Dimsdale and Langford. To be sure, Thompson
relies in part on his friend Langford's *Vigilante Days and Ways*
for matters of fact concerning events he did not witness, and so
we may impugn the firsthand authenticity of his narrative to this
degree. Moreover, as quoted above, he states in no uncertain
terms his admiration for the leadership role of Sanders, whose

friendship Thompson continued to cherish to the end of his days. Yet the bulk of what he writes is based on direct personal observation, reported with a conscious attempt to avoid overstatement and sensationalizing.

Careful in his use of language and judicious in temperament, Frank Thompson helps assure us that the vigilante movement met a real challenge with a practical solution, severe but unavoidable given all the circumstances. Thompson is fully believable. His narrative strongly reinforces the conclusion that Henry Plummer was indeed guilty of murder and robbery and that he was the head of some sort of a criminal conspiracy. He describes in full particulars the evidence that led him and others to these conclusions, based both on strong circumstantial evidence and eyewitness reports, independent of political motives or personal bias.

Thompson helps us see that Henry Plummer was a man far more complex than the stereotyped villain portrayed by Dimsdale and Langford. But in his narrative, Sheriff Plummer appears more culpable than simply misunderstood. He was not the tragically unfortunate figure who emerges in the revisionist, deliberately challenging accounts by R. E. Mather and F. E. Boswell. These modern authors claim that "though there is no evidence that the Bannack sheriff headed an outlaw gang, posterity believed the charge simply because the vigilantes hanged him."[23] Frank Thompson might argue, pointedly, that he and other responsible residents in Bannack had irrefutable evidence to uphold that charge before the vigilantes organized to end Montana's gold rush crime wave. Thompson also helps us understand the role of Wilbur Sanders, Plummer's nemesis. He was the key figure who set in motion the events that brought about the sheriff's execution, who ordered his men to do their duty and drop the sheriff from the gallows, and who then became the master apologist for the course of action taken by the vigilantes.

When another account of the 1864 Montana vigilante movement is written, its credibility will depend on the willingness of the
author to gather all the relevant evidence and evaluate it with an
impartial eye. In this evaluation, for very good reasons, Frank
Thompson's testimony will prove crucial.[24]

IN THE PREFACE TO HIS REMINISCENCES, Frank Thompson declared
that his old Montana friends, especially Wilbur Sanders, had at last
persuaded him to set aside his scruples "against making public, in
so personal a manner, these events of my otherwise prosaic life."
From the perspective of half a century, Judge Thompson must have
relived his experiences in early Montana with great emotion. If his
life was otherwise prosaic—as all our biographical information tends
to confirm—he remained still a man with an interesting, exciting
past. His fond remembrance of this past was a personal legacy,
but one imbued with more than strictly personal significance. Now,
all these years later, when we are well beyond any direct connection with Thompson's era, this new edition offers the opportunity
to see those memorable events once more through the eyes of a
Montana tenderfoot we can truly esteem.

EDITORIAL NOTE

WITH FEW EXCEPTIONS, I have intended to reproduce the text of Thompson's original publication with exact fidelity. I have corrected a few insignificant typographical errors and adopted consistent spellings of rare words not treated consistently by Thompson and his original editor. Because Thompson occasionally adopted a passive construction that obscured his meaning, here and there I have supplied a bracketed subject word or phrase for clarification. Otherwise, punctuation and capitalization remain as they appear in the original.

Thompson's language illustrates certain locutions common during the nineteenth century and early twentieth century that modern readers may identify as racist terminology. For example, he writes of Indian bucks and squaws and expresses his New England white cultural values in commenting on native cultural practices or the appearances of native peoples he encountered in the Northwest. I have not altered these passages, nor have I made any change in his references to a "nigger" engine, the steam-driven capstan he saw in use aboard the Missouri River steamships. A reflection of both the man and his times, this language conveys a complex of attitudes that we judge to be appalling today, but that, so we may yet need to be reminded, are no less historically authentic.

THE WESTERN TRAVELS OF FRANK THOMPSON

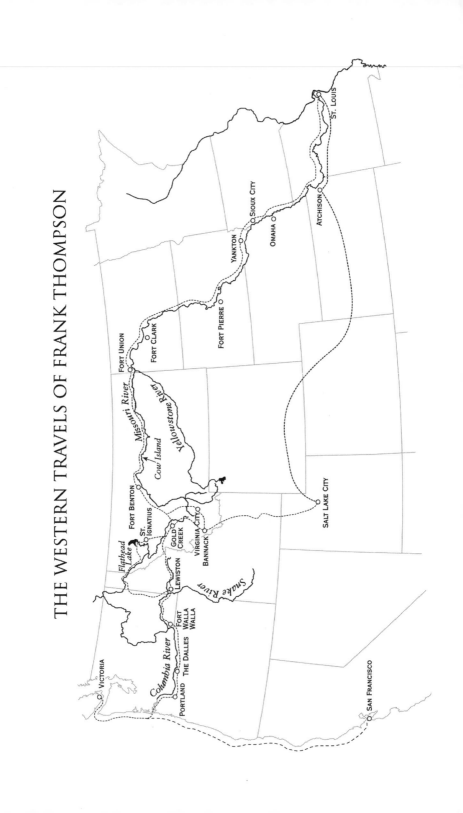

AUTHOR'S PREFACE

Often a thing trivial in itself affects a man's whole after life and brings about in his future career, results neither planned by or for him.

In my own case without doubt, the reading of a sensational story when I was yet a boy and attending the district school, affected my whole after life. The writer of this wonderful story described, as I then thought in a most fascinating manner, the capture of a beautiful maid from an Oregon emigrant train, by Indians and half breeds, the pursuit and rescue of her by her brave and gallant lover, their refuge at a trading post upon the Missouri, and their return to civilization by the fur trader's boats down that stream.

This exciting story created in me a strong desire to read all the books of travel and adventure which I could obtain relating to the great Northwest, the result being, that I was determined that if circumstances ever permitted, I would visit this wonderful and mysterious country.

I was, therefore, readily interested, when, after my return to Chicago and while on account of the outbreak of the war I hesitated to re-enter business, my brother, Hugh M. Thompson, a mineralogist in that city, wrote me of the discovery of gold near the head waters of the Missouri and the proposed organization

of a company there to send out an exploring party. The St. Louis
press, always alert to advance the interests of that city, amplified
all direct information concerning the discoveries at Florence and
Oro Fino, and extravagant rumors became, to the newspaper
men, well established facts.[1] So much interest was created in the
matter that no trouble was found in organizing a company with
means sufficient to send our party of a dozen men with ample
supplies for a year's prospecting. I was elected secretary and treasurer of the prospecting party, and it became my duty to keep an
official journal of its transactions.

It had always been the policy of the American Fur company,
who owned the trading stations among the fur capturing Indians,
to oppose any emigration to the fur-producing region, but excitement regarding the discovery of gold near the headwaters of
the Missouri had caused them to change their tactics, and they
advertised their willingness to take passengers for the Rocky
mountains, in their boats, the *Spread Eagle* and the *Key West*,
and both left St. Louis heavily laden with passengers and freight
for the mountains. Those sterling old river men, Joseph and John
La Barge had for years been in command of the Fur company's
boats, taking supplies up to the trading posts and bringing down
the furs, and well knew the immense profits in the trade. So an
opposition company was organized to take a share of the Indian
trade. The new firm of La Barge, Harkness & Co., advertised
the *Shreveport*, a light stern wheel boat commanded by Captain
John La Barge, and the *Emilie*, a fine four hundred ton side
wheeler, under command of Captain Joseph La Barge, for the
Missouri river trip.[2]

Our party joined the opposition, and we took passage on the
Emilie, which sailed May 14, 1862, the smaller boat having left
late in April. Each member paid one hundred dollars for board
and accommodations from St. Louis to Fort Benton. With the

FRANK THOMPSON'S MONTANA

MILES

10 20 30 40

Teton River

FORT BENTON

Mullan Road

Sun River

SUN RIVER FARM

↖ *Great Falls of the Missouri*

Dearborn River

Missouri River

Hell Gate River (Clark Fork)

HELL GATE (MISSOULA)

GOLD CREEK   MARYSVILLE

○ DIAMOND CITY

○ FORT OWEN

Deer Lodge River

HELENA

○ DEER LODGE

Bitterroot River

BUTTE CITY

WHITE HALL

THREE FORKS   GALLATIN CITY

Big Hole River

Jefferson River

○ BOZEMAN

SILVER STAR

Madison River

Gallatin River

Beaverhead Rock

VIRGINIA CITY

RATTLESNAKE RANCH

DEMPSEY'S RANCH

Beaverhead River

Stinking Water (Ruby River)

BANNACK ○

Grasshopper Creek

exception of horses or mules to haul our goods after leaving the boat, we were well equipped for a year's field work. With great expectations, we set out upon our journey, willing to face all the dangers of the navigation of the "Big Muddy" and all the savages which inhabited its shores.

Having thus become a pioneer in the country which is now Montana, and having later assisted in the erection of the original territorial government, and having as a member of the first legislature drawn the bill and aided in chartering the Historical Society of Montana, I have often been urged by its officers, and by my contemporaries to put in permanent form my journal and recollections of the strenuous days through which we passed.

The personal solicitation of my companion of those days, the late Wilbur F. Sanders, former senator from Montana, has been of much weight in overcoming my scruples against making public, in so personal a manner, these events of my otherwise prosaic life.

In a recent letter from Hon. Nathaniel P. Langford of St. Paul, he says "I am very glad that you are putting your pioneer experiences in form of preservation, for every item of our early history that can be rescued from oblivion is so much gained to all who may come after us."

F. M. T.
Greenfield, Mass.

ONE

The Missouri River

THE HONOR OF THE FIRST exploration of the upper Missouri must be credited to Pierre Gaultier de Varennes, (Sieur de la Verendrye) who with his sons, reached the *mauvaises terres* (bad lands) in 1742, and passed over to the Yellowstone. Verendrye was the son of Lt. Rene Gaultier Varennes and Marie Boucher, who were married at Three Rivers, Canada, Sept. 26, 1667. She was but twelve years old at the time. These French adventurers were several years making their approach to the Rocky mountains, and spent several more in their explorations. The father died on the Saskatchewan in 1749.

A Scotch half-breed called "Benetsee" from the Red river, whose real name was Francois Finlay, has the distinction of having first discovered gold in what is now Montana, at Gold creek, in 1852, but to James and Granville Stuart belongs the honor of turning the discovery to any practical account. Obtaining an outfit at the Salmon river mines in 1858 they began sluicing in Pioneer gulch and were successfully operating the mines at that place when our party reached that location in July, 1862. The Stuart brothers were the pioneer miners of what is now Montana.[1]

A friend who was a passenger on the *Shreveport*, which left St. Louis April 30, 1862, gives us the particulars of the journey of that boat up the "Big Muddy."[2]

A good deal of excitement existed as the *Shreveport* lay at the St. Louis levee, with steam up, ready to begin her journey of thirty-two hundred miles up the Missouri, to the Rocky mountains. Captain John La Barge is in command, and the boat is loaded down with Indian goods, provisions, arms, machinery, mining implements, and a full supply of whiskey and store goods. In order to command respect from the wild Indians of the upper river, two small brass field pieces grace the forward deck.

When all was ready for the start, a salute was attempted, when by a premature discharge, a member of the crew was severely wounded, and the poor fellow injured thereby had to be sent to a hospital. Off at last amid the shouts and cheers of the multitude, and the waving of hats and handkerchiefs of friends left behind. We stopped at the powder magazine and took on a full supply of war material. About dark we left the clear waters of the Mississippi, and entered the muddy, swirling waters of the Missouri, and soon after tied up to the bank, to await day light in which to pick our dangerous way among the snaggy river bars and shallows.[3] During the night a youthful somnambulist walked overboard. His cries roused all the people on the boat, and he was fished out without apparent damage, except to his pride. Charles Conoyer met us at St. Charles and we took on a lot of corn. While the steamer was being wooded, a young fellow-passenger thought he would take a run upon the river bank. Soon the overhanging turf gave way, and the sprinter dropped into the stream between the boat and the shore. He crawled out bearing a decidedly sheepish appearance. The day was bright and beautiful, as

May-day always should be, and all felt its cheering influence. We ran until midnight and tied up at Miller's landing. We have already met the *Sunshine, S. B. Madison, Isabella,* and the *Russell,* bound down the river. As we arrived at Lexington near midnight and left at daybreak, the passengers were disappointed in not seeing the battle ground where a few months before McCulloch with 28,000 Confederates compelled Col. Mulligan to surrender 3,000 Union men, and the city.[4] At Richland we met the *Florence* at the wood yard, and she had as passengers some mountaineers who had left Fort Benton April 5th, in a Mackinaw boat.[5] They gave glowing accounts of the new mines, and we all felt assured of soon having all the gold we cared for.

Near Wyandotte the steamer had to lay up and have the boilers cleaned. The passengers built a great bonfire in the woods and spent a long evening in games and singing. The next day a broken mud valve caused a detention of twelve hours, and we arrived at St. Joseph, Mo., May 7th, where we received letters, and took on several passengers. We have on board seventy-five cabin passengers and a goodly number of deck men, some of whom are working their way. Soon after leaving St. Joseph we met the regular packet *Omaha,* and among her passengers was Mr. William [Charles] Galpin, who for many years had been a prominent man of the American Fur company, but who had recently joined the La Barge, Harkness Co. The two steamers tied up to the bank and Capt. La Barge and Mr. Galpin had a short interview.[6]

At Omaha we took on Mr. Galpin's horse, and two passengers for Fort Berthold.[7] Sunday dawned bright and pleasant, and many of the passengers made a display of clean linen and store clothes, but otherwise it was the same old story—steaming on up the river. At a stopping place today we saw a few Omaha Indians, the first red men we have seen. At Sioux city, which is quite a town, Gen. [John Blair Smith]

Todd and other prominent men came on board and drank to the success of the expedition.[8] We also took on five additional passengers. At Yankton, the capital of Dakota Territory, we found the legislature in session, and governor Jayne and judges Williston and Bliss, and Mr. Trask (editor of the *Dakotian*) and most of the members of the legislature came on board the steamer, and with common consent and enthusiasm, joined in drinking success to Capt. La Barge, the *Shreveport*, the new trading company, and the expedition in general.[9] The town has its Broadway and its Fifth Avenue, and its great expectations. At supper our wag suggested that if practice at the *bar* would aid in making good lawyers, our visitors might be certain of success.

At the Yankton agency, Dr. Burleigh, the Indian agent visited the steamer accompanied by old Strike-the-Ree, Longfoot, and other less noted chiefs.[10] We were informed that Smutty-Bear, the head man of the Yanktons, had attended two feasts in one week, a few months before, which indiscretion resulted in his death. The agency Indians were anxiously awaiting the arrival of their annuities, which were on the Fur companies steamers. A party consisting of Capt. Pattee, Lt. Rutan, Mrs. Dr. Burleigh and her sister, took passage with us for Fort Randall. Arriving at that post, we were greeted by the huzzas of the men of the 14th. Iowa volunteers of the garrison, and after taking on freight and a supply of ice, they gave us a salute, as we steamed away up the crooked river.

Sunday again, and we spent the most of a cold and rainy day on a sand bar in the river, repairing a broken rudder. At Feinsy's island, we took on all the wood which the boat could hold, as this is the last place at which we expect to find cord wood. Henceforth we must cut our own fuel. There was a heavy frost this morning and overcoats are in demand. About noon today we reached the Big bend, and twenty passengers landed to walk across the four miles of hills, while the steamer took its forty-mile round-a-bout course to meet them. The hunters had hardly got out of hailing distance when the officers in the wheel house, discovered a herd of buffalo quietly feeding in a hollow not a mile from the straggling footmen.[11] It was eleven o'clock at night before the *Shreveport* reached the camp fire of the hunters, who had surrounded and captured a solitary buffalo calf, each man of the party claiming that he "did it." It is now the 20th of May, and we are getting into a country alive with game. While the boat was wooding, some passenger killed another buffalo calf, which we find is very savory meat.

It was very cold, wet, and disagreeable when we arrived opposite Fort Pierre, a trading station.[12] The water was too shallow near the fort to permit the boat to land near the Indian village. The boat's clerk and an interpreter went over in the yawl, while the expectant Indians lined the shore, dressed in their bright and varied costumes, giving a very pleasing effect. They found the camp under great excitement, as a few days before, a war party of Rees had killed their herdsman and stolen twenty horses. The body of the dead warrior was wrapped in a robe and placed on a raised scaffold, while the squaws with slashed and bleeding legs and arms wailed forth their tribute to the virtues and courage of the dead warrior. The braves left the mourning to the squaws, while they daubed their faces and bodies with vermillion and lamp-black, and made preparation to take the war path and avenge their losses. The whites at the trading post, as well as the Indians, had for a long time been expecting the arrival of the company stores, and in order to convince the Indians that there was no deception, and prevent any difficulty, the chiefs, Big Head, Black Eye, White Bear and an interpreter, were invited to cross over to the *Shreveport* and partake of hospitalities. Taking with them the father of the dead warrior, they entered the boat, and the clerk said that he felt of his scalp several times in crossing, to see if it was in place. The bereaved father was covered from head to foot with clay, as a sign of mourning, and if dirt is a symbol of grief, he must have been inconsolable.

Seated in the steamer's cabin around Capt. La Barge, each in turn took a whiff of smoke from the pipe of peace, and then in the sweet and melifluous accents peculiar to the race, announced with the usual amount of verbiage that they were glad to see us, that they were glad that there was to be opposition to the Fur company, that they had abundance of robes which they wished to trade for provisions and ammunition. They concluded their talk through Beaure [G. P. Beauvais?] as interpreter, by shaking the hand of the Captain, calling him "Father."[13] He in duty bound, made them the usual presents of tobacco and trinkets. These noble men of the plains looked at the peace offering with critical eyes, and then like Oliver Twist, asked for more; they could not afford to shake hands and go through with all this palaver so cheaply as that. But they didn't get any more, and were sent back in the yawl and we sailed on, happy to be relieved of them. We landed four passengers who intended to hunt all night and get on board before we sailed in the morning. The boat laid up at the mouth of the Cheyenne river, and our hunters came up having secured three antelopes and one buffalo. Plenty of fresh meat for the present.

In the morning we met a Mackinaw boat commanded by Jeff. Smith, from Fort Benton loaded with robes.[14] They were out of provisions which the boat furnished them with. They told us of the approach of a war party of Rees, going down to attack the Yankton Sioux, again. Some of our rebel sympathizers advised the party in the boat to be careful how they shouted for "Jeff" [Davis] unless they wished to get into some military prison down the river. Soon after supper we met the Sioux war party, in eight bull-boats. They fired a salute as a sign of peace and dexterously brought their rude boat along side the steamer, and all came on board. Several passengers thinking that we were attacked, were sprawled upon the cabin floor for safety from any stray shots. When they learned the true state of affairs, they loudly disclaimed being frightened, but did not like the careless manner in which the red-skins managed their guns. Red Fox, the Ree chief, said that the Sioux had stolen many of their horses, and he was going down to get even with them. They went through with the usual palaver with Capt. La Barge, who told them of the great benefit of the opposition company, gave them some presents, and they expressed their satisfaction by joining in a dance in the cabin. We improve the opportunity to study naval architecture as represented by Bull-boats.

A round crate of green willows is constructed like the frame work of a big basket, with a rim around the top formed by weaving in the pliable tops of the willows. Over this frame is tightly drawn a whole buffalo skin, flesh side out, which is carefully turned in at the top and securely fastened with sinews, thus forming a water-tight bowl, probably just like the one in which Mother Goose's "three wise men of Gotham" went to sea in. When thoroughly dry these are very light and serviceable, and large ones will carry three men. When on a horse stealing expedition the Indians take the greatest caution, lying concealed in the day time, and traveling by night. They take great risks, as if they are not successful in getting horses they are obliged to take the foot-path home.

Twenty-five days out finds us at Cannon Ball river, so named because of numberless perfectly round stones found in the stream, formed by action of the water upon a curious formation of rock. At deserted old Fort Clark, once the seat of the Mandans, with whom Lewis and Clark spent the winter of 1803-4 we pulled down one or two deserted cabins and took them on board for fuel.[15] We are meeting the carcasses of many dead buffalo floating down the stream with the floodwood, they having been drowned while trying to swim the river. We were favored with the company of another war party of Rees going down to entertain the Sioux near Yankton. They drank many cups of strong coffee, and one bold warrior complained of not feeling very well and deserting his companions, remained on board the steamer. While tied up for the night a few miles below Fort Berthold, three more bull boats under the command of a chief named Napoleon, took up their quarters with us. Napoleon was a fine looking and appearing fellow, dressed in a white shirt and straw hat, and had with him his son, Napoleon, Jr., a fine specimen of uncultivated *genus homo*. This party with their boats remained on the steamer until we reached Berthold, where upon our arrival we found a great gathering of Indians of many different tribes assembled to do us honor. Many of the big men came on board, held a pow-wow, drank immense quantities of coffee, and smoked the pipe of peace. The people were entirely out of coffee and sugar, and we left a large stock to be traded for. Many Indians crowded on board to cross the river to the Ree village, where we were compelled to go through the usual performance, and as we at last resumed our journey, were thankful that we were not likely to see any more Indians until we reached Fort Union.

The river is rising very fast and is full of driftwood. Game of many varieties is very plentiful and we are feasting upon antelope, venison, buffalo hump and tongue, beaver tail, catfish, whitefish and other delicacies of the country and season. June 2nd, we ran into vast numbers of buffalo swimming across the river. There was much excitement and every man on board killed a buffalo, or said that he had; but as only three were secured, some people must have been mistaken. That night we tied up at the mouth of the Yellowstone [River]. Undoubtedly some time in the future here will be a large city. The location is all that

Fort Union. Described in 1843 as "the principal and handsomest Trading post on the Missouri," Fort Union was located about six river miles above the mouth of the Yellowstone River and about nine hundred miles below Fort Benton, the destination of the steamer Emilie *taken by Thompson and his mining partners. An American Fur Company employee painted this pre-1860 view of the company headquarters.*

Montana Historical Society Photograph Archives, Helena

could be desired, and happy would be the man who knew just where to locate town lots. Before breakfast we tied up at Fort Union, finding but few Indians at this post.[16] We were soon on our way up the river, Fort Benton being but nine hundred miles distant. At old Fort Stewart we found Lemon & Larpenteur, the traders, in dire distress.[17] They had a Mackinaw boat all loaded with furs to send down the river. They had been having hard lines; had lost all their stock and were entirely out of provision. Said they had been living of late on boiled hides and other delicacies of like nature. Capt. La Barge left them a temporary supply, which they thankfully received. A few miles above, we passed the wreckage of the Fur company steamer *Chippewa*, which burned last year, together with the supplies for the upper fort.[18] At Fort Charles, a new post built by the Fur company in 1861, we lay all day, waiting for the companion steamer, the *Emilie*. Our men cut and piled a large lot of wood on the bank of the river, for the use of the boats. Finding a large pair of elk horns, some of the men nailed them to a tree and put up a notice that the wood was for the *Emilie*, and that the place was "Elkhorn Landing."

The bright and beautiful Sabbath morning of June 8th, finds us far away from any sanctuary but the noble cottonwoods, which are "God's first temples, not made with human hands." The sanctity of the day meets with due respect from the passengers, and many of them who never trouble themselves about attending divine service when at home, would be very glad to listen to even a dull sermon today. No signs of the *Emilie*, and we push on up a beautiful river now enshrined in most wonderful scenery. The indescribable bluffs and hills which have hemmed us in for several days have receded from the immediate banks, and we have beautiful sloping banks between which runs a swift flowing stream of clear water, and the days are warm and pleasant. The eternal hills are still within sight and more mountainous in their aspect, assuring us that we are gradually nearing the end of our journey, *the mountains*.

This morning we discovered a mother elk and her kid swimming the river. We secured the young one alive, and it will make a fine pet. The scenery daily grows in beauty. Of late we have been steaming southerly, and the season seems much more advanced. Wild roses are in bloom, goose-berries are ripe, and every green thing bears evidence of a warmer clime. The river grows more and more narrow and flows with more rapid current, but the water is clear and deep, and no one would suspect that it is a portion of the "Big Muddy." The hill tops are decked with pines, which largely cover their native ugliness. Elk, deer, buffalo and antelope are in abundance, and now and then a huge grizzly shows his form, or a mountain sheep springs nimbly up the mountain side. Those outcasts of creation, the sneaking wolves, are seen everywhere, and follow closely after every herd of buffalo seeking the calves or the wounded. We passed one some days since floating down the river on the carcass of a dead buffalo, Robinson Crusoe like, "he was monarch of all he surveyed."

We have lost our beautiful scenery and have entered into the *mauvaises terres* or 'bad lands.' The river makes its winding way through grim and barren hills circling under bold bluffs whose stained and broken fronts show the remains of layers of coal burned out in ages past. The side canyons support stunted pines, and luxuriant prickly pears which produce wax-like flowers both crimson and white. The river is high and it is with difficulty we are able to stem the tide. After a hard struggle we brought up at the foot of Bird's rapids, where we were compelled to cordelle up the yawl containing an anchor which was planted in the river above the falls, and from it a line was attached to a keg which floated to the steamer, and by the aid of the "nigger" engine she slowly made her way over the rushing waters.[19] It was a hard job, and to add to its discomforts it rained hard and was very cold and disagreeable weather. The Captain having his fighting spirit up, steamed on twelve miles to Dauphin's rapids and pulled over them in the same manner. While [we were] resting after these heavy labors, a Mackinaw boat hove in sight containing men from Captain John Mullan's command, at Bitter Root valley.[20] They declared that experienced miners were taking out from an ounce to an ounce and a half per day, which was elating news to us.

Sunday, June 15th was a cold rainy day, and we lay at the foot of Dead Man's rapids, dreading the day's work. All at once a mighty yell went up, as we heard the boom of cannon, and we saw the *Emilie* with colors flying come around the point below. Her pilot had seen the smoke of the *Shreveport* far ahead.

TWO

On the *Emilie*

THE FINE FOUR HUNDRED TON side wheel steamer, *EMILIE*, Captain Joseph La Barge, sailed from St. Louis Wednesday, May 14th, 1862, bound for the extreme head of navigation upon the Missouri river. Her commander had for years been in charge of boats of the American Fur company, and knew all the freaks and fancies of that changeable stream, and being financially interested in the result of his undertaking, we felt that we were setting out upon our long voyage under most encouraging conditions. It was near four o'clock in the afternoon before the last passenger and the last dray load of freight, came on board. The levee was crowded with friends of the one hundred and fifty passengers on the boat, and the idlers of the city had gathered in great numbers, as the press had given much publicity to the novel undertaking. Amid the cheers of the people, the booming of cannon, the waving of hats and handkerchiefs, the *Emilie* slowly moved out into the Mississippi, and began her three thousand mile trip.

The steamer carried three hundred tons of Indian goods, general merchandise, miners tools, implements and provisions, wagons, horses and mules, and generally, things which were thought to be most desirable in opening up a new country. The exploring party of The American Exploring and Mineral Company, consisted of Thomas C. Willard, George P. King, Henry King, Henry C. Lynch, Edward H. Mead,[1] Henry B. Bryan, Frank R. Madison, Prof. Wm. H. Bell, Henry B. Watkins, George McLagan, Wm. C. Gould, and Francis M. Thompson. Mr. Gould was accompanied by his wife. We had a complete mining outfit, a year's supply of clothing and provisions, a good Studebaker wagon, two sets of double harness, but no horses or mules.

There were several smaller parties on the steamer, that of Chapman, Clow and Jones being admirably fitted out, and they were wise enough to take four good mules along with them. Col. [Darius] Hunkins also had a good team with him.[2] The trip along the lower river was not of unusual interest, excepting that the burned and ruined buildings along the river banks brought altogether too forcibly to mind, the terrible contest in which the government was engaged for the preservation of the union. As secretary of the expedition I kept an official diary of the trip, but as its publication would be largely a repetition of the account already given of the trip of our consort, the *Shreveport*, its insertion is omitted.

Whenever necessity required, the *Emilie* would run her nose into the bank at some wood yard, and off would file forty or fifty roustabouts, dressed in fancy shirts of rainbow hues, which are destined ere long to charm the eye of many a squaw, and as they toted on board huge backloads of wood, pop! pop! would go the revolvers and rifles of the valorous would-be hunters and miners, who shot at every conceivable object which presented itself as a target. Wood was very scarce, and the price seemed high, but as the men were largely in the rebel or the Union armies, there was no relief. The situation reminded me of a story of early days on the Ohio river, when wild cat money was used as currency, the larger portion being almost worthless. The captain of an Ohio river boat seeing a fine lot of wood on the river bank, hailed the supposed proprietor; "Is that wood for sale?" "Yes!" "How much a cord?" The granger asked "What ye going to pay in?" "Oh! Gallipolis money!" "Then it's cord for cord!" We came to St. Joseph on Sunday morning, and the boom of our cannon brought to the levee so many people that but few could have been left in attendance at divine service. Another salute was given as we steamed up the river.

At Omaha we found encamped about eighty teams, the owners being bound overland to Oregon and Washington territories. We are told that fifteen hundred teams have already crossed the river, bound for the new mines. We learn that the Fur company steamer is but two days ahead of us, and we feel certain to overtake her very soon. At a wooding place on the Iowa side of the river, I found in the woods a log house, the owner of which told me he was from Virginia. He said that he had never seen a railroad engine, but that a telegraph line did once overtake him, but he sold out and moved away. He "reckoned" that if the gold mines paid, he would have to move on; too many people for him; they scared all the game.

We stopped at the Omaha Indian agency—Blackbird landing— a beautiful place. Many mounted Indians dressed in all their finery, came cantering down to the boat, but having no interpreter we could not talk with them. There are beautiful bluffs on the Nebraska side, and upon the very highest point, is the grave of the great chief Black Bird. He died in 1800 and was buried upright upon his horse. He was held in the utmost awe by his nation, for it was observed that he could foretell the approaching death of any member of the tribe without fail. The secret of his power lay in a quantity of arsenic supplied to him by a merciless trader.[3]

At another wooding place, I learned from the old lady occupying the woodman's cabin, that they were from Marlow, New Hampshire. She said that the Indians made them no trouble, but that wolves and wild cats played havoc with their small stock. Not far below Sioux city we saw on the Iowa side of the river, standing upon a steep bluff, a post placed there to mark the spot where Sergeant Floyd of Lewis and Clark's expedition was buried.[4] The government agent, Mr. Hedges [Cornelius Hedges?], from Cincinnati was our fellow passenger and we had on board of large lot of goods for his Indians. Here, for the first time, I saw the progeny of a negro and an Indian squaw, a most interesting specimen of humanity. The agent informed me that the head chief of the Indians had recently died, and that while he was very sick he had sent for him, and asked that he might be buried like a Christian. The chief's son was away on a war expedition when his father died, and the agent, true to his promise had a good casket prepared for the burial of the chief and his remains received Christian burial. A few weeks after, the son returned and immediately had his father's remains disinterred, and wrapping the body in skins and a buffalo robe, he placed them upon a high scaffold which he had prepared, according to the custom of the tribe. At Fort Randall we were welcomed by the garrison composed of Iowa volunteers.[5] Here the government had a good steam saw mill and a grist mill in operation. We crossed the river and tied up for the night near an encampment of one hundred lodges of Sioux. Madison Carr, a half breed, and claiming to be a sub-chief of these Indians had been a passenger on the *Emilie*, and he visited many of the lodges with us. I greatly amused the little Indian boys by playing on a big jews-harp, and finally got a number to dance to my music. The men were finely formed, strong and lusty, and were clothed with breech-cloth and a robe thrown over their shoulders, so arranged as to show any scars they had received in battle. The squaws wore cloth or skin shirts and leggings, sometimes ornamented with porcupine quills, or beads, or both. I was surprised and somewhat disappointed not to find among the many whom I saw, a single squaw who could lay any claim to even passable good looks. We encountered many severe wind storms and during the trip were several times compelled to tie up to escape danger of being wrecked. During one storm our old dog Jack was so frightened that we had to take him into our state room in order to pacify him. The river is full of small islands and it was very difficult to decide which was the proper channel to undertake to ascend, and after running up a certain one for an hour, it was frequently necessary to return and try another. High bluffs along the river abound, barren and streaked with burned out layers of coal. I climbed to the top of a high barren bluff, only to find other similar ones beyond of greater height. At the "great bend" fifty bold pioneers took to the cut off, the captain assuring us that he would meet us by sunset. A stray Indian went along, and after a four-mile march we came to the river without seeing so much as a jack-rabbit for our pains. No boat appeared and building a floodwood fire we spent a cold, hungry, miserable night. Many were frightened because the Indian abandoned the camp, he evidently fearing that our big fire would attract hostile Indians. On the fertile bottom across the river, we saw a large herd of wild ponies, and we picked up many fine specimens of fossil fishes. When the *Emilie* came to us about nine o'clock in the morning, she was enthusiastically greeted by a hungry set of explorers. She had been lying on a sand bar the greater part of the night.

Just above old Fort Medicine, of which nothing remained but an old chimney and one or two cabins nearly undermined by the falling banks of the river, we ran on a sand bar at the head of an island, and after getting free we were obliged to tie up for the night. In the morning another chute was tried with no better success. The captain was only too glad to run ashore and let forty passengers and all the live stock disembark to march twelve miles across a neck of land to a point opposite Fort Pierre, where the boat would land and take us on board. Each man took his gun and started. I thought that it would be a fine thing to ride one of the big mules. Catching him and fixing the halter he wore into a kind of bridle, I mounted, and my steed was off in a moment to join his mate who had got some distance ahead. I had no control over him whatever, but thought I could ride as fast as he could run. The grass was quite high on the river bottom, and unexpectedly to the mule as well as myself, we came to the edge of a deep cut in the sod and the mule stopped as suddenly as though dead, while his rider still continued his journey for many feet, rolling over and over as he struck the turf. The result to the rider was a badly sprained ankle, and to the mule freedom and the gleeful greeting of his mate. I turned to look for the steamer, but she had gone down the river to hunt up a new channel. Nothing remained for me but to hobble the twelve miles to the appointed rendezvous. Using my rifle as a crutch, I made the painful journey lagging far behind my companions. The people at Fort Pierre having discovered us, we waved peace signals, and a boat came over in which was La Troube, a half breed, and the big Indians Bare-foot, Starving-man, Bear that Surprises, Dirty-leg, Man-who-sits-high-in-the-tree, and another whose name I have forgotten. When they found that we were from the *Emilie*, LaTroube said they would go down and meet her. All my companions insisted that I should go with them that I might get treatment for my ankle which was giving me intense pain. Joining the Sioux party we struck across the river and kept under the right bank, only one pair of oars being worked, and all the other Indians sitting with their guns cocked and their sharp eyes watching for a war party of Rees who had a day or two before killed one of their men and stolen about twenty horses. I hardly enjoyed the situation, and was heartily glad to discover their lights burning on the *Emilie*, which was several miles below where she had been when we left her.

It had begun to rain, and our humane captain ordered a boat's crew to take blankets and provisions and find the hungry, tentless, passengers at "starvation camp" but the boat returned about three o'clock in the morning having been unable to discover the location. The *Emilie* had good luck in the morning finding a way over the shoals, and we were most warmly received by our starving comrades. Taking them on, we crossed over to Fort Pierre, a Fur company post, where we found about 1600 Indians of mixed Sioux tribes. While lying here our old dog Jack pitched on to an Indian cur which ventured on board the boat, and during the melee Captain La Barge got badly bitten, and in his rage he pitched the old dog overboard and shot at him as he swam, but he reached the shore and probably had many stout battles before he established himself as a Sioux leader.

The next day buffalo were discovered, and one came slowly down to the river and plunged in, and was nearly half across the river before the boat came up with him. The fusillade was enormous and each 'man behind the gun' claimed that his was the fatal shot. Being in want of meat, the captain tied up and by the help of the "nigger" [engine] the huge beast was hoisted on board. Only seven shots had struck the brute among the hundreds which were fired. The careless shooting resulted in the calling of a mass meeting of the passengers and the choice of Captain Galpin to enforce more safe and sane conditions. Sundays were passed in comparative quiet, and the passengers were apparently generally interested in religious services held by Rev. John Francis, a Welsh preacher of great merit, who was a fellow passenger, and well adapted to make himself popular with a mixed assembly, like that gathered on the *Emilie*.

One day we discovered on the river bank ahead, a large party of the Indians, who desired the boat to stop and take them on board. The captain considering that we were two hundred miles from any aid in case of trouble, kept on his way. The Indians showed their displeasure by aiming their guns at us and brandishing their tomahawks, but when they saw the men getting the cannons ready for action, they showed peace signals. They may wreak their vengeance upon some other party not so well prepared to resist their demands. Prof. Bell of our party killed an elk which was swimming the river, and the boat was stopped to take this addition to our larder on board.

June 4th, we were awakened at day-light by the cry, "buffalo!" "buffalo!" and immediately the boat ran into a herd containing hundreds swimming the river. The water seemed alive with them, old bulls, cows, and calves swimming in the eddy formed by the body of their mother, and the wheels of the steamer had to be stopped, lest the paddles be broken on the horns of the animals. The shooting was kept under control, and only seven were killed, four of which were secured and hoisted on board. A yearling was taken on board alive, but proved so full of fight, that the captain fearing that some person would be hurt by it, had it butchered. Numerous wolves followed the herd and furnished legitimate targets for the marksmen. At old Fort Clark we pulled down two of the deserted houses for fuel.[6] There were several large circular pole and dirt houses still standing, each large enough to hold twenty or thirty Indians and four or five horses. Nearly the whole nation of the Mandans were swept away by smallpox a few years since.[7] The elevated platforms where the dead had been buried had rotted away, and skulls and other bones lay scattered about the prairie.

At Fort Berthold we overtook the Fur company boat, *Spread Eagle*, on which was Mr. Reed the Indian agent, to the upper river tribes.[8] He was holding a grand council, which I attended and heard an impassioned speech from Running Antelope, a famous Indian orator. He stoutly objected to having the boats take arms, ammunition, and supplies, to the upper Indians who came down and made war upon the lower tribes. A half breed, Charlie, leaves us here and is to go overland to the Milk river, and gather in a lot of Indian ponies on the way, to trade to the tenderfeet.[9] On June 6th, the *Spread Eagle* and her companion, the *Key West*, and the *Emilie* all lay together at night. The Fur Company boats had killed but one buffalo and we supplied them with meat. Indians, squaws and bucks, on our boat ate the raw livers and unborn fawn of elk and deer, and men familiar with their habits declare that when short of meat they leave absolutely nothing but skin and bones of such game as they may secure.

There is much jealousy between the two fur companies, the American Fur company feeling that La Barge Harkness & Co., are intruding upon their established rights. Not much respect for law exists in these wild regions, and some are apprehending serious trouble. The feeling culminated to-day. The *Spread Eagle* got away a few minutes before the *Emilie*, which was followed by the *Key West*. After running a few miles the *Emilie* passed the *Spread Eagle*, but running on to a sand bar, some time was lost, and she again had to fall behind her rival. Going over to the side of the river where the *Spread Eagle* was, the *Emilie* putting on full speed soon came along side, and the two boats kept side by side for a mile or more, but reaching a bend in the river favorable for the *Spread Eagle* (or "Buzzard" as we called her) she forged ahead, but the *Emilie* kept her nose close to the stern of the *S. E.* She could not run as fast as the *Emilie*, and her pilot knew it, so to keep her in the rear, the channel

being narrow, he kept his boat running in a zig-zag course so
as to occupy the channel. At last Capt. La Barge seeing a chance
pushed the *Emilie* along side the *Spread Eagle*, when the pilot
of that boat turned her nose against the *Emilie* and nearly
crowded her on shore. Capt. La Barge swore a big French oath
and grasping his rifle aimed it at the offending pilot's head, but
his son caught it from him, the *Emilie*'s wheels stopped and the
Spread Eagle had the river for a short time.[10] The *Emilie* ran
until later in the evening [again passing the *Spread Eagle*?] and
we saw no more of the *Spread Eagle* until we had been some
time at Fort Benton. Reports are rife that Fur company men
have said that the *Emilie* would be sunk before she reached
Fort Benton. The French blood of Captain La Barge took fire,
and he declared that he would fill the next man with buck shot,
who undertook to wreck his boat. Thousands of buffalo are to
be seen upon the river banks and crossing from one side to the
other. The wheels are often stopped out of pity for the beasts as
well as to save injury to the boat. A huge grizzly, awkwardly
ambled away from the river bank, and an eagle surveyed us
from her nest in the Vermillion cliffs.

June 7th we met a Mackinaw boat containing ten men and a
large lot of furs. The crew were anxious for war news, having
heard nothing for a year. Three days later we passed the mouth
of the Yellowstone and tied up at Fort Union. The post has done
but little trading for a year, and only four Indians were present
at the camp. While here, Mr. Francis held another of his popular
services. At the mouth of Milk river, Mr. Galpin and four others
with five horses, two mules and a wagon, left the steamer to
drive 275 miles to Fort Benton. They hope to meet Indians and
trade for ponies to sell to the *to be* stranded passengers.

One day a nice looking log cabin was discovered on the southerly side of the river, and landing, it was found to be the home of

Dubois, a Frenchman noted as an expert hunter.[11] Captain La Barge purchased all his furs and taking him, his squaw, papoose, horses, cart, and a buffalo calf on board steamed on up the river. He had killed during the winter eleven hundred wolves by poison, and bear, beaver, buffalo, elk and deer in large numbers. I killed a buffalo which was swimming in the river, and others some on the shore. The one I shot drifted away down the river, but as soon as the boat struck the river bank, a young Indian who was on board, leaped ashore and running down the stream, jumped in and was soon on the floating carcass, and lashed it to some overhanging brush. Soon after the steamer dropped down the stream and took both the dead buffalo and the living Indian on board. Just above, we came upon five more, swimming the river, one of which was wounded before reaching the river bank, but still able to run as fast as a horse. As the steamer turned to the shore, a stag hound owned by a passenger was let loose, and away he went after the frightened buffalo and soon had him at bay. Some person killed the monster with a revolver, and a long line was brought from the boat and the carcass was snaked by willing men to the boat.

As we sailed up the never-ending river, one day excitement arose, caused by some sharp-eyed tenderfoot sighting a bear swimming the stream far ahead of the boat. A fusillade began and the supposed bear made for the shore, bullets dropping all around him in the river. Reaching the shore as he rose from the water the *bear* was discovered to be a buffalo calf. His lucky escape was greeted with shouts and cheers, while his discoverer felt exceedingly small. The weather for the last few days has been horrid, wet, and cold. Venison has been plenty for some days past, an agreeable change from buffalo hump and steak. An epidemic of fishing has struck the passengers, and some fished all night, catching over 300 pounds.[12]

A Mackinaw boat which passed down the river reported the *Shreveport* about fifty miles ahead of us. The hills have closed down upon the river and the magnificent bluffs are several hundred feet in height. The clear and sparkling water runs very swiftly, and small rapids are met at every turn. We reached the first important rapids near night, and the *Emilie* trembling under the heavy head of steam, bravely entered the fight. For a half hour at a time she hardly gained a foot in her progress, but by the free use of tar and rosin under her boilers she finally succeeded in passing over the crest of the fall, the victory being cheered by all on board. Tying up for the night ten miles above the rapid some forty or fifty of the passengers climbed to the top of one of the high hills. The view from the summit was marvelous, but no snowy mountains could be seen. The winding river looked like a canal.

Sunday morning the 15th of June, the good ship *Emilie* worked her way over the second rapids before her passengers were up, and soon after breakfast the pilot announced that he saw the smoke of the *Shreveport*. Cheers broke forth from the weary passengers, and the cannon was fired to give notice of our approach. The *Shreveport* was lying at the foot of the third rapids, and when the *Emilie* came alongside, mingled greetings, hootings, howlings, and cannon firing, ended in a general pow-wow. After an hour of visiting, preparations were made for getting the boats over the rapids. The steamers lay at the foot of a long steep sliding bank with a buffalo trail running above the river which was several inches deep with mud, and a cold rain was adding to disagreeable conditions. Without complaint, in order to lighten the boat, at least 200 men took to the path at the captain's request, and standing in the mud and rain we watched the efforts made to run the rapids. Using rosin and pitch, the smoke from which belched forth from the tall funnels of the *Emilie*, she made satisfactory progress until she reached the very swiftest part, then

Fort Benton. Thompson describes their historic arrival at Fort Benton, an American Fur Company trading post: "About two o'clock in the afternoon of June 17th, 1862, the Emilie *and the* Shreveport *ran their noses upon the bank of the Missouri at Fort Benton, the first steamers ever reaching that point."*

From Thomas F. Meagher, "Rides through Montana,"
Harper's Monthly, October 1867, 570

wavered and fell back. By signs we finally induced the pilot to work the boat over toward us and to throw us a line, which strategy having been accomplished, the half frozen men easily cordelled the boat over the crest into stiller water. The *Emilie* then dropped an anchor and attaching a long line to a keg, let it float down to the *Shreveport*, which came over by the aid of her "nigger" engine. The same tactics were repeated at the dreaded "Dead Man's Rapids" and again repeated the next day at the rapids a mile or two below Fort Benton. That evening, Mr. Francis preached to us, his appropriate theme being "Faith and Works." We were a sorry looking lot of first-class passengers when we filed on board the boats, after playing canal horse in the rain and mud.

About two o'clock in the afternoon of June 17th, 1862, the *Emilie* and the *Shreveport* ran their noses upon the bank of the Missouri at Fort Benton, the first steamers ever reaching that point. A hundred Indians on horseback had come down to meet us, when our boats were discovered below the rapids, and riding along the river bank escorted us to the landing. The young bucks, gaily decked out and bedaubed with ochre and lampblack, exhibited masterly feats of horseman-ship, and the old battle-scarred warriors rode along in conscious dignity. After an hour's stop at [Fort] Benton, the *Emilie* moved up above the ruins of old Fort Campbell, (perhaps a mile above the first landing,) and began to unload her cargo. Here La Barge, Harkness & Co., propose to build a trading house, the adobe walls of old Fort Campbell being a safe place of retreat, in case of hostile attack.[13]

Among the passengers who made the trip with no expectation of remaining in the country, was Chancellor Hoyt, the honored chief of the Washington University of St. Louis.[14] Accompanied by his good wife, he made the excursion by the advice of his physician, seeking rest for an overworked body and brain. In order to add to their comfort, Captain La Barge erected a temporary partition across the rear of the long cabin, so as to secure privacy and abundant room for his distinguished guests. President Hoyt gave his impressions of the long journey in a letter to the *St. Louis Democrat*, which was as follows:—

TRIP TO THE HEAD WATERS OF THE MISSOURI

Editors Missouri Democrat:—

A voyage in a first-class steamer of three thousand one hundred miles on one of the *branches* of an American river, is an event in the history of navigation of sufficient interest, perhaps, to justify us in saying a few words about it in the DEMOCRAT.

OUR BOAT,

The *Emilie*, of four hundred tons burthen by measurement, and drawing about three and a half feet of water, is the first side-wheel steamer which ever found its way to the head waters of the Missouri. She carried up eighty-five cabin passengers at one hundred dollars per head, and fifty-three on the deck, at a rate which we did not learn, together with three hundred tons of freight at ten cents per pound. The boat must have paid for itself, and will henceforth "run on velvet."

The Captain, Joseph La Barge, is a skillful navigator and a courteous gentleman, and his subordinate officers thoroughly competent to their places.

THE PASSENGERS,

aside from a few invalids, were gold seekers, as fine a set of men, with a few whiskey-loving exceptions, as were ever seen together on a steamboat. They were generally united in companies for mutual assistance and protection, though occasionally one went resolutely "on his own personal curve." The American Mining and Exploring Company, under the leadership of Captain Willard, contains twelve active members and one of Cicero's *impedimenta*.[15] The outfit of this company is very good with the important exception of means of transportation; but we presume that this lack may be supplied, though perhaps at exorbitant cost, from the Indian ponies with which the country abounds.

We can hardly imagine that a company containing such men as the high-minded and efficient Thompson, the good-natured and energetic Meade, the versatile Watkins, and reliable Gould, should fail in their undertakings unless there should prove to be some radical defect in the constitution which holds them together. A small company, consisting of Messrs. Chapman,

Clow and Jones, is undoubtedly the best-fitted in all respects for the work before them. They had no whisky in their spacious tent, but they had four stalwart mules picketed in the grass waiting to take them and their baggage to their place of destination. When we say that their outfit was provided by Giles F. Filley, Esq., of this city, it will readily be inferred that not a single article necessary for use or comfort was omitted.[16] They will be accompanied by Rev. Mr. Francis, a Welsh clergyman of rare powers of adaptation, who conducted our Sabbath exercises on the boat, and who goes to the mines with the unselfish hope of doing good.

This company will act in concert with another company under the lead of a Mr. Hurlbut, an intelligent miner of large experience. If there is any gold in this far-off mountain region, these men, we predict, will find it. There were several other companies, but we did not get sufficiently acquainted with their members to be able to speak of them intelligently. We remember there was a company with a large outfit, led by a Colonel Hunkins. There was another consisting of Messrs. Lansing, Arnold, and others.

Mr. Arnold, an exceedingly ingenious mechanic in wood and iron, takes with him to the mines his wife, a most genial and accomplished lady, and his little daughter, who was the pet of the boat. Besides the gold seekers, there was a Mr. Vail, who, with his family, was going to oversee the government farm, an establishment on Sun river, about sixty miles from Fort La Barge, intended to be an agent in civilizing the Indians, especially the Black Feet, Piegans and Bloods, who speak a common dialect. We have little faith in the success of the enterprise.

THE MISSOURI

Is, undoubtedly, the muddiest, and crookedest, and swiftest, and snaggiest river on the globe. The clayey banks are constantly falling in, and mingling with the water, render it as impervious to human vision as mush and molasses. Some of the bends form peninsulas, not more than five miles across the isthmus or neck, while it is thirty-five by the river. Several of the passengers at different times varied the monotony of the voyage by shouldering their rifles and taking these short cuts. On one occasion some thirty of them, after completing their march, were compelled to spend the night on a bleak bluff, supperless and unblanketed, in a violent thunder storm, the boat failing to reach them in consequence of getting "stalled" on a sand-bar. We observed that these adventurers the next morning ate their fried bacon and corn bread with unusual relish and in fabulous quantity.

The swiftness of the current, coupled with opposing snags and sand bars, and the necessity of stopping to chop our own wood for the engine more than half the way, prevented us from making much more than ninety miles per day, so that the voyage up occupied us nearly thirty-four days—a time sufficient for three voyages across the Atlantic. We reached home, after remaining two days at Fort Benton, July 2d, the thirteenth day from starting. The whole trip, therefore, making no deductions for delays at trading posts and for involuntary detentions from accidents, was just seven weeks long. We lay more than a day on one sand bar somewhere in the region of Fort Pierre, and spent at least half a day in mending a rivet hole in the boiler. We "tied up" every night. On our return we came at railroad speed, some days making three hundred miles.

THE SCENERY

along the river is not unworthy of notice. The banks in Missouri, Kansas, Iowa, Nebraska, and for a considerable distance in the immense Territory of Dacotah, are not very grand, but they are exceedingly green. Everything indicates a region of unsurpassed fertility, waiting in its primeval solitudes for the industrious hand of the white man. From this point to a point

some two or three hundred miles above the mouth of the Yellow
Stone, a distance of more than a thousand miles, the river banks
are high and precipitous bluffs, bold and barren, looking down
upon the *voyageur* morning, noon and night, in dull and ever-
lasting monotony. There may be productive lands beyond them,
but we infer from the epithet, *mauvaise terres*, applied by the
French explorers to a large portion of this region, that it is com-
paratively worthless for cultivation. Throughout the last five
hundred miles of our trip, the scenery is grand and striking beyond description. Nature seems to have wrought with human
hands, and with the implements of human art. Red sandstone
urns of various sizes, apparently as perfect in form as if chiseled
under the eye of Powers or Story, crown the apex of conical hills
on each side of the river.[17] Castellated turrets and frowning battle-
ments, partially crumbled, beguile you for the moment into the
belief that you are traveling amidst the ruins of dilapidated for-
tresses and castles in the old world. The river, in two or three
instances, seems, in some remote period, to have broken through
remarkable stone walls, running across the river at right angles,
and extending indefinitely over the bluffs into the prairie. These
walls are about three feet thick, with smooth parallel faces, as if
hammered, and sometimes reaching a height of twenty or thirty
feet. Whether nature, in some masonic freak, or man in the times
beyond the flood, built these walls, we can only say that the
master-builder, whoever he was, "broke joints," and did his work
well.[18] The bottom lands are frequently covered with the inevitable cottonwood, a species of poplar, filled at maturity with
little green bolls, which open in June and whiten the air with
their thistle-like down. A sort of red willow far up the river supplies the Indians with a tobacco which they call "Kinnikinick."
Prickly pear abounds in infinite varieties, to the great disgust of
the Indians, whose moccasins are a poor defense against their

terrible spikes. We observed on the banks, among other flowers, modest mountain lilies and the showy porcupine plant; but we learned little of the geology of the country, and still less of its flora.

OF THE FAUNA

of the country, we saw specimens of almost every variety known in North America. We shot at least thirty buffaloes from the boat, and lassoed and brought home eight calves. The buffalo is a magnificent beast, physically, but, like some large men, does not shine intellectually.

The net weight of one big bull dressed on the boat was estimated at twelve hundred pounds They will cross the river at improper times, and that, too, in front of the boat. Some of the droves on the bottoms and adjoining slopes must have numbered nearly two thousand. The elk, with its broad-branching antlers, the antelope, with "its soft dark eye;" the wolf, both mountain and prairie, over whose sneaking pursuit of some wounded or defenceless animal, the turkey buzzard hovers and circles with unflagging interest; the beaver, whose two chisel-like teeth will fell a cotton-wood tree a foot in diameter, as handsomely, if not quite as quickly, as the wood chopper; the black-tailed deer, with its scentless hind-feet—all alike fell before the deadly aim of our sportsmen. We were also visited by the black bear and the mountain sheep, with its enormous horns, upon which he hurls himself when springing from peak to peak among the precipitous heights which he frequents. We brought back with us to St. Joe, a grizzly bear, the most vicious brute on the globe, and took home three amiable young wolves, a prairie dog looking more like a huge aldermanic grey squirrel than it does like a dog, two cat-owls, the sharp-sightedness of whose great yellow eyes in the dark furnished Homer with an epithet for his Atheme—"the bright-eyed," not the "blue-eyed Minerva."

THE ATMOSPHERE

Is exceedingly dry and pure. Buffalo tongues and strips of meat hung in the sun will be dried through and thoroughly cured in a few days without a speck of salt. So far as our observation went, the air is too bracing for pulmonary invalids, irritating instead of soothing the lungs. We say most earnestly to all sick men, especially to those troubled with organic difficulties in the chest, disbelieve all the stories told you by kind friends of marvelous cures effected by change of air, and *stay at home.* You cannot heal an old fever-sore by fanning it with a new fan.

THE FORTS,

so-called, are, with the exception of the Government fort, Randall, mere trading posts, occupied by the Indians, half breeds, horses and wolf dogs, living together within the same high inclosure in *fragrant* and harmonious fellowship. There is not a livery stable in this city which is not a more desirable place to live in than either Fort Benton, Fort Union or Fort Berthold. About a mile above Fort Benton we dedicated, in honor of our worthy captain, a new fort—Fort La Barge—which, we trust will be in point of neatness and comfort, an exception to the filthy lairs to which we have referred. The passengers of the *Shreveport,* which we had overtaken and brought along with us, assisted at the rites. Dr. McKellops presided, and brief speeches, under the quiet stars, amid the white tents of the gold seekers dotting the bottom lands, were made by Rev. Mr. Francis and Messrs. Barrell, Meade, Chapman, and others, and the whole affair passed off pleasantly, with hearty cheers for the new fort, the captain, the Union, and the old flag waving over us.[19] From the bluffs of this point the Rocky Mountain chain is distinctly visible, its snowy peaks looming up in the western horizon in solitary and majestic grandeur.

INDIANS

of numerous tribes were constantly visiting the boat after we reached the Yanckton Sioux reservation. The chiefs and braves of the Sioux, Mandans, Ricarees, *Gros Ventres*, Crows, Bloods, Piegans, Blackfeet, and others, came on board and accompanied us, in greater or less numbers, throughout our voyage. The *Gros Ventre* chief and squaw who came to this city are the best specimens we saw on the trip. At all the principal ports the boat was thronged by the inevitable red-skins. Their black eyes were peering into every nook and cranny, and their light fingers did not fail to appropriate any attractive articles which might be "lying round loose." Our own room, which had been made by parting off the after cabin, contained three windows, all of which were turned into *tableaux* frames, each being filled with swart, curious faces, whose imperturbable stare after a few hours became disagreeable. The personal appearance of the Indians is in the highest degree grotesque and fantastic. There is with them no fashion in dress, no aping of upper tendom, but each one arrays himself as seemeth best in his own eyes. One wraps a bead-bespangled government blanket about him and lies down to pleasant dreams; another disports himself in the sultry noon in a huge buffalo robe; another exults in a bobtailed military coat buttoned up to his chin with brass buttons, and reaching almost down to his hips; another rejoices in a pair of leggings and wolf-skin cap; another struts about in a breech-cloth of limited dimensions and uncertain tenure of position, and another riots in un-fig-leafed Paradisaical freedom. The women are as brawny and muscular as their stalwart lords, and dress themselves with as little taste and decency. Pigments are in great demand. The squaws, instead of *rouging* their cheeks like civilized ladies, bedaub their foreheads and eyebrows with a fiery red paint. This is the favorite color of the braves, and they spread it on thick just before starting on a war expedition. We noticed one great bare-chested fellow, whose ugly face was painted a coal black, his arms and breast being striped with the same color, like a gridiron. He looked like the devil as represented in the ancient Mysteries.

The food of the Indians consists largely of wild meat, which, without the intervention of knives, forks or tables, they devour both cooked and raw. We saw them ourselves, on several occasions, gobble down raw, the half washed tripe and liver, still palpitating with the life of animals shot from the boat. A hole in the ground or in the center of a log serves as a cooking stove, which, together with a large tin pan, into which they throw their broiled meat, and out of which they eat it, constitutes the bulk of their household furniture. The squaws also raise some corn, which they dry on a scaffolding above their hovels and then bury it in holes in the ground. When they wish to use it they grind or pound it with a large pestle and mortar, a good specimen of which, found at an abandoned fort, has been presented by Mr. Clow, to Washington University. The lodges scattered along the river banks, whether mud huts or tents, are almost invariably dens of filth and vermin. When the heads of the inmates become over populous, they hunt each other's domain, and devour, uncooked, the prey which they capture. An exhibition of this sort on the boat, reminded us of the famous riddle proposed by some fisher-man to old Homer, who is said to die of vexation, because he could not guess it. The morals of the Indians according to any standard with which we are acquainted is far below zero. With no delicacy, no sense of beauty and purity, no conception of self-sacrifice and forgiveness, they are gross in all their appetites, revengeful, treacherous and bloody. We saw a half-breed trying to sell his two daughters to a negro servant on the boat, for a certain amount of whisky, and the bar-keeper was offered the squaw of a Blackfoot for a single glass of "rot-gut."

But if we should discuss, however briefly, all the Indian characteristics which attracted our attention, we should write a volume. We will only say, in conclusion, that, in our judgment, sympathy and sentiment are wasted upon them, and that the narratives of Catlin and Bryant, and the poetry of Longfellow and Colton, are alike the unreal and delusive creations of a riotous imagination.[20]

THREE

Fort Benton and the
Head Waters of the Missouri

FORT BENTON, OWNED BY THE American Fur Company, is the head-quarters of the Indian trade in this region, and thus a place of much importance. It is built of adobies, with bastions and port holes, and a few determined men ought to be able to defend it against any force which the Indians can bring against it.[1] This region abounds in tales of tragic and romantic events. Once the country of the Flatheads, now domiciled west of the Rocky mountains, by conquest, it became the home of the related tribes known as Bloods, Piegans and Blackfeet. The *Gros Ventres* living below the mouth of Milk river, are also related to these tribes, and speak the same language. Lewis and Clark were probably the first white men who came in contact with these people, and their acquaintance commenced with tragedy. The first party they met boldly took possession of two of Captain Lewis's horses and in the struggle for their recovery, two Indians were killed.[2]

In 1810, two venturesome traders, named Ashley and Henry, erected a defensible trading post near the Three Forks of the Missouri, expecting a large trade with the Crows and Blackfeet, but their venture was a failure, as was also a similar attempt made in 1822 by others for the establishment of trade in this region.[3] But in 1831, James Kipp, a trader at Fort Union, filling Mackinaws with "trade goods" enlisted seventy-five men in his service and they trailed their boats to the mouth of the Marias (about 30 miles below Benton) where they built a post and called it Fort Piegan, in honor of the local Indians, and succeeded in establishing a very profitable business. In the spring [Kipp] returned to Fort Union, with the peltries he had gathered, and re-loading his boats with Indian goods he with sixty men started upon his return up the river. Ill luck attended him, and by a sudden storm his boats were wrecked and all his goods were lost. Runners were sent to Fort Union and a new stock in trade was dispatched up the river under charge of David D. Mitchell, who succeeded Kipp as chief trader. Not liking the location of Kipp's fort, he built a new one on the south side of the Missouri and named it Fort McKenzie.[4] With Mitchell, at this time went Major Alexander Culbertson, whose advent proved an important factor in subsequent events in the valley of the upper Missouri, as, for thirty years he was the most important man in the whole region.[5] Maximillian, prince of Weid [Wied], and his suite, made Fort McKenzie their head-quarters for a season, and while here they had opportunity to witness and take part in an Indian battle. Thirty lodges of Piegan's had pitched their lodges near the walls of the fort, and were busily engaged in exchanging their furs for such articles of trade as they desired. All at once fifteen hundred Assiniboines came rushing toward the fort, the inmates of which thought they were the party to be attacked, and opened upon the raiders with seventy five guns. Seizing the first gun at hand the prince rammed down a big charge, put the piece to his shoulder and sighting through a port hole at a hideously painted warrior, fired. The recoil of the double loaded gun knocked the prince across the bastion and striking the opposite wall he was for a few moments stunned, but recovered consciousness and found that his gun was already loaded when he took it. One Assiniboine was killed, perhaps by the excited prince. It was soon apparent that the attack was upon the Piegan camp, and the entrance gate was thrown open, and in the rush for safety, the Piegan squaws loaded down with saddles and household utensils, so blocked up the way that twenty-five men, women and children of the tribe were slaughtered at the very gate of the fort. The Piegans traded at the fort; the Assiniboines did not; therefore it was good policy for the traders to aid the Piegans; so Culbertson and Mitchell with some of their men joined a large party who were camped nearby at Cracon-du Nez, in an attack upon the Assiniboine camp.[6] The battle lasted amid the broken grounds all day, and when the Assiniboines withdrew they took with them forty Piegan scalps, and left but eight of their own in the hands of their enemies. The whites escaped injury.[7]

The next year Major Culbertson was in charge of Fort McKinzie. One day three Blood warriors and a squaw came to the fort on a journey to the Crow country to steal horses. The Major discouraged them and they concluded to abandon the expedition and return home. While camped at Cracon-du-Nez they were surprised by a party of Crows who dashed upon them and killed two of the Bloods and wounded the other. He made a supreme effort and knocked a Crow from his horse, seized his enemies' spear and leaping on the horse escaped to the fort. The sister of the Crow [Blood] warrior was taken captive and the Crows started for their own country. The wounded Blood piloted Major Culbertson and a party to the battleground, and the

Major Alexander Culbertson, his wife Natawista, and son Joe, circa 1863.
An American Fur Company employee, Culbertson founded several trading
posts on the upper Missouri and fostered good relations with area Indians,
earning Thompson's praise that "for thirty years he was the most important
man in the whole region."

Montana Historical Society Photograph Archives, Helena

bodies of the slain were taken to the fort and decently buried. A few days after the Major thought he saw some person in the bushes on the opposite side of the Missouri river, and crossed in a canoe to reconnoiter. He discovered the squaw, entirely naked but for some twigs bound round her body and recognized her as the sister of the brave Blood warrior. The Crows had stripped off her clothing so as to prevent her escape and placed her in care of a lynx-eyed old squaw, from whom she escaped. Traveling night and day without food or clothing, she had been fortunate enough to reach a place of safety. Her arrival at the fort was opportune, as she had learned of a plan of the Crows to attack the trading post in large numbers. Forewarned, preparations to receive the Crows were rapidly made, but no time could be spared to increase their supply of meat, before a large body of Crows swept down and captured all the horses belonging to the fort. They went into the camp near the fort and then asked for a parley. Major Culbertson told them to return the horses and then he would talk with them. He talked with friends, not with enemies. The Crows would not return the captured stock, and kept the fort in a state of siege. The garrison dug a well inside the stockade finding a supply of water, but their food entirely failed and they were obliged to kill their dogs for sustenance. The men were in a rebellious mood because they were not allowed to attack the savages. The sagacious Major, true to his policy of making and keeping friends, forbade the men to fire upon the Indians. Learning that there was a conspiracy among his men to steal a mackinaw and abandon the fort at night, he told the Crows that if they did not depart before noon of the next day he would send a thunder-bolt among them. He accordingly trained his cannon in the bastion upon their camp, and calmly awaited the time limit. Exactly upon the hour fixed, the thunder broke forth and cannon balls went plowing through the Crow camp, and the frightened red-skins lost no time in pulling down their wickiups and the big chief Rotten Belly and all his young braves, who had driven him into this attack upon the fort, skedaddled, crestfallen away over the hills. To wipe out this disgrace a war party was made up to find and make attack upon the Piegans, the friends of the whites. At the Goose bill, just above the site of Benton, these Crows discovered a party of twelve *Gros Ventres* in camp. Rotten Belly was a brave man and a great chief. He said to his party, "Now we shall see who are brave men. I shall lead the attack though I feel that I am to fall in

it." The Crows swept into the fight and killed the entire party of
Gros Ventres, but Rotten Belly was, as he had predicted, mortally
wounded. He called his warriors around him and said, "Go back
to my people with my dying words. Tell them ever hereafter to
keep the peace with the white men."[8]

In 1837 the Fur company's boat *The Trapper*, brought with it
to Fort Union a man sick with smallpox. An Indian carried off
an infected blanket, and the dread disease spread with terrible
rapidity. The Assiniboines were reduced from twelve hundred
fighting men to eighty. The Minneteres lost one half their number. The Mandans with whom Lewis & Clark wintered, in 1804-5,
the best Indians in the western country, were nearly wiped out;
from six hundred warriors they were reduced to thirty. Five hundred lodges of Piegans and Bloods were camped near Fort
McKenzie. Major Culbertson warned the Indians of the fatality
of the dread scourge, but they insisted upon receiving the goods
which were to come by the boat, assuming all responsibility for
their action, much against the active protest of Culbertson. The
result was, that nearly every one of the ninety employees of the
fort and the Major himself, had the disease, with the peculiarity
that of the twenty-seven who died, twenty-six were squaws. Six
thousand Bloods, Blackfeet and Piegans died of the disease; two
thirds in number of the allied tribes.[9]

Major Culbertson had been called to the head office at St. Louis.
For ten years Fort McKinzie had held a large and profitable trade,
but the new managers, [Francois] Chardon and [Alexander]
Harvey, by their want of consideration and both being possessed
with ungovernable tempers, ruined its prospects and caused its
destruction. In 1842 a war party of twenty Bloods came to the
fort and demanded admittance, which was refused. Angered at
their treatment they shot a pig which belonged to the fort, and
went on their way. Chardon took six men and went after the

angry Bloods, and as one of his men named Reese (a negro) climbed to the top of a bluff and looked over, he was shot by the Bloods. Maddened by their experience, the whites returned to the fort and Chardon and Harvey secretly resolved to take vengeance on the first party of Indians who came to the fort, thus adopting the Indian way of payment of old scores. They loaded the cannon in the upper bastion of the fort with musket balls and trained it upon the center of the main entrance to the fort. Not long after, a large party of Blackfeet arrived and the three chiefs were at once admitted through the small door, and the others were directed to gather at the main gate, which would soon be opened. When all was ready, Chardon threw open the gate, and as he did so, Harvey with fiendish satisfaction fired his pistol into the priming on the cannon and a hundred musket balls crashed into the crowd at the open gate. Twenty-one dead Indians strewed the ground, many wounded ones straggled away, several being killed as they ran. The three chiefs in the confusion, climbed the walls and escaped.[10] When reason returned to the murderers, they became alarmed, and making up a working party, Chardon dispatched them by night with orders to build a new fort in the Crow country, at the mouth of the Judith river. Keeping close through the winter, Chardon loaded his goods on board some boats and with the opening of spring, safely dropped down to his new fort, called "F. A. C." the initial letters of his name. No trade came to the new post, and the Indians kept it beleaguered the most of the time. Neither Chardon nor Harvey dared show themselves outside the walls of the fort.

The St. Louis managers at last persuaded Major Culbertson to return to the upper river and negotiate a peace. As the boat which bore Major Culbertson and the supply of goods approached Fort F. A. C. it was hailed and Malcolm Clarke and James Lee came on board.[11] Finding Harvey on the boat, with

whom they had a feud, they attacked him with hatchets, but
Major Culbertson interfered and saved his life. At the next wooding place, Harvey and Culbertson landed and reached the fort
before the boat arrived, and Culbertson managed to send Harvey
down the river in a canoe before Clarke and Lee arrived. The
Major did not approve of the location of Fort F. A. C. and taking
five men with him in a Mackinaw with stores and material, he
left Malcolm Clarke in command of the fort and went up the
Missouri to find a new location. He decided to locate a few miles
below the great falls of the Missouri, on the south bank of the
river. He was so anxious to get under cover of his wooden walls,
before any Indians discovered him, that he forbade hunting, and
his seventy men had to feed on dog flesh. Early in January in
1844 he felt himself prepared to receive company and sent out a
party of hunters who returned with plenty of meat and brought
with them an old Blackfoot man whom they had discovered,
who told them that the tribe was encamped on Belley river in the
British possessions. Furnishing him with provisions and presents
he sent him to his tribe with an invitation for them to come to
the fort and hold a council. In due time Ah-Kow-Mah-Ki, (the
Big Swan,) appeared with fifty of his head men. Major Culbertson
told them that the bad men had been discharged by the company and that he would remain at the head of affairs and that he
desired peace. Big Swan in reply, speaking to his own people,
told them that if there were any present who had lost friends in
the massacre of Fort F. A. C. [Fort McKenzie] they must bury
animosity and take good heart; that from this time forward there
should be no stealing of the horses of the white men; no killing
of white men, and no molesting of the fort so long as the bad
Chardon and Harvey remained away; that the ground had been
made good again by Major Culbertson's return, and that the
Blackfeet must not be the first to stain it with blood.

Peace having been concluded the Major gave each of the six principal men a rifle and distributed to others blankets and tobacco, and ever after, until the arrival of emigration, the Blackfeet kept faith with the whites, with the exception of some individual encounters. For this peculiarly valuable service Major Culbertson would not accept pecuniary remuneration, but the American Fur Company found a way to remunerate him by increasing his salary from $2000 to $3000 a year, and after a time to $5000.

The Indians disliked the location of Fort Lewis, as at times it was dangerous to cross the Missouri; they wished a trading post near the Teton river, where was always plenty of grass, wood and water. So Major Culbertson sought a new location, and pitched upon the spot where Fort Benton was built, which was but a few miles from the Teton river. In 1846 Fort Lewis was moved by piecemeal down to the new location, and when finished named after in honor of that noble old Roman, Thomas H. Benton.[12] In 1845 Harvey again appeared in the country as manager of an opposition post and taking a Piegan wife, built a fort just above the Cracon du Nez where he secured some trade from his wife's tribe. He died in 1853 and the station was abandoned.

In 1854 Andrew Dawson came to Fort Benton and was in charge when the *Emilie* arrived with its crowd of immigrants. Dawson was a strong and able man, and managed the Fur company interests with great skill and judgment.[13] The ensuing year Governor Isaac I. Stevens of Washington Territory and Col. Alfred Cummings [Cumming], were appointed commissioners by the United States government to negotiate treaties between the different Indian tribes occupying the country about the sources of the Missouri and Columbia rivers, and between all the Indians and the whites.[14] The council met on the north bank of the Missouri, opposite the mouth of Judith river, and the negotiations were so long continued that Col. Cummings feared that the river might be closed by ice before his Mackinaw could reach civilization. He put his ambulance [wagon] on board a boat and sent his mules overland along the river. The river closed in before he had reached Fort Pierre, at which point he learned that his mules had been stolen by the Indians.

He made application to General Harney who was arranging his winter camp near the fort, for mules to haul his ambulance.[15] The bluff old Indian fighter, who was no believer in peace agreements with the savages, answered: "Yes, Colonel Cummings, I have plenty of mules, but you can't have one; I only regret that when the Indians got your mules, they didn't get your scalp also. Here all summer I and my men have suffered and broiled, to chastise these wretches, while you have been patching another of your sham treaties, to be broken tomorrow and give us more work."

Col. Cummings secured his team from private parties and made his way across the country. Getting near the camp of Little Soldier, a noted Sioux chief, the Colonel thought it good policy to make him a ceremonial visit. Finding himself thoroughly winded when he arrived at the village located upon the top of a high bluff, (as he weighed about three hundred pounds) he declared that he never would go down that hill. A quick-witted squaw helped him out of his dilemma by seizing a large buffalo robe and spreading it upon the ground persuaded the doughty colonel to be seated in the middle of it, when she and a dozen other squaws seized the edges of the robe and safely with great hilarity transported the United States official to his ambulance, free from any injury with the exception of his wounded dignity.

Within a day or two after our arrival at Fort Benton the goods brought by the *Emilie* and the *Shreveport* were piled upon the river bank, and the passengers who decided to remain in the country were turned loose to shift for themselves. Our party were kept busy getting together our belongings, and we engaged a young fellow whom we called "Little Stewart" who had worked his passage on the *Emilie*, as cook, and pitched our camp on the prairie, and for a few days the whole company were together, but for a few days only. A very few Indians were camped in the vicinity of the fort, but horses were very scarce and high priced. I obtained a nice pony for which I paid sixty dollars, which ordinarily would have sold for twenty-five. The *Emilie* hastened upon her return trip, for fear of low water, and we were forced to bid good-by to Professor and Mrs. Hoyt, and some others who at the last moment had weakened as pioneers and turned their faces homeward.

We engaged the services of a mountaineer called "Big Gwynn," to obtain for us four horses to haul our wagon and supplies to the mines at Gold creek.[16] The big prairie was none too large to contain those four ponies and their long-haired driver during the few days when they were changing from saddle horses into draught animals. The first appearance of our turn-out in public was as good as a circus, and the driver had the assistance of all the emigrants and Indians at the landing, but in the course of a week we were able to move our wagon from Benton about seven miles over on the Teton river where was plenty of wood, water and grass. It proved a lucky move for us, for riding over to the fort the next day, to purchase more ponies, we learned that the *Gros Ventres* had made a raid there and stolen eighty horses. Our fellow passengers, the Risby party, lost six, which cost them $550.

In order to facilitate the surveys for a Pacific railroad undertaken by Gov. Stevens in the fifties, that portion of the United States army which acted as guard for the surveying parties, under command of Lt. John Mullan, laid out and constructed what was known as the "Mullan Road" between Fort Benton and the Dalles, in Oregon.[17] It was when first constructed passable for loaded wagons, but led over steep mountains and through rocky canons, and at the time of our use of it, very many of the log

bridges over the mountain streams had washed away. The Gray
party, having a fine mule team, soon were ready to start for the
mountains and invited me to join them. A party was soon made
up, consisting of Mr. Filley and son of St. Louis, Major Reed,
the Indian agent, Mr. and Mrs. [James] Vail, their two children
and Miss [Electa] Bryan, a sister of Mrs. Vail, and myself, and
we pushed on to overtake the Gray party. The Vails were from
Iowa, and were in the employ of Mr. Reed, the Indian agent, to
reside upon and manage the "Government farm," established to
educate the surrounding Indians in the mysteries of farming.[18]
We rode thirty-five miles and camped at a place called "the
springs" on a high prairie which reached to the foot hills of the
Rocky mountains. The next day we overtook the Gray party
and kept with them until we reached "the farm" on Sun river.
The Sun river is a beautiful mountain stream, and on its banks
stand the palisaded farm buildings, built of hewed cotton-wood
logs. At the station were many cattle, a few horses, but no Indians
were taking lessons in agriculture. The valley was large and beautiful, and was the home of numberless deer and antelope. Camped
at the fort we labored hard to recover and repair the ferry boat
owned by the government, in order to take the wagons over the
river. When the ferry was ready, it was discovered that Gray's
team was missing. After a long search the strays were found far
up the valley, and being recovered we safely took over the river
all the wagons, the stock being compelled to swim. We bade
farewell to our fellow passengers, the Vails, and camped that
night at Bird Tail rock; a most curious freak of nature. An immense rock covering many acres rises from the plain, resembling
a turkey's tail when spread.[19] A few miles distant stands Crown
Butte, covering a large territory, its perpendicular walls rising
hundreds of feet above the surrounding plain. Its top appears to
be level, and I could not learn that it had ever been ascended by

Bird-Tail Mountain, *by A. E. Mathews. Thompson observed "Bird Tail Rock" on the Mullan Road while traveling between Fort Benton and the gold-mining country of western Montana.*

From A. E. Mathews, *Pencil Sketches of Montana* (New York, 1868), plate 22

man. Crossing the Dearborn, a fine clear mountain stream, not far from its junction with the Missouri, we met many teams from the west side of the Rocky mountains on their way to Fort Benton for goods. We camped on Wolf creek and the baying of wolves upon our unsophisticated ears, kept us awake a good part of the night. In the morning we found that the thieves had gnawed off the raw-hide lariats which picketed our horses, and let them loose.

July 1st, we met Giles Filley's team at Little Prickley Pear creek, which enabled us to forward letters homeward. We learned by them that several bridges were washed away in the canon ahead of us, and we were compelled to cross over Medicine Rock hill, which was a heavy pull for our teams. On the summit of the mountain rises a wall of white quartz extending for a long distance. Such a freak of nature has great significance with the Indians, and they hold the place in great reverence.[20]

We were up and off at three o'clock the next morning, hoping to cross the summit of the Rocky's that day, but we had a rough trail and were compelled to camp upon a branch of the Big Prickley Pear creek which sends it waters to the Gulf of Mexico. We had followed the Missouri to its source. At ten o'clock, July 3d, 1862, we carved our names on Mullan's mile post, had a game of snow balling, waved the "Star-spangled Banner," and gave three cheers for the Union. At this place the summit was grass covered and to the west we could see the little stream, which we were afterward destined to follow until it emptied its waters into the Pacific, down which we took our winding way.[21] When we made camp, Bryan and I caught plenty of fine trout to furnish the whole party with supper.[22] The night was very cold and ice a half inch in thickness formed in camp. Following down the Little Blackfoot which soon became a sizeable stream, we crossed the north end of Deer Lodge prairie and following down the Hell Gate river, about night came opposite the mouth of Gold creek, but finding the waters too strong for fording, we camped on the north side. By noon the next day we had the pack train and goods safely over the Hell Gate, a feat accomplished with some difficulty. A little Frenchman who had walked and carried his own pack all the way from Benton, undertook to follow the train in the ford, with his pack strapped upon his back, but reaching swift water his feet were swept from under him and he rolled in the stream, sometimes the Frenchman and sometimes the pack uppermost, but by good luck he regained the shore from which he started. Although we all feared that he would drown, we could not help but laugh at his comical appearance. I hired an Indian to lead my horse over and bring him across. We found about twenty of our fellow passengers already at work in the mines, and some claimed that they were getting out about ten or twelve dollars per day. We saw one man who had been at work in the mines about two months, clean up his day's work by which he realized an ounce of gold worth nearly twenty dollars. Our party went some distance up the stream and staked out some claims, and we did a little prospecting, getting the color of gold in each pan of gravel.[23]

Monday morning July 7th. [Frank] Madison of our party came in from Fort Benton and the next day we and some members of the Gray party took blankets and provisions and crossing the hills toward the east struck Rock creek, in a tramp of four or five miles. We found in almost all the prospect holes we opened, a few specks of fine gold. At night we wrapped ourselves in our blankets and without shelter of any kind slept like old mountaineers.

Continuing down the creek the next day, we came to a small circular valley in the midst of which was tall rank grass, service berry bushes, and willows, and in the thicket we heard the "whisk" of white tailed deer. Although still quite lame from my wrenched ankle, I slipped from my horse to look for game, while Madison mounted my horse and rode on down the trail. I had the only rifle in the party, and soon heard Madison shouting "Come on, Thompson! here's a bear!" I hobbled down the trail as fast as possible, and caught sight of the bear climbing the bank on the opposite side of the stream, while the boys were firing at him with their revolvers. Without much regard to my game leg, I climbed through the canon and caught sight of Bruin as he ran into a little thicket in a hollow. As I approached the thicket he ran out from it up a hill opposite where I stood. I fired at him while he was running, and as the bullet struck him he clawed the wound, and then ran over the hill out of my sight. I thought that I had lost him, but loaded my rifle as I ran, and in so doing lost the little brass false muzzle, used in starting the bullet. As I came to the hill-top, down the slope, stood several immense rough barked pines, and I soon saw the bear shinning up one of them. He walked out on one of the large limbs until it forked, where he turned himself around, and laid down with his head upon his fore paws, like a big dog. I remember saying aloud, to myself, "Now Thompson, keep cool, don't get rattled; that's your bear."

I undertook to start a bullet into the muzzle of my rifle with the cleaning rod, but could not do it, and was compelled to hunt a dry stick of service berry bush and whittle out a starter. Pounding the bullet in with a rock, I succeeded in loading my gun, and creeping up to the side of a big pine I took good aim and fired. At first the bear did not move and I feared that I had missed my aim, then came a sort of shudder, and the big creature fell more than fifty feet to the ground. Before approaching him I reloaded my rifle and being ready to fire at any hostile movement, I moved toward my victim, finding him stone dead. Our party had made camp about a mile away, but my lungs were good, and I yelled so loudly that Madison came up, and cutting a stick we arranged it gambrel-like in the bear's hind legs, but found it hard to draw the brute against the fur, so cutting off the top of my moccasins we tied the stick to the bear's nose, and dragged him with comparative ease to the camp. We *guessed* he would weigh two hundred pounds, and found bear steak an enjoyable change from side bacon. The next day one of the boys loaded the horse with bear meat and returned to the home camp at Gold creek, while the rest of us continued to prospect Rock creek. When we reached home, I was hailed as "Bear Killer," a distinction which I intensely enjoyed.

On the 13th of July, Rev. Mr. Francis held service at Gold creek, possibly the first time that a Protestant service was ever held at any settlement in what is now Montana. I organized a choir for the occasion. We received word that our man "Big Gwynn" had succeeded in getting our wagon into the Deer Lodge valley, and we rented from Johnny Grant, the owner, a deserted log cabin standing at the junction of the Little Blackfoot and Deer Lodge rivers as our headquarters. Grant had moved several miles up the Deer Lodge, and built new houses near Cotton-wood. At our place was a good corral, and hundreds of cattle were grazing in the valley.[24]

Noticing some wild cows with calves nearby, with the aid of others I succeeded in capturing two calves and putting them into the corral, the mothers were also taken. By gentle usage I became able to calm the fears of the mothers to such an extent that I could milk them. At least twice each day the cows came to their calves and thus I obtained a sufficient supply of milk for our camp, churning the cream by shaking it in a pickle jar. The two rivers in our front yard were alive with fine large mountain trout, and with an occasional antelope for change, we lived on the fat of the land. The two rivers by their junction formed the Hell Gate, a large swift flowing stream, and Gold creek, or American fork, entered about twenty miles below. James and Granville Stuart had at that point opened up some good paying mines, showing from seven to twenty dollars per day for each man. But the bed rock lay from twelve to fifteen feet below the surface, and the time necessary, and the cost of doing this stripping, before reaching pay dirt, discouraged those who had seemingly expected to pick up nuggets upon the bars in the streams. The Gray party decided to sell out their surplus supplies and move on over the mountains to Walla Walla, or some other good point, and purchase a hotel.

After several days spent in fishing, hunting and prospecting, Bryan, myself and eleven others organized a party to go to the "Beaver-Head country" on a prospecting tour.[25] We had heard exciting stories of United States soldiers finding rich prospects while marching through that region.

We hired John W. Powell as guide and July 21st we gathered
and rode up the Deer Lodge camping two miles above Johnny
Grant's houses.[26] The Deer Lodge valley is a beautiful park, some
thirty miles in length and of varying width, surrounded by high
mountains, and at that time was full of game. We took our noon
lunch at the Hot Springs, having killed an antelope as we rode.[27]
In the midst of the prairie there rises a conical mound some sixty
feet across its base and about thirty-five feet high, built up by
the mineral salts contained in the boiling hot water bubbling
and sizzling in a cavity at the apex of the mound. Near by, flows
the clear cool waters of the Deer Lodge, and at the base of the
cone are basins a few feet deep containing water of various de-
grees of temperature. It is a wonderful exhibition of the works
of nature. In the early evening we had a big scare. Far up the
creek we saw forms moving about among the low shrubbery
and all were sure that they saw Indians. We organized our forces
in military fashion, Major William Graham being chosen commander, and voted to set regular guards, changing at midnight.[28]
Upon a thorough examination with a field glass, we found our
enemies to be a pack of wolves. Our guide knew of a pass in the
main chain of the Rocky mountains, more to the east than the
trail toward Salt Lake then ran, which he said would bring us
out near the "Three Forks." As we made our way up the Deer
Lodge, some one discovered a large animal upon a bench of land
far ahead. Powell thought it was a grizzly bear, and Parker,
Mandeville and I, prepared to go in pursuit. Powell warned us
of the danger, but we determined to hunt the bear. As we rode
deep in the valley we could not see the animal, but we fixed
upon the spot where the high bench pushed out into the valley,
and when we came to it my companions followed up a small run
which came down from the bench, while I continued around the
nose of the hill, and followed up another similar run. When at

the height of land I raised myself and about twenty rods away stood an immense buffalo, the largest I ever saw. Across the bench I saw Parker and signaled him to shoot, which he did. Immediately the big beast headed toward me on a gallop. I slunk back into my ditch, with nerves at highest tension, and ready to fire in an instant. After waiting seemingly ten minutes, no buffalo appearing, I ventured to take another view. The big brute stood not far distant on the plain, turned around once or twice and laid himself down as would an ox. I approached with rifle ready for instant use, but the beast was dead. Mandeville was the butcher and we found that Parker's bullet had passed through his heart. Cutting out the choice pieces we left a mountain of meat to the wolves and turkey buzzards. He was of the species called a Wood Buffalo, and his head would have been a prize for any museum. His head and fore locks were so full of teazles, burrs and seeds, that he must have been blind for years.[29]

From all the information which I can gather, the city or mines of Butte stand upon the spot where we killed the buffalo. The next day we passed through the mountains and traveling down a branch of Whitetail Deer creek, we came across a real grizzly, but he was on the farther side of the creek and the canon was so deep that we could not cross to attack him. Camping in a small park filled with beaver dams, we were driven nearly wild by mosquitoes. In fact they did stampede the horses and we had a long hunt for them in the morning. After a twenty-five mile ride we made camp in a pretty park filled with dry, tall grass. In the morning all the party but Rawlings, an Englishman, and I, started out to prospect a small creek we had passed. We were to keep camp and bake bread. I built a fire under the shade of some bushes to protect it from the wind while Rawlings went into the grass and digging out a little hole without scattering the fresh earth over the grass about his fire place, started it and went to the creek for water. In a few minutes a gust of wind sent the fire into the grass and the whole country was on fire. I fired guns to bring in the men, and lugged all the saddles, blankets and camp material on to a burned spot where I had spread down blankets, while Rawlings jumped up and down and yelled like a crazy man, giving no aid whatever. An immense cloud of smoke rolled up and that night we set extra guard, for fear that the Indians would find our camp by the great smoke. We followed north on the foot hills of the range, having a hard ride over a very rocky trail, but camped in a beautiful valley filled with game. I killed two wolves which were lurking near our camp.

The next morning not a horse was to be found in camp. The horse guard followed the trail back to our dinner camp of the day before and found the missing animals luxuriating in an acreage of sweet grass which they had discovered on their previous visit. He also found that two Indians had occupied our abandoned camp. How they missed our stray horses we cannot imagine. As we are watched we will have to be more careful of our horses in the future. Being very fond of shooting I am privileged to ride in front with the guide. Today as we came out of a deep canon we ran onto two mountain sheep. Powell whispered to me "take the left one." I slipped off my horse and under great excitement fired at the big fellow not ten rods away standing broad side toward me. Off up the mountain side he ran while I let go the bullet in my smooth-bore barrel, which only added to his speed. This was the only time I ever had an attack of *buck fever*. I don't suppose that I saw the forward sight on my rifle during the whole incident. Powell's sheep rolled over and died. We were sure he would weigh 250 pounds, and with great regret were obliged to abandon a fine set of horns at least five inches in diameter at the base. Gathered around the camp-fire that evening we found roast mountain sheep fine eating.

The following day we continued north on the east side of the main Rocky-Mountain range for 25 miles and camped on Crow creek. Powell claimed that the previous year he had found a good showing of gold at this place. We killed an antelope just as we made camp. Cutting off what our immediate necessities required, by using a pole we hung the remainder of the carcass so high on a tree that flies would not find it, where it might, even without salt, safely remain until cured by the dry air. We have killed an antelope every day since we started, excepting the first.

After two days prospecting on Crow creek we concluded that although a color of fine gold was found in nearly every pan of earth, that it was too much diffused to warrant us in taking up claims. After a conference we decided to return to the large creek (Boulder) where we had recently camped. Riding in advance I killed a two-year-old buffalo heifer which proved the sweetest meat I ever tasted. The unshod feet of my pony had become very sore, and taking the scalp of the buffalo I made it into moccasins for my horse which did good service. While carelessly riding with my bridle reins lying on the horse's neck, using both hands in loading my revolver, as I passed close by an old buffalo skull a rattlesnake suddenly sounded his alarm, and the horse jumping [to] one side pitched me off. I fell upon the sharp buffalo horn cutting a deep hole in my right elbow, the scar of which I carry today. Which was the more frightened, the rattler or myself I hardly know, but his rattles were added to a score or more in my possession. My pony took a long circuit and recovering from his fright returned to me. It was our custom when we made camp at places which we suspected were infested with rattlesnakes, to coil around our sleeping places a lariat made from buffalo hair, and I never knew of a snake crossing such a barrier. We made camp upon a little creek making into the large stream, where there was good feed for the horses. At midnight it became my turn to stand on guard. I went out a few rods from camp and lay down in some high grass. Perhaps I had fallen asleep, but raising my head cautiously I was sure that I saw Indians creeping toward camp in the tall grass. How a man's heart will throb under such circumstances. My first thought was to fire at the moving creatures as shown by the moving grass. Then it occurred to me that if it was a false alarm, that I would be the laughing stock of the party. As I lay upon my stomach, every nerve and sense was under the most intense strain. The light in the east grew more and more powerful as I watched the moving grass, ready to fire at any instant, my nerves calmed, and I determined to kill at least one of those Indians before alarming my comrades. All my dreams of glory suddenly faded as up bobbed the ears of a prairie wolf. I let the boys sleep 'till morning.

We moved camp some eight miles to the mouth of the canyon, where we prospected, finding indications of gold scattered through the gravel. Moving up the river over a very rough trail at a distance of perhaps twelve miles we camped for dinner upon a small creek coming in from the north.[30] While the cook was busy, Powell sunk a shallow prospect hole and taking a pan of dirt washed from it a fine showing of gold. Immediately all were excited, and before dinner was ready, we were sure that we had made a valuable discovery. A mining district was organized, Maj. W. Graham being chosen president and myself recorder. The creek was named for Dr. Atkinson (now Boulder) and the small one Powell's Run. The Boulder Mining District being organized, claims up and down the streams were recorded, and all joined in working on a prospect hole begun by my partner, [Henry] Bryan. We went down some ten feet, finding gold all the way, some pans showing as much as half a penny-weight, but we did not find bed rock.

Our provisions were exhausted and we struck across the mountain for Deer Lodge. We camped on the summit August

6th, it being bitter cold and ice formed a half inch in thickness.

We reached our home camp at the Johnny Grant houses to find that during our absence of sixteen days, at least a hundred of old miners had arrived from "Pike's Peak" the most of whom were dead broke—without money or provisions.[31] Capt. [Thomas] Willard, who had remained in camp had welcomed them all, had dealt out our stores with a most liberal hand to all who would promise to secure us claims in any discoveries which they should make. His methods were not approved by most of his associates, and much friction was the result. Those of our party who had remained in camp had plotted "Deer Lodge city" at the junction of the Little Blackfoot and Deer Lodge rivers, and it looked like some newly projected Kansas town. When Deer Lodge city really materialized, its location was several miles up the valley. During the two days I spent at the home camp I was kept busy answering the questions of the "Pike's Peakers" concerning the new discoveries. When three of our party set out to return to Boulder, we were followed by a crowd of the new comers anxious to find some placer where they could get sufficient gold to keep them through the approaching winter. We camped again at the summit, (my fourth crossing) and once more suffered with cold. The same day Mr. and Mrs. Gould of our party left for Fort Benton upon their way to St. Louis. When, traveling down the creek I told the "Peakers" that the discovery was but a mile ahead, away they went with a yell each determined to get nearest the discovery claim. Before I could unsaddle my horse some beset me to record their claims.

Immediately work commenced. Exciting reports came in of fine prospects, but ten, fifteen and twenty feet were reached, showing large boulders, and no bed rock could be found. The situation was exciting and desperate. These old experienced miners were without resources, could not get through the winter unless they could find ready gold, which they could not secure from ground which they thought to be rich, but was too deep and too full of great boulders to be worked to success before winter closed in. Immediate results could not be assured, and it was evident that all must go or all stay, as we were in the midst of the country of the wicked Crows who would surely rob any small party. Great tumult prevailed, and some of the rabble began to find fault with me for having led them into such a country. The more reasonable ones declared that I was free from blame, that the country was rich in gold, but that it would require too much money and time to reap results from it this season.

I pleaded with our men to stay, but they had decided to go to the Beaver Head country near the Three Forks of the Missouri. Some who had lost their horses were compelled to stay a few days, and one of our party took out a dollar and a half worth of gold in one pan of gravel. I told our men that we had supplies in plenty, and that we ought to take our chances with the Crows, and stay by the mines; but I was compelled to go with the others. We again crossed the main range, meeting many men hunting for the new mines.

On the 15th of August I reached the home camp, sore and vexed that our men had abandoned the Boulder. Most of them are bound for the Beaver Head, but I decided to remain at camp until they got located somewhere. I again corralled two of Johnny Grant's cows with their calves, and I was thus enabled to luxuriate in fresh milk and butter. The two mountain streams which united in our door yard, were filled with fine trout. What we did not need while fresh we corned a little [with salt or a brine solution] and then nailed them to the cabin walls to dry. I find that within two months I have ridden my black pony which was never shod, over seven hundred miles. After Bryan and the others of our party had started with the wagon for Beaver Head, Capt. Willard and I only remained at the home station. On a visit to Pioneer Gulch I found forty men working, claiming to average five dollars per day each. On the 19th of August fifty-two wagons came into Deer Lodge under command of Capt. James L. Fisk, having come overland from St. Paul, following near the British line.[32] In the party I found an old friend, Nathaniel P. Langford, afterward appointed governor of Montana.[33]

One day some deer hunters came to our cabin from up the Little Blackfoot, under considerable excitement, saying that just above they had seen a grizzly bear which was so large they did not dare to attack him. Five of us armed with heavy rifles started to bag that bear. We reached an island in the creek which was covered with immense bear tracks and followed a fresh trail leading into some tall willows. I was in the rear. Soon the trail failed, and the leader shouted to turn and go the other way. This change brought me to the front, and picking my way along in a new direction, all at once the immense brute rose up within six feet of me from behind a clump of willows which he could see over, and giving one roar, he left those parts and so did we. Which was the most frightened I did not stop to enquire. Evidently he was not the bear we wanted. When telling the story to old Malcolm Clarke, who had been scalped by a grizzly, he said that we were mighty lucky to be scared for that if had we wounded him there, we would have been in great danger. Our small army returned to camp, one at least conning the old couplet:—

> "He who fights and runs away
> May live to fight some other day."

About the last of August a man came to our camp and told the following story, which afterwards proved to be true. A few days ago three men came into Gold Creek diggings having an outfit of three horses and two mules. They appeared to be desperate characters and were gamblers, and gave their names as

William Arnett, C. W. Spillman and B. F. Jernagin, and said they were from the west side. About a week after their arrival two strangers who said their names were Fox and Bull slipped into the settlement in the edge of the evening and finding James Stuart they told him they were from Elk City, that the three gamblers had stolen their [Fox and Bull's] outfit there, and that they had followed them to secure their arrest and regain the property, and asked that the citizens aid them. Stuart promised all necessary co-operation. The searching party organized at once, and finding Jernagin in Worden & Co.'s store covered him with their shot guns and ordered him to throw up his hands and surrender, which he did without a murmur. Placing him under guard they traced the other two to a saloon where they were engaged in a monte game. Barnett was dealing the cards, and as the party stepped inside the door, and shouted, "Hold up your hands!" he instinctively grabbed for his pistol which was lying in his lap, when Bull shot him through the breast with a charge of buckshot, killing him instantly. Jernagin ran into a corner shouting, "Don't shoot, I surrender." The two were kept under guard until morning. The next morning Barnett was buried, the cards which he was dealing being stoutly clenched in his hand. A jury of twenty-four men was then organized to try the prisoners. Each had a separate hearing and Spillman was convicted and Jernagin acquitted, but ordered to quit the country in six hours, but he was sure that he did not need so much time. Spillman was a fine manly looking fellow of about twenty-five years and made no defence at his trial, but said that Jernagin was innocent, that he was only to be blamed for being in bad company. When informed that he was to be hung in half an hour's time, he simply said that he would like to write a letter, and in a firm hand he addressed one to his father which he left unsealed, in which he recited the circumstances, and declared that his ruin was owing to keeping bad company, that he hoped his father would forgive him for the stain he had brought upon his family, and that his fate might be a warning to other young men on the road to perdition. When asked if he had any other request to make, he said that he had not, and was ready for the end, although the time given him had not expired. He walked to the place of execution with firm tread, apparently less concerned than any spectator. These proceedings gave the settlement the name of "Hangtown" which clung to it for many years.[34] A Mr. Wood came to our cabin from the Beaverhead mines bearing favorable reports from the discoveries. The next day Capt. Willard, [Henry] Watkins and I of our company, and John Cummings, rode up the Deer Lodge valley bound for the Grasshopper mines. Antelope are seen in abundance near the foothills, but are very wild. The third day out we met Mr. [George] King and Mr. Henry [King?] without our team, going to our camp for provisions. They had been surrounded by a war party of fifteen Flathead Indians who had been quite saucy and searched them for provisions. These Indians would hardly attack a white party, but there are mighty few Indians who will not steal anything they wish from a weaker party than themselves. The Snakes and Bannacks who infest the country between here and Salt Lake will attack any weak party they meet, when they think they will not get whipped. They have already killed some fifteen whites and destroyed several loaded wagons. The Bannacks say there are but a few hundred whites and that they are all squaws—i. e., will not fight. One great trouble is to distinguish between the friendlies and the bad ones. At night we sleep with our guns beside us, and when particularly fearful we bring up our horses and tie the lariats to a corner of our blankets. Crossed the Rockies for the sixth time next day, and camped near the Wisdom or Jefferson Fork. Here we met [Henry] Lynch, [Edward] Mead and Eads [William Gould?] of our party, bound for St. Louis. They had been cleaned out of provisions by the Indians, and we had to divide our scanty stock with them. They reported that our partners, [William] Bell, [Frank] Madison, [Henry] Bryan and [George] McLagan had drawn out of the company and taken a large part of the outfit. Willard, Watkins and I left the team with some others, and rode ahead for the mines. We made a secret camp way up in the mountain, after a long ride. While following an Indian trail in the hills away from the traveled road, in coming down a slope toward a creek we saw approaching a single horseman who did not discover us. Willard and I stopped at the creek, while Watkins in trying to cross some distance below, got mixed up in beaver dams, and at last coming out of the brush saw the single horseman, and thinking it was one of us, halloed and started on a gallop to catch up. The stranger thought Watkins an Indian and put his horse into a run in order to save his scalp. Away he went without looking back, and for forty years I have wondered who he was. On the 3d of September, 1862, we reached the mines and found our men getting dirt from a bluff about sixty feet above the Grasshopper which they pulled down the hill in rawhide bags, and washed in a rocker. They were getting from $5 to $12 each per day, while many who found pockets in the bed rock secured fabulous amounts. The next day I purchased eighteen feet of whip sawed boards, and made me a rocker, paying $7.20 for the lumber.[35]

John White of Capt. Jack Russell's Denver party, first discovered gold on the Grasshopper. The party were on their way to Florence and Oro Fino, and had reached Fort Lemhi, a Mormon station on a branch of the Snake river, but found the season so far advanced that they dare not proceed, and turning eastward crossed the divide striking the Grasshopper.[36] They were in that chronic state of miners, out of provisions, and knowing they could not live on gold, were just starting for Salt Lake when a

Mr. Woodmansee rolled into the valley with several wagon loads
of provisions, including a full supply of "Valley Tan," or Mormon
whiskey, which, a writer says, "caused the camp to become
hilarious with joy."

The discovery of rich mines in the northern country was of
immense benefit to the Mormons.[37] They found a much needed
market for their surplus produce and provisions of which they
had great abundance, and of which the destitute miners stood in
much need. Four hundred miles through an entirely unsettled
country was a long haul, but the prices they realized made the
venture very profitable to them. I find accounts of purchases for
my retail trade of eggs (frozen as hard as rocks) at $1 per dozen,
butter at $1 per pound and flour and other articles at propor-
tionate prices. In 1862 on the Salt Lake trail at the junction of
two creeks, nailed to a tree, was a board bearing the following
lucid directions:—

> Tu grass Hop Per diggins
> 30 myle
> keap the Trale nex the blufe
> Tu jonni grants
> one Hunderd & twenti myle

Just as Watkins, myself and three others had begun mining
operations I was taken suddenly ill, the first sick day I had experienced since I left St. Louis, but happily it was not of long continuance. We hired a team and hauled dirt from Buffalo gulch,
about a mile and a half distant, on the mountain, and washed it
out in my rocker. From ten buckets full we cleaned up $2 and felt
encouraged. On Sunday we suspended our work, but all around
the camp were men trading, drawing dirt in wagons, packing it
in bags on mules or donkeys and even on their own backs, while
some worked their rockers by the stream. The shoemaker across
the way has a side of sole leather drawn before the opening of

his tent and is showing his respect for the day. A miners' meeting has been held to elect officers for the district. On Monday we put in a hard day's work. When we all gathered around the cleaning up pan and weighed the fine gold we found we had $9 for our work. The results the two following days were no better. We did some serious thinking. We could not expect to secure enough to carry us through the fast approaching long winter, and taking counsel of Bill Hamilton, an old mountain man, (who said that very likely the Indians would drive us out before spring, if we succeeded in getting in a winter's supply of provisions,) I finally decided to go to San Francisco for the winter, where I could be in communication with the company in St. Louis. Hamilton loaned me a horse to ride to Deer Lodge in his company, and with Watkins we set out, I riding a pack saddle for want of something better. I realized quite a little sum from the sale of my surplus provisions, at prices about five times those of the St. Louis market. Our cook, a young fellow whom we had found working his passage on the steamer and took into our employ largely from compassion, begged of me not to leave him at the mines. I was fearful that he might suffer and took him along, though my means were quite limited. The Indians along the route were reported robbing all small parties, but we had full faith that Hamilton, with his well known skill would take us through, all right. On this occasion Hamilton much desired to take with him a big bull dog which he had purchased of some "tenderfoot." He said that he thought the ugly looking beast would "do up" the dog of a neighbor of his at Deer Lodge. This would amply repay for all his trouble and cost. We took a lively gait and the dog came on very well until tired out. After a little rest Hamilton attached a long lariat to the dog's collar, and all went well until the poor dog got his feet full of the long spines of the prickly pear.

The dog's condition compelled a half hour's stop for the removal of the thorns in his feet, and the escape of naughty words on the master's part, when we again took the trail. Soon, we saw Hamilton and the dog far ahead, the poor beast rolling and tumbling along the trail, dragged by the lariat, the master in worse temper than the dog, and as we came up he drew his pistol and threatened to shoot the beast. I put in a plea for the forlorn looking brute and by Hamilton's leave boosted him up upon the pommel of my saddle, or rather where the pommel should have been. In this way we got on ten or fifteen miles, and thus rested, the old fellow would run for a few miles, but either Hamilton or I carried him a large share of the 120 miles, which for fear of Indians we accomplished inside of 48 hours, but on our arrival at the Cottonwood ranch, we were in about as collapsed a condition as was the dog.

While in camp William T. Hamilton told me of himself.[38] He was of a Scotch and English blood, born near the Cheviot Hills in 1822. He joined at St. Louis in an expedition for trade with the Cheyennes when about twenty years of age. He found the tribe encamped near where the city of Denver now stands. Learning that all the Indians from Mexico to the far north understood a sign language, he applied himself to mastering its mysteries, and so well succeeded, that when he became attached to the army, he was acknowledged to be the most skillful in this particular of any scout in the service. Employed under Col. Wright in the Spokane and Palouse war in 1858, he was present when the eleven chiefs were hung by him [Wright] on the Spokane plain.[39] At that time Col. Wright detained nine other chiefs as hostages for the good conduct of their tribesmen.

At a council of war it was decided that some knowledge of the condition and feelings of the tribes about the headwaters of the Missouri was most desirable, and Hamilton was asked if he would visit that region, make examination and report. He told his commander that if he would detain the nine chiefs until his return, that he would gladly undertake the scout. To this Col. Wright agreed, and gave the proper officers orders to supply all Hamilton's demands. Taking with him one Alex McKay, whom he knew he could rely upon in any emergency, they set out upon their perilous expedition. They took with them five pack horses loaded with Indian goods, for trade and presents, and selected two of the best riding horses and the best equipments the camp offered. Hamilton took the precaution to obtain from Col. Wright a circular letter addressed to all Indian agents, directing them to supply him with any articles or aid which he might desire.

These instructions he placed in a large packet, sealed with the largest golden wafer that he could find at head-quarters, which he was certain would be looked upon as "big medicine" by all the surly Indians.

For the first two hundred miles his route lay through the country of those Indians whom Col. Wright had so recently thrashed, and had it not been for their knowledge that their chiefs were detained by him [Wright] as hostages, the journey of those two scouts would have quickly ended. When detained by bands of warriors, Hamilton with great dignity and solemnity would produce his mysterious package, and proceed to read orders from Col. Wright such as he thought would best be suited to his surroundings. The name of Col. Wright commanded great respect among the rebel tribes at this time, and Hamilton generally soothed the wounded passions of the chiefs by suitable presents. His route was up the Clark Fork of the Columbia, and he reached the Flatheads, who were always friendly to the whites, without serious trouble. They warned him to beware of war parties of Blackfeet, who could not be trusted in the least when in an enemy's country. In fact, a war party of young bucks when in any enemy's country will often attack white men, when they would not dare to do so in their own country. At that time the Blackfeet, Piegans and Bloods were in league, as one people, yet with a tribal distinction, and the Flatheads were at peace with the two first named tribes, but at war with the Bloods.

Two Flatheads chiefs announced their determination to go with Hamilton to the Piegan Agency, at the government farm on Sun river. Col. [Alfred] Vaughan, the agent, welcomed them and gave Hamilton all the information he was able to, regarding the Missouri river tribes, and advised him to visit the camp of Little Dog, head chief of the Piegans, then to the northward on the head waters of the Marias river.[40] Striking the Marias, one afternoon Hamilton discovered three Indian hunters, who also discovered his party and fled to the northward. The two scouts and their Flathead guests immediately made camp, and the scouts, casting off their soiled clothing arrayed themselves in their finest, and awaited visitors. Soon twenty-five horsemen finely mounted and elegantly made up, according to Piegan fashions, came riding towards them at full gallop. When a quarter of a mile away, they fired their guns into the air, which is a universal sign of peace, and when thirty paces away they all "halted at a jump" as the trappers say. Little Dog and Hamilton advanced and shaking hands, greeted each other with the usual "How! How!"

Little Dog arrayed in his war bonnet and all his war equipments, impressed Hamilton as being one of the finest appearing warriors he had ever seen, and when he presented to him his son Fringe, a fine young fellow of nineteen, Hamilton was so impressed that he gave to each a fine blanket.[41] Distributing tobacco and other presents to be divided among the others of the party, he held a long conversation by means of signs with Little Dog, and producing the big packet with its golden seal he interpreted from it

the request of Col. Vaughan, that being his friend he should also
be the friend of Hamilton.

After a "square meal" the big chief and most of his followers
departed, leaving Fringe and two other Indians to keep guard
and bring the party to his camp in the morning. There was a
feast in Little Dog's camp that night, largely consisting of dain-
ties presented by Hamilton. The proud Fringe and his guests
were received with much ceremony in the morning, when he
conducted them to his father's camp. The "Haranguer" was sent
out to give the news brought by the scout, the people being eager
to learn the result of the Spokane war. The announcement that
eleven chiefs had been hung to wagon poles, was received with a
loud grunt. Hamilton was given the name of "The Sign-talking
White Man." Valuable presents were exchanged and then
Hamilton exposed his goods and trinkets for exchange for robes
and furs. His transportation outfit being quite limited he refused
to trade for anything but the very choicest furs, selected from
those offered him, for which he paid good prices. He felt it to be
his duty to visit the northern Blackfeet, before his return to Walla
Walla, but knew that he was taking large risks in so doing. Little
Dog warned Hamilton that the Blackfeet could not be trusted,
and said that while he might get out of their country alive, he did
not think they would ever permit his outfit of goods to be taken
away. Seeing Hamilton determined to go north, Little Dog sent
Fringe and three other Piegans to accompany him, professedly
as guides, but Hamilton felt that they were to protect him if
necessary. In due time the little cavalcade reached the joint village of "Calf-shirt" and "Father of all Children," and were received by those noted chiefs by ugly grunts, and hostile signs
(well understood by Hamilton) to their retainers.[42]

After a little time Hamilton brought forth his mysterious
packet and although he eloquently interpreted the message of

Col. Wright to his friends, the Blackfeet, he could not wholly gain the confidence of these wily chiefs. He talked with them by signs, told them of the Palouse war and its ending, made some presents, opened his goods for trade, and got in some fine skins and robes, but the surroundings were all hostile. He told the chiefs that he should leave in the morning, and they were anxious to know the route he intended to take, but he claimed that he had not decided.

Fringe, while all were seated in the wigwam of Calf-shirt thought he saw a hostile movement and throwing off his blanket drew his revolver and launched out into an impassioned speech, and before he had finished the Blackfoot leaders bowed their heads in shame. Fringe and his men promised Hamilton that they would go with him to the summit of the mountains, and the party got out of the hostile camp without an out-break, but it was evident that only fear of punishment by Little Dog and Fringe saved Hamilton from serious trouble.

Hamilton gave Fringe and his faithful friends each a revolver and ammunition when he parted from them at the divide, and not stopping to eat pushed on down the Big Blackfoot in order to put as much space as was possible between themselves and the ugly Blackfeet, before night overtook them. Hardly three hours of hard riding had passed when they were fired upon by three Blackfeet lying in ambush, but without effect, and the smoke had hardly risen above the bushes when Hamilton and McKay were upon their enemies with revolver and knife, and McKay seemed happy as he tucked three Blackfeet scalps under his belt. Before dark they ran upon a camp of friendly Kootnai, who were at war with the Blackfeet, and upon seeing the bloody scalps of their enemies, whom they knew had been spying about their camp, the village was turned into pandemonium of joy and the scouts were warmly welcomed.[43]

Early the next morning the Kootnai village was attacked by a
large party of Blackfeet who had followed the trail of Hamilton,
and he and McKay were then able to repay with interest, for the
insults which they had received in the Blackfoot camp and upon
their march. Although McKay and twenty Kootnai were wounded
and four killed, they gathered thirty-five scalps from their dead
enemies left on the battle field. The Kootnai moved westward to
the Tobacco Plains, where they were again attacked by a large
number of Blackfeet who were partially concealed in a "draw"
and some woods, where the young Kootnai warriors attacked
them in return, but could not induce them to come out and fight
in the open.

Hamilton directed the squaws to soak a number of blankets
for use in protecting the camp from fire, and told them to set the
leaves and grass in the draw on fire, which strategy was a success, for as the Blackfeet fled from the flames the Kootnai with
Hamilton and the wounded McKay rode down upon the disor-
derly mass, doing great execution. Exchanging presents with the
delighted Kootnai, and securing a valuable addition to their stock
of furs by barter, the scouts again took up their march toward the
hostile Spokane and Palouse camps. By making a long detour
known to McKay, they escaped collision with any hostile Indians
until they had almost reached the Nez Pierces, who were friendly
Indians. Here they met three Spokane warriors who seemed un-
decided whether to stampede their train, or not. Hamilton showed
them his packet, and told them he was Col. Wright's scout, and
that if they did not go about their business that he would arrest
them, when they made off, and left him to proceed on his journey. Soon after they found the camp of Lawyer, a Nez Pierce
chief, who assisted them in crossing the Snake river, and without
further adventure they reached Col. Wright's headquarters at
Walla Walla, much to the relief of the officers of the post.[44] They

returned with two hundred selected robes, many elegant small furs, buffalo tongues, and Indian curios of great value. Col. Wright urged Hamilton to remain in the service, but he had his heart set upon the Bitter Root country, and immediately made arrangements to return to it. Securing two years' supply of Indian goods, he soon retraced his steps, entering the Bitter Root valley by the St. Regis trail. After the organization of Montana, he served with credit as sheriff of Choteau county, and for a season as deputy United States marshal. This short sketch does scant justice to the life and services of "Wild Cat Bill."

The wild ride from the mines to Deer Lodge was too much for our charge, Little Stewart; and we left him at Johnny Grant's while the rest of us went to our old camp, where we found Messrs. Clow, Jones, Rev. Francis, and Mr. Mead of our party just starting for Walla Walla. They consented to wait two days at Gold Creek for me to join them. They next day I went to Johnny Grant's for Stewart, and found him pretty sick, but fearing to be left, he mustered up courage to return with me to our home camp. He seemed to be suffering from some internal inflammation, and heating a camp kettle of water I secured a barrel, and putting into it a package of mustard I gave him a hot bath, and coming out as red as an Indian, I put him to bed and he was soon asleep, sweating profusely. In the morning he was so much improved that he thought he could ride the twenty miles to Gold Creek, and we abandoned our cabin and started out for the Pacific coast.

At the summit of the first hill on our route, I discovered a herd of antelope, and stalking them succeeded in killing a large buck. While [I was] busy trying to fasten the undressed carcass to my riding saddle, a half dozen Indians appeared and assisted me, and were made happy by receiving a few fish hooks. I saved my venison, but to do so, had to lead my horse and trudge on foot a dozen miles.

On the 20th of September, 1862, we were fairly started on our long journey. The party consisted of Messrs. Clow, Jones, Watkins, Mead, Stewart and I, on horseback, and Mr. Francis, Dr. Riley and Stevenson in the wagons. Two yokes of oxen drew the large wagon, and four horses the light one. At the tail end of the latter a good cow was tethered. Stewart is glad to exchange places with Mr. Francis, and he and I ride ahead to secure game and select camping places. Once, riding down the Hell Gate, we saw some distance ahead, an Indian fishing. The noise of the river prevented his hearing our approach, and we were right upon him before he saw us. Completely surprised he dropped his fish pole and ran like a deer into the woods. Traveling through a pine forest, we found no feed for the stock, and when turned loose at night they often wandered long distances and we were often delayed in searching for them. We came at length to Mullan's long bridge over the Big Blackfoot [River], which was a picturesque piece of architecture. Built of large pine logs, its flooring was of split saplings, but it well answered the purpose for which it was built. Near here we met a large party of Flatheads on their way to the Missouri to hunt buffalo. The whole tribe seemed to be on the journey of a thousand miles, taking horses, dogs, women, children, and all camping outfits, to secure a supply of jerked buffalo meat and skins for robes and wigwams. No buffalo are found west of the Rocky Mountains, and these western tribes run great risk of attack by hostile Indians in the buffalo country.[45] Watkins traded ponies with the Indians.

We reached the Bitter Root valley settlements September 24th, and purchasing potatoes at three dollars per bushel, onions at seven, turnips at two and a half, and parsnips at four, we feasted on vegetables, the first we have had since we left the *Emilie*. Camped at a French settlement and have adopted a Pen d-Oreille Indian as a herdsman. Had shoes put upon my horse, as he was foot-sore. While waiting, the Indian stole my overcoat and ran away with unknown articles in the pockets. Made camp on the Shak-o-tay, having come but twelve miles. The Mullan road followed along the banks of the Bitter Root river, sometimes running up some little canyon, or over some rocky point which could not well be otherwise passed. The scenery was most beautiful and the waters so clear that from high bluffs fish could be seen swimming in the stream, and Mr. Francis and I were able to keep the camp well supplied with beautiful trout. Every mile is blazed upon a post or tree with the letters "M R" and the number of miles distant from Fort Benton; the work of Governor Stevens' surveyors, for the Pacific rail-road. At times the road was very rough, and led over the tops of high mountains, and we often were obliged to camp in the thick forest. Having no forage we were obliged to turn our stock loose so that they might find feed, and in search of it they would stray, causing much vexatious delay. One day I rode on alone in order to obtain a supply of fish for dinner. The river ran in a deep canyon, but finding a ravine making down to it, I tied my horse and leaving my rifle near by, clambered down and working up the stream found a good place, and while intent on fishing, was startled by a war whoop. Two Indians were running up the other side of the river with guns in their hands. I concluded them to be Snakes, and abandoned my nice string of trout and scrambled up the side of the bluff displacing stones and brush and wounding my hands on thorns and briers, reached the top and regained my rifle. Then each party called across the river and abused the other, to their hearts' content, neither understanding a word that was said. Finding a suitable camping place I built a fire and waited for the train. Getting very hungry I ventured to catch some more fish, and broiling them, satisfied my hunger on fish alone. At dark no train having appeared, I curled myself up in my blanket in the roots of a big pine tree and slept, the train coming up late in the evening, having had a breakdown. They were much relieved to find me in such good quarters. They had picked up a Flathead on the way and he camped with us. Saturday night we were compelled to camp in a deep forest, and the next morning Mr. Francis and I struck out to find a camping place where feed could be found for the stock. After a "Sabbath day's journey," as Mr. Francis remarked, we struck Brown's prairie, finding every requisite for a perfect camping place. Building a fire, Mr. Francis and I caught a fine mess of splendid trout, this being the only time I ever went fishing on Sunday, with a Baptist minister. Three parties passed us as we lay in camp, bound for the new mines. Near night, Major John Owen, proprietor of Fort Owen in the Bitter Root valley, made his camp with us, and when we became acquainted he found that he had letters for Mr. Mead and myself.[46] Mine was from my brother in St. Louis, and gave me the first information from home since I left in May.

While lying in camp Major Owen told me of a trip he made to his fort from the Dalles, in 1858, just after the Indians had heard of the defeat of Col. Steptoe, and the death of Captain [Oliver] Taylor and Lieut. [William] Gaston, and the retreat of the army to Walla Walla.[47] He was at that time government agent of the Flatheads, Pend-Oreilles, and Kootnai Indians, and had with him twenty-five pack animals carrying valuable supplies. One evening seven or eight canoe loads of Yakima Indians made their appearance near their camp, all painted and rigged up for war, and evidently anxious to be insulted. The interpreter advised making a bluff, and so they built an immense camp fire, and all hands, himself included, caught hold of a dried hide and danced around the fire, beating the hide with billets of wood until they were nearly exhausted. Thus they showed their visitors that they were not afraid of them and were ready to fight at any minute. Much to their relief their visitors left, going down the river in their canoes before break of day. At another camp, when they started out in the morning, they were escorted by twenty-five or thirty warriors riding either side, keeping up a constant war-whoop, but finally leaving them without making an attack. He had with him Tom Harris and Henry M. Chase and their families, as well as his own, and also Charley Frush. A war party of Spokanes overtook them and they had a long "waw-waw" about Major Owen, debating whether to keep him, or kill him, as they said he "had big eyes and big hands, and that he wrote bad things about them to the 'Great Father' at Washington," but they kindly concluded to let him proceed on his way.

After a camp in the deep forest and hunting up our strayed stock, we came to the Bitter Root river where some "firster" had established a ramshackle ferry. We paid him eighteen dollars for our ride over, and the privilege of working our own passage. Here we caught a quantity of fine salmon trout very large and toothsome. They resemble in form the brook trout of New England, but are built upon a larger scale.[48] Two miles beyond the ferry, we went into camp and loaded our wagons with grass, as we now leave the Bitter Root valley and cross the high range of mountains of that name. There was no feed for our stock for the next seventy miles. In a drenching rain we set out to follow up the St. Regis Borgia river into the mountains, and were soon traveling in woods so dense that the road seemed walled in by immense trees. In this wilderness I killed many beautiful mountain pheasants, which were very gamey and much enjoyed by our party. Many of Captain Mullan's bridges had been washed away by the tumultuous stream, and progress up the mountain was slow and sloppy. We stopped at the forty-sixth crossing, and camped in a drizzle of rain and snow, listening nearly all night to the howling of a pack of timber wolves who lacked courage to come into camp.

Watkins' horse was missing in the morning, and he and I, after two hours' search, found the beast snubbed by his trailing lariat. An Indian whom we met said the snow was deep upon the summit, which, after crossing the river twenty-seven times in our day's march, we failed to reach, and were compelled to pitch our tents in the road. Six inches of snow fell in the night, and some faint hearted ones wished to turn back. A rousing fire and a good brook trout breakfast, however, cheered them up, and we kept on our way, crossing the small stream nineteen additional times during the day. I rode ahead in order to hunt, but toward night, being cold, wet and stiff, in dismounting from my horse, the saddle turned, and my frightened horse ran down the mountain bucking and kicking, and nearly ruining my saddle. The men secured my horse while I tramped on and reaching the tall pole marked in feet, placed there by Captain Mullan, found but eight inches of snow. Waiting for the train I shot some birds and warmed myself at a huge fire, and measured some magnificent pines and cedars, over forty-five feet in circumference. The western slope of the road is a dugway cut through these splendid trees for two miles of sharp descent. Quickly descending this grade we soon made camp in a little round valley, containing everything needful for an exhausted party. We are now at the head of the Coeur d'Alene river. Rain—rain—rain—all day and all night. In the morning Watkins' horse was missing and we discovered the reason that the Indians had for trading off that animal.

Traveling through a magnificent forest we crossed the stream twenty-seven times in fourteen miles. At one point the road ran across the top of a stump which was so broad that all four of the wheels of the ox wagon stood upon it at the same time. We have hardly seen the sun for weeks and the stock have had little feed and are nearly starved, drowned, and frozen out. We have crossed the Coeur d'Alene river fifty-three times in traveling thirty-two miles. Arriving at a little prairie which contained good feed for the stock, we made camp and the blessed sun broke forth in all its glory. Mr. Francis and I soon caught a plentiful supply of trout and we are a happy crew. The approach to the Coeur d'Alene Mission, furnishes a most delightful landscape. The little church stands upon a slight elevation, and to us, who have not seen anything larger than a log cabin for months, the priests houses seem palatial.[49] Near by, built of anything which could be used for shelter, are fifteen or twenty huts occupied by the mission Indians. The Indians are outwardly devoted, but we were warned by a good father to take good care of our belongings, as they were obliged to keep everything under lock and key, even the vegetables in the garden. A few of the Indians cultivate small plots of land, but this and an outward show of sanctity is apparently about all that the twenty-five years' service of the devoted priests has been able to accomplish in the civilization of these mild mannered natives. These earnest Christian men, who sacrifice themselves in their efforts to promote the welfare of these people, deserve a crown of glory, whatever may be their present success. We bartered all our surplus clothing with the Indians and purchased from the fathers a fine lot of vegetables and a young heifer for our commissary department. The next day was the most trying of our trip. It rained incessantly and we were obliged to cross the Coeur d'Alene mountains through thick timber with no feed for the stock. But the camp in Wolf's Lodge prairie turned our despondency into joy, at finding plenty of grass, wood and water. Game was scarce and we found it necessary to kill our heifer for food. One of our camps was beautiful beyond description. The mountains seem to flatten out, and in the midst there lies the picturesque Pend-Orielle lake, perhaps twenty-five miles in length and of varying width, the water being intensely blue and reflecting the woods and mountains by which it is surrounded.

Into this lake flows the Coeur d'Alene river, and its outlet is the Spokane, down which we make our way. A party of Spokane Indians camp near us, out on a bear hunt. I found that I could communicate with them by signs and what little Chinook I knew, and was much interested in their description of a successful horse stealing raid upon the Snakes. They had with them the skin of a wolf stuffed with straw, in the belly of which a hole was cut to fit the head of the owner. An Indian put this upon his head and acting with the utmost caution crept to the summit of a little hill close by, and pretended as he peered over that he saw one Snake Indian guarding twenty horses on the plain below. By his signs it was easy to imagine that the party after traveling on foot several hundred miles had reach the outskirts of a large camp of their enemies, and were lying low in order to stampede a band of horses, and escape without loss to themselves. The wolf's head upon the hill, would to the horse guard be nothing unusual, and would create no suspicion of the proximity of an enemy. The war party go on foot, because the failure of their plans impose upon them a return on foot, which whets their boldness and daring. In this instance the skilled actor describes the discovery of the lone horse guard, and a satisfactory band of horses, and marks out the way of covered approach within striking distance of the guard. Then on hands and knees the whole party creep towards the ravine leading to the plain on which the horses are grazing. Pointing to the sun they indicate that they are several hours in waylaying the guard, before they let go a half dozen arrows into his body. An Indian mounts the dead guard's horse and with a lariat captures one of the best in the herd, which is mounted in turn by a comrade, and others are caught until all are mounted and the whole band having stampeded the grazing herd started at full gallop for the Spokane country. They ride all night, and with much humor the relator tells of getting asleep and nodding as he rides, and when waking, shouting "Snake! Snake!" when all pushed on at a gallop until obliged to stop from exhaustion. Our entertainer pictured in strong colors their safe arrival at their home village, the people shouting at the waving of the Snake scalp, and the exhibition of the captured horses. The whole scene, lighted up by the great fire in the forest was weird and picturesque. An Indian is trying to trade me two horses for my gun, using signs and Chinook jargon, of which they know a little, and I not quite so much. The horses are "Nah-took-tchin-klas-klas" and my gun is "So-lo-la-me."

Following down the north bank of the Spokane we found a place which seemed fordable by the train. I rode in, to examine, but soon my horse was swimming. Having started in, I was bound to cross, which feat I accomplished, but my experience kept the others from the attempt to follow a fool leader. Some miles below, a bar was found where the wagons were crossed in safety, and we thus cheated some progressive ferryman out of eighteen dollars. Soon after crossing we found the prairie covered with bones, which we afterwards learned were the remains of about eight hundred horses, which Col. Wright had killed at the time he hung the rebellious Spokane chiefs to his wagon poles, which strenuousity brought the humbled warriors to a lasting peace. We are traveling over a high volcanic plain, and standing by the roadside is a tree on which is cut "M R—144" indicating that old Fort Walla Walla is still that distance from us. In what seems to be an old crater is a beautiful blue lake, (Medicine Lake) but the surrounding country having lately been burned over, there is no feed for our stock. We are traveling over a country covered with sharp volcanic rocks, and our poor cattle suffer terribly both for food and good water, nearly all the streams we have found being strong of alkali. On the road we met a half dozen squaws with a pack train loaded with dried salmon from the Columbia. The lordly bucks compel the women to do all the packing, they coming along when they please. A lusty squaw sits astride a big pack and from a pocket hanging by her side peers a "little Indian" whose keen black eyes glitter like those of a snake. As the leading squaw came over the hill ahead of us, she had a papoose board on her back projecting far above her head, and her appearance suggested to me the Queen of Sheba. What water there is on this volcanic plain runs in cracks deep down in the rock and is hard to get at. As I sit alone in utter desolation, the whole country having been burned over, these words of Shelley cross my mind,

> "Is this the scene
> Where the old Earthquake-demon taught her young
> Ruin? Were these her joys?"

Camped on the "Oraytayoose" which I take it must mean "The little alkali creek which runs in the crack in the ground." Watkins' horse for the twentieth time is again missing. Mead, Steward and Watkins hunted him in vain, and came into camp at night without tidings of him, and are sure that he has been stolen. After a weary time we reached the Palouse river and caught a fine lot of trout for supper. We passed the Palouse falls after dark and came to Snake river late at night. Tying the stock to the wagons we went supperless to our blankets and at daylight found that we were along side the graves of a lot of Indians who were killed in the Indian war, the graves being surrounded by an apology for a fence, and upon the rails were stretched the dried and shriveled remains of the dead warriors. After ferrying across the Snake river we went into camp a mile or more from the ferry ranch, where our stock could find feed. Here Mr. Mead and I determined to exchange our horses for a Hudson Bay Company batteau, and take our chances in navigating the Columbia and Snake rivers to Portland.

FOUR

River, Ocean, and Wilderness

SUNDAY, OCTOBER 18TH, 1862, our party spent in camp together, for the last time. Being assured by the men at the ferry that there was no danger in descending the Snake river, excepting at the Pine Tree rapids, Mr. Mead and I exchanged our horses for a well built lap-streak Hudson Bay batteau, which would carry about six tons and seemed tight and seaworthy. We had seen in a Portland paper accounts of boats being wrecked in the river, and the drowning of several returning miners, but when Rev. Mr. Francis decided to join our party, we felt sure that we would escape all danger. He was a most practical man and had crossed the ocean some fourteen times, and had for many years been a dweller on the New Found Land coast. He declined to take command of our ship and I was elected captain, Watkins was engineer and was to keep the ark dry, Mead was cook, Reverend Francis, chaplain, and all hands oarsmen.

We stocked the ship with provisions sufficient to take us to old Fort Walla Walla (now Wallula) where we hoped to find less extravagant prices. The next day we bade farewell to the Clow-Jones party, who continued their overland journey toward Fort Walla Walla, and we were soon swiftly floating down the treacherous Snake river, which seems to run in a great crack in the earth's surface, and there is scarcely a bush or green thing to be seen for miles and miles. We passed down several pretty rough waters during the day, and often wondered how much worse than these the dreaded Pine Tree rapids were. I found that the rudder, hung in the usual way, gave me no control of the boat in very swift water, and when we camped having found the ruins of a broken boat, I decked over a standing place in the stern of the ship and substituted a long sweep for the rudder. I now had an extended view of the river and perfect control of the boat and full confidence that I could safely guide the craft under any circumstances, and I have no doubt but this change saved our lives. Being in a deep canon, at night we were forced to tie our boat to a big rock and pass the hours in rather close quarters, on board. Having no way of cooking on board we kept on our way in the morning until we saw the mist rolling up from the great rapids. Landing, while breakfast was being prepared, Mr. Francis and I climbed up the walls of the canon and I made a chart of the channel, as it wound from side to side of the river. There were several ledges, some projecting from one side of the river and some from the other. There seemed a safe passage way, if we could only keep in it. The upper rapid was on our side of the river and with all the men at the oars, we started in, and with our hearts in our mouths ran the torturous channel with perfect safety, the only mishap being a wetting from the spray caused by the bow of the boat splashing down upon the rough water. Our confidence in our boat and in each other was vastly improved.

Tired and weak from our excitement after a short day's travel we made camp upon a sandy beach, where we hoped to bake some potatoes in the hot sand. A strong wind sucked up through the canon, and Watkins, our clown, remarked as the sand sifted in all our food, "We have sand-wiches enough to make us all crazy." Our wit responded,

> "The world which knows itself too sad,
> Is proud to keep some faces glad."

The next day brought its full measure of dangerous rapids, but by use of the long sweep and the quick response of the man at the oars, we passed them all in safety, and about three o'clock came to the junction of the Snake and the Columbia. Mead dipped water from the great river and in grandiloquent speech, dubbed the ship *The Novice*, and captain, chaplain, and crew joined in three hearty cheers. Before dark we reached Wallula and took up our lodgings in an old boat drawn up on the shore. The wind blew a gale up the canon, and we spent the hours of waiting in gaining information about the river. It is one hundred and ten miles to Deschutes, the first large rapids, but just above the mouths of all large rivers entering the Columbia, there are dangerous rapids. Stocking up our craft for a week's travel, and taking on a passenger, we renewed our journey, in a stiff head wind. Camping on a sandy beach, the wind nearly covered us with drifting sand during the night. When, during the next day, we neared the head of the Umatilla rapids, we hauled to the shore and I climbed to the bluff and made a chart of the river. There were five reefs stretching across the river within a few miles, with the deep water winding from side to side above each. I put Mead in the bow of the boat to look out for sunken rocks, and we started into the path from which there was no turning. At times, the boys had to pull for their lives to escape some big rock, but we came through safe and sound, though poor Mead was drenched from head to foot. The shooting of these rapids is as exciting as a ball game or horse race. Every nerve and muscle is at extreme tension, and the spice of real danger adds interest to the occasion. After passing Grande Ronde landing we made camp on a beautiful grassy slope and slept well after our exciting day. With the morning's sun a most magnificent scene broke upon our view. Mount Hood with its eternal cap of snow loomed up in the south-west, piercing the clouds. Along the river were many Indian camps, and the natives were out in their canoes busily engaged in picking up the dead salmon which float in the stream by hundreds. Unless too rotten, they dry them for food.

Sailing against strong head winds, we made slow progress but near night came to a point where we could hear the roar of rapids which we knew extended for fifteen miles. Near by, the crew of another boat were camped, but having no provisions they were up and off at daylight. After climbing the bluff and sketching the river as far as I could, we entered into the Rock Creek rapids and flying through them passed Squally Hook, then the Indian rapids, and at last the great John Day rapids.

Between the John Day's and the Deschutes rivers we had a strong head wind, and were compelled to cordelle the boat for some miles, and near sunset reached Klik-i-tat landing, when our passenger said that he knew the river well from there to Deschutes. I told him to come up and take the helm, and I took his place at an oar. As we approached the rapids, the river being in a deep canyon and taking a sudden turn, the stranger turned white as a sheet and called out to me to "come up." Mr. Francis shouted "get up there, Thompson." I saw in an instant that we were close upon the falls and on the wrong side of the river; that the reef ran quartering across the river, in which great breaks existed, through which the water poured in mighty sluiceways. I told the men they must pull for their lives, this time, and headed the boat toward a raging torrent which ran close beside an immense rock. I could not see what was below the reef, but it was our only chance, and as we shot over the crest the boat just grazed upon the standing rock and down we went in a fall of at least ten feet, the *Novice* riding the falls and the big waves below, like a thing of life. When he could stand, Mr. Francis arose and spreading out his hands as in a blessing, reverently said, "Thank God!" It was a close shave and we all joined in the "Amen!" It was pitch dark when we made our camp on a little island in the mouth of the Deschutes river. The next day we continued our journey to Celilo, a little village at the head of the Dalles.

We could not pay the exorbitant fare for conveyance by stage to the Dalles, so we sent our baggage by wagon and footed the fifteen miles over the foothills. We abandoned the *Novice* with great regret, but the stage of the water was such that she could not be taken through the Dalles, so we left her in the hands of an agent to be sold. Reaching the Dalles before sunset we made camp near the steamer landing, beside a pile of railroad ties. During the night thieving Indians crawled up toward our camp and when I whispered to Watkins, loud enough so that I knew they could hear, "Hand me my pistol," the miscreants gathered themselves up and ran like deer.

The fare to Portland the next day we found to be $5, while the opposition boat due the second day carried passengers for $2, so considering that our lodgings were free, we camped another night. We think that this place will sometime in the future be an important point, when time shall come that the immense water power is developed, and the trade of the rich mining and agricultural valleys established as they surely will be in the near future.[1]

Taking the little opposition steamer *Dalles*, at five o'clock in the morning we made our way down the mighty river, which runs in a deep canon with almost perpendicular wall rocks. Now and then there are a few acres of bottom land lying in some bend of the river, on which some settler has built a log house. Being hemmed in by the rocky walls they seem to have no outlet but by

The Dalles. *In the fall of 1862 Frank Thompson crossed the mountains and descended the Snake and Columbia Rivers en route to San Francisco to spend the winter. The Dalles on the Columbia was one of the many places he noted on his passage to the coast.*

From *Explorations and Surveys for a Railroad Route from the Mississippi River to the Pacific Ocean, 1853–55,* vol. 12, book I (Washington, D.C., 1860), opp. 154

the river. A few miles above the Cascades, in the lake-like river, are standing the petrified trunks of immense trees, sometimes reaching thirty or forty feet above the waters. Many seem to have been broken off by the water, perhaps by some flood occurring centuries ago. These seem to add credence to the Indian legend that formerly the river ran beneath the Cascade range, and that the mountains, Hood and St. Helens fought each other with fire, the effect of which was to break down the bridge. The scenery of the Sierra Nevada [Cascade] gorge and mountains is sublime. Reaching the landing at the head of the Cascades, we walked the four miles to the foot of the rapids, rather than pay a dollar for a ride upon the apology for a railroad. We thus had a magnificent view of the angry river as it reached the brackish waters of the sea. How a reckless steamer captain, anxious to escape service of papers by an officer of the law, ever brought his boat down those fearful rapids, remains an unsolved mystery, but such is the fact.

> "And the river leaps and whirls and swings,
> To the changeless song the great cliff sings."
>
> van Beuren.

At the landing, we found an ancient scow upon whose deck an upright boiler had been placed, and on it were crowded about forty horses and four loaded wagons, and sandwiched in, were some fifty passengers. Some of these climbed upon the roof of what the captain called the cabin, but were ordered down, as the captain said the boat was "top heavy anyway." As she rolled to one side and the other, when she got under way, one man offered the captain five dollars if he would put him and his horse on shore. We declined the venture, and waited better accommodations.

October 31st, 1862, we reached Portland, having come from the Cascades in the *Leviathan* a staunch little steamer fifty-two feet in length. Our minds can hardly conceive more magnificent scenery than that of the Columbia below the Cascades. Nine miles below the rapids on the Washington side of the river, stands Castle Rock, covering four or five acres, with perpendicular walls eight hundred feet in height.[2] We pass the celebrated Multnomah falls, and the beautiful Bridal Veil, which is the most bewitching of all. A small rivulet in its course reaches the top of the cliff on the Oregon side of the Columbia, and leaps a distance of four hundred and fifty feet, almost into the river at the foot of the great precipice. Tall trees standing at the base of the falls seem like small bushes, so high is the white sheet of water above their tops. Cape Horn, on the opposite side of the river is a bold promintory of great height and majesty.[3] On our arrival at Portland late in the evening we once more succumbed to the influences of civilization, and put up at the What Cheer house.

On the first of November we took an account of stock and after selling all our saddles, blankets, and other impedimenta, and getting about six ounces of gold assayed at the United States mint, which produced nineteen dollars and a half per ounce, we found that we could no longer provide for our companions, Mr. Francis and the faithful little Stewart; but good luck attended both us and them, for we were able to obtain from good Governor Gibbs, for Mr. Francis the office of chaplain, and for Stewart the appointment as guard, in the Oregon State Penitentiary.[4] Having put our friends in a safe place for the winter, we paid forty-five dollars each for steamer tickets to San Francisco. Our steamer—the old *Pacific*—was largely loaded with apples—and such big ones—some specimens would nearly fill a man's hat, but they lack the New England flavor. Running upon a sand bar in the Willamette [River], we remained fast until high tide in the morning. A strong west wind had worked up a wicked sea, and when outside, out of two hundred passengers only eighteen thought they needed any supper. I was a business man most of the afternoon. Thousands of white pelicans were to be seen at the mouth of the Columbia. The next morning found the steamer in the beautiful straits of Juan de Fuca, with a calm sea and restful scenery. The shores are heavily timbered and there are many beautiful islands in a sea varying from five or six to ten or fifteen miles in width. Far away to the east Mount Baker lifts its helmet of snow which glistens in the sunlight. Threading the channel among the beautiful islands in Puget sound, we reached Victoria, B. C., about noon, and had plenty of time to visit the town and the great British naval station called the Esquimalt. For three days [following] we were at sea, no land in sight. A single ship appears on the western horizon. A large whale spouts near the ship. A few porpoises tumble and play at a little distance. The ship rolls heavily, and I don't like it.

Nov. 8, 1862. We approach the Golden Gate, which seems to be a mile or more in width and is flanked on either side by high headlands. There is an extensive fortress at Fort Point, but we have learned that its walls would be little protection from the new iron-clads. The soldiers' barracks upon the hill-side look very neat and cozy. The grim guns threaten us as we pass Alcatraz Island, but we make our way to the wharf and are safely quartered in another "What Cheer House" before night.

During my stay of three months in San Francisco, I had the company of an old St. Louis friend, C. E. Wheeler, and also an acquaintance with P. C. Dart, a 'Frisco merchant, and Captain Henry W. Kellogg of the United States Army, a native of Shelburne, Mass. I was thus enabled to pass the rainy season with enjoyment after I had established communication with St. Louis and the East. I was a constant attendant with the congregation of T. Starr King, a man of great talent, and heard with great pleasure his sermon preached Feb. 1, 1863, from the text "The Lord reigneth! Let the earth rejoice," having relation to President Lincoln's proclamation of freedom.[5] Having completed arrangements with my brother in St. Louis to send me a general stock of merchandise to Fort Benton by steamer in the spring, my friend Wheeler and I left Feb. 8, by steamer for Portland, where we arrived in due time after a very stormy passage. Here I found Messers. Clow, Jones, Curley, Stewart and others who had been companions the year before on the voyage up the Missouri. Rev. Mr. Francis was in Oregon city, and supplying also Salem. One day early in March while I was awaiting information from St. Louis, Dr. Hicklin and I went out on the mountain to visit a friend of his. Arriving at a little log hut, we found his friend with his wife and nine children, the oldest being twelve years old. Where we were all to sleep I could not imagine, but come night, the doctor and I were given the trundle bed in which we curled up, spoon fashion. Here I learned a new method of making a clearing in a heavy forest. The settler bores a hole on a level into the center of a great pine tree, and then beginning two or three feet above, bores another on an angle downward to meet the first one, at the tree center. Into these holes he pokes a few coals of fire, where it smoulders until the tree burns off and falls to the ground. Then he bores similar holes in the prostrate body of the tree in lengths suitable for handling with a team and when the tree is burned into logs, piles them up and burns them. The waste of fine timber is wicked. On my return to the city, I shot a large American eagle which I presented to my friend A. J. Butler, who had it mounted. Mr. Francis having friends upon the steamer *Sierra Nevada*, which was aground in the river below the city, we visited a Mrs. Very and her daughter, who were on their way to Port Townshend, and helped them while away the weary hours of their delay, much to our pleasure. On the 19th of March I bade goodbye to Mr. Francis and little Stewart, having decided to return to Beaver Head, while Mr. Francis, goes to San Francisco and from thence to New York. He is a fine old Welshman, and knows more of human nature than most men of his profession. The next day Wheeler and I left Portland on the steamer *Wilson G. Hunt* for the Cascades. We landed at the lower landing on the Oregon side and walked the five miles to the head of the Cascades, thus cheating the horse railroad out of two dollars. A steam railroad was being built on the opposite side of the river, running near an old blockhouse. Taking passage on the *Idaho* we passed the petrified trees, the grave yard island where bleach the corded up bones of hundreds of Indian small pox victims, and now and then saw a hewn log house built on the bottom lands, with projecting upper story for defensive purposes, against possible

Indian enemies. The Dalles was a busy little town, large parties of miners and freighters fitting out for the newly discovered mines on John Day's river and the Blue mountains. The Portage railroad through the Dalles gorge to Celilo had just been built, and by the polite invitation of the Oregon Steam Navigation Company I had the pleasure of a trip over the romantic way.[6] The road runs near the river and about five miles above the village, in its construction through the sand heaps, numerous Indian skeletons were unearthed and skulls and other bones lay exposed upon the embankment. The river at this point seems to have been turned up edge-wise, and the waters of a large territory pour through a seemingly small crack in the rocks, but of unknown depth. To stand upon the elevated rocks above the tumultuous waters across which one feels himself able to toss a stone, produces a most unusual sensation, long to be remembered. This is the great fishing place of the natives, and all along in the sand can be seen the *caches* in which the dried salmon have been stored.[7] The excavation is made in the shape of a jug, sometimes ten or twelve feet in depth and from four to six feet in diameter, the entrance at the top being just large enough for a person to get in to pack the fish. The sides are carefully lined with tules, and in these the fish are safely kept for many months. I left [The] Dalles on my long journey the third of April, going to Celilo by stage, where I took the opposition boat *Kiyus* for Wallula. On our way up the Columbia we had several races with the regular boat, *Spray*, in which we were elated to be able to come in ahead. We were obliged to tie up over night at the Umatilla rapids, over which we were compelled to wind up by a tow line. We came to Wallula an hour and a half before the *Spray*.[8]

The government abandoned old Fort Walla Walla some years since, and built anew in a beautiful valley, some thirty miles up the Walla Walla river, and a mile or more away from the army buildings there was located quite a nice little village. Here I was joined by Mr. Wheeler who decided to accompany me to the Beaver Head mines. Mr. Terry, an old mountain man, advises us to go to the Bitter Root valley, by the Pend-Orille trail.

The 10th of April we took the stage at 3 o'clock in the morning and after an eighty-three mile ride, arrived at Lewiston situated at the junction of the Clearwater and the Snake rivers. Our very pleasant traveling companions were Major Francis, Captain Truax and Lt. Hammer of the army, and Mr. Woodward agent of Wells Fargo & Co. The steamer *Kiyus* passed above Lewiston on the Snake river the same day. The next day Mr. Haggard with express matter from Fort Benton came in, bringing news from my companions at Beaver Head. Having purchased a good sized American horse for riding, and a pack animal, and Mr. Wheeler having bought a riding pony, on the 10th [12th?] of April we crossed the Clearwater on a ferry-boat and climbed the high hill lying northward of the town. We were followed by about a dozen of as rough looking specimens of the human species as ever I saw, who announce their intention of keeping us company to the Beaver Head mines.

If the old saying that "a bad beginning makes a good ending" proves to be true, then we will be happy indeed; for as we made our way up the mountain side from the ferry, we met a half dozen green pack horses, running and kicking and bucking off their packs, and our horses joined in with the rest and away the crazy brutes went down the mountain, scattering the contents of the champaign basket which we called our "kitchen" along the hill side; and butter, beans and bacon, cheese, candles and coffee, onions, potatoes, pepper and sardines strewed the way for a mile, while the flapping frying pan and coffee pot, added frenzy to the demoralized *Kiyus*. It was a discouraging start, but we gathered up the fragments and capturing our four footed helper we repacked the remnants, and led the beast for the rest of the day. We carry no tent but sleep under the roof of heaven and pay no rent. The first day we made but six miles, and it rained and snowed during the night, but we traveled twenty-five miles the second day, during which I was compelled to lead our pack animal. A party of three overtook us before making camp, and one of them whom I took to be a woman, though dressed in men's clothing including boots and hat, announced that she was a "Scotch man, and wasn't married to no man!" She rode astride her horse as all women should. As we pull out of camp and ride off down the trail in Indian file, with our fifteen or twenty pack horses we make quite a formidable looking party. For two days it rained and snowed and we remained in camp, and made ourselves as comfortable by big fires as circumstances would permit. We have had an Indian guide, but being disgruntled at something, he undertook to run away, but I took after him and by giving him "chickamin" (money) persuaded him to stay with us.

As we came to the Palouse river I killed three grouse which furnished us fine food. Another party who camped near us got but one grouse, but had killed a large owl. Dressing it they put it into the camp kettle with the grouse, but after cooking it for a long time it still remained so tough that they could not eat it. Building a raft we attached our lariats to it and hauled it over and back to bring across all the packs and people. The horses were made to swim the river. One of our followers lost his pack horse this morning. Our guide has disappeared, and the rabble all depend upon following my lead. Steptoe's Butte is my objective point, a well known land mark, as near by [Lt. Col. Edward J.] Steptoe was defeated by the Indians a few years since [May 16, 1858]. One day we traveled through deep snow on the northerly side of a mountain, and our delightful traveling companions cursed loud and deep concerning my leadership. It was at times hard to keep control of my speech, but I realized the danger of a wrangle with such a crew. After a hard ride of twenty-five miles we came out on Camas Prairie creek, where we found good camping grounds. Some of the men ascending a small hill, discovered that just beyond there was a large Indian camp.

I immediately told our people to make into heaps all articles in the camp and cover them with blankets, and advised them to have a man sit on each pile. Soon came up a hundred Indians, their sharp eyes looking for any article which they could lay their hands upon. They were anxious to exchange potatoes and dried salmon for sugar, coffee, or any thing else which they fancied. Some of the young bucks were very pert and quite saucy. While I was palavering with an old Indian, a young fellow came near, and as quick as a cat snatched from my belt a small self cocking French revolver; I looked at him and smiled, and as he put it up before his face to examine it, he unwittingly caused it to explode, and the bullet passed through the brim of an old soft hat he was wearing. A more astonished looking fellow I never saw, and after a moment he meekly handed back the little pistol and departed much subdued in manner.

In this party was an old man remarkable in appearance by reason of wearing quite a full beard. He came up in front of me and saluting "How! How!" pointed to his breast and said, "Me, Clark; me Clark." What the celebrated early explorer would have said about the claimant of his name, I know not, but it is an old saying that "It is a wise son who knows his own father."[9] But not all Indians are truthful. Again we were compelled to build a raft to cross this narrow but very deep and rapid creek.

One morning after it had rained all night and everybody was out of sorts, I struck off down a creek and the hangers on began to grumble. I told them to go where they pleased, but they followed on. After a while we found that the trail led across the creek, when the rabble broke out again. I "answered them not" but struck off toward Steptoe's mountain, abandoning the trail, and after four pathless miles struck a broad trail which I followed until our horses could go no farther, and we made a dry camp in a thick forest. Soon the big camp fires lighted up the great pine trees most beautifully, and we feasted on broiled grouse but with nothing to drink. After a most tiresome day we reached the top of a high hill from which we could see a large valley, which I knew to be the Spokane prairie, so we hurried on down the mountain, coming on a wide gravel plain, the river seeming to be about five miles away.[10] Continuing on our way hoping to reach water, the day waned with the river apparently as distant as hours before, and we felt compelled to make another dry camp, which is a most discouraging thing to do. We were in a scattered forest of pine, and while I was busy getting supper, Wheeler, remembering that he had passed some snow at the foot of the hill, started to find some for tea. With not the slightest idea of locality, he was soon lost. I fired guns hoping to direct him to camp, but when I discovered him after two hours search, he was going directly away from camp, completely bewildered. An Indian came to our camp in the morning and guided us to the ferry owned by Antoine Plante, and crossing the Spokane [River] we made our camp a mile above, hoping here to escape our quandom friends.[11]

We purchased fine vegetables from an Indian who told us that the Hudson Bay brigade passed up the valley the day before, on their way to the Flathead country. I immediately conceived the idea of overtaking this party and traveling with them. Mr. Wheeler and I had taken a fancy to a man among our followers by the name of Cook, and invited him to join us in the capacity of cook. He was glad to come with us and I bought a pony of our Indian friend for his use. Very early the next morning we three stole from camp and pushed on to overtake the Hudson Bay people, which we accomplished, and found Captain McLaren very cordial in his invitation to join his party.[12] They had some sixty pack horses and about ten or twelve Indian and half breed servants. The commander told us to turn our stock in with the others and his men would care for them. On our way we met Major Owen, and Mr. McDonald, agent for the Hudson Bay Company, at Colville, on their way to Portland. Our brigade was bound for St. Ignatius Mission, and at night we met and camped with a brigade loaded with furs bound from Colville to Portland, where they would purchase and bring back a season's supply. We here left the Spokane and struck across to the Pend Orielle lake, making a march of twenty-five miles. On the south side of the lake outlet, we found an old chief and a few followers, who had a boat made of the bark of an immense pine tree, the brasing out of the middle of the boat cocking up the two ends above the water line. No one was permitted to enter this frail craft without first removing his shoes, for fear of puncturing the bark. The old Pend-Orielle chief took a great fancy to my big horse, and as we bargained for the transportation across the lake, of our party, he importuned me to sell him my coal black "Colonel." He offered three good ponies, but I made him understand that I only needed the one horse and would not sell him. As a final inducement he led out from his wickiup a young girl some sixteen or seventeen years of age, of comely and modest appearance, and offered her to me in exchange for my horse. He seemed struck with amazement when I would not exchange my horse, even for a princess. Captain McLaren informed me that the probabilities were against my having the Colonel in the morning, unless I held his lariat all night.

The horses of the brigade were driven into the lake twenty-five at a time, and before they reached the opposite shore the noise of the puffing and blowing of the swimming horses, reminded me of the noise of a big mill. When our turn came, the old chief sat in the stern of the boat and carefully held the Colonel's head above water as he swam by the side of the bark canoe. Once in camp and supper eaten, I stole away alone with my valuable horse and made a secret camp, that the Colonel and I might still be traveling companions. We traveled up the northeastern side of the lake, where in ordinary stages of water there is a fine beach, but all the rivers now putting into the lake are running banks full, and the water is so high that we are compelled to take to the woods.[13] Scrambling over fallen timber, scratching through thick brush and climbing over rocky points jutting out into the lake, we find most wearisome and trying to both nerves and temper. It was most interesting to watch our long string of pack horses, as they filed through the woods. They were led by a wise old bell mare who would carefully climb along the side of a large tree, when it had fallen across the trail, until she reached the end, and then go around it and follow back to the trail, while some green horse, seeing another a little way ahead, would undertake to leap over the trunk and come to disaster, frequently rolling over down the hill. After ten miles of such travel we again took to the lake shore, often finding deep water as we wallowed around the ends of tall trees fallen into the lake.

Coming to an impetuous mountain stream running into the lake, and fearing that the packs would get soaked if remaining upon the horses, we stripped off our clothes and, each rider taking a pack before him, forded the icy river and returning for another continued until a hundred packs had been safely transferred.[14] We met with a large party of Pend-Orielle Indians returning from a buffalo hunt, and took some lessons in "simple life," as they camped near us. All the streams running down from the mountains are at flood stage and we are greatly hindered at their crossing.

Reaching Pack river, we were lucky enough to find three Indians who had a boat and for some trifling presents they took our packs over. Made camp and Captain McLaren opened some goods and traded with the Indians. For a little tobacco we obtained some large salmon trout and a beaver's tail, of which delicacy I could not persuade Wheeler to partake.

We had hardly proceeded a mile, in the morning, before we came to a river too deep to be forded, and a messenger was dispatched for the Indians to come with their boat, and again they helped us in a crossing.[15] Cedar river proved so deep and the current so swift, that both horses and men were nearly exhausted when we made camp high up on the mountain side, where we not only found good feed for the horses, but a magnificent view of the lake and river. Soon after starting in the morning a half blind horse was made wholly so, and had to be abandoned. The green horse substituted ran away with his pack, and the French half breed who brought him in, rode up to Captain McLaren and said, "How much 'e price dat hoss? I buy him and kill dam fool." The trail along the river is overflowed, and we are compelled to take to the brush and timber along the mountain side, and both men and horses suffer terribly. We are following up the Pend-Orielle river and coming to the Bull's head river, found it running a torrent.[16] We found a narrow place and felled a tree which luckily reached across and caught on some floodwood upon the opposite shore. The middle of the tree was a foot under water, but some limbs helped us to preserve our balance and the men carried over the whole camp outfit. We then undertook to compel the horses to swim the raging flood, an Indian leading the way with my big horse, but he was the only one which made the passage; some of the others landing on the shore they started from, and some washing down to the big river and reaching an island, from which Indians were sent to drive them to the home

camp. I crossed over the tree to get to my horse and finding that
we were on an island I attempted to cross a slough on the
Colonel's back, but the water proved so deep that we both had
to swim. It was raining hard and very cold, and after much trouble
I succeeded in starting a fire, and my horse and I stood close by
and shivered. I gave the horse a half loaf of wet bread as there
was no feed, and we both had a miserable night. In the morning
we recrossed the river and driving the horses a mile above camp
found a place where we thought they might ford. Stationing men
with long poles on the rocks, an Indian mounted a pony and
rode in, the men rushing the other horses after him. He succeeded in getting across and as the others came stumbling within
reach of the poles they were frightened over toward the other
shore, and at last all gained the solid land. We only marched
seven miles and camped in a little prairie, close by an Indian
grave. The next day we made a long march, and some of the
horses being weak and underfed fell out and an Indian was left
to bring in the stragglers. We camped beside Vermillion river
and I found a good prospect of gold in the gravel.[17]

On Thompson's prairie, where a few years before the Hudson
Bay Company had a fort, we laid for two days, that men and
beasts might recruit, and that washing, mending and baking might
be done. I caught a great quantity of large salmon trout, which
when broiled on the coals, was a most agreeable change in our
diet.[18] Here we toted our packs across on a log which we were so
fortunate as to fall across the river. Driving in the horses, some
were nearly drowned as they passed under the tree which we
had used as a bridge, but we saved them all. Crossing a very
steep point some eight hundred feet in height, composed of sharp
loose stone, called Cabinet mountain, was a very severe trial for
the stock, but the trials of the day were forgotten when we made
camp in beautiful Horse prairie.[19] It was the 8th of May but

water froze in our camp. Here we abandoned the river, and after clambering over a trail strewn with sharp rocks for ten miles reached a camas prairie which extended to the Flathead river, just below the Flathead lake.[20] Six Flathead Indians from a camp near by, are our guests for the night. The tribe are digging camas, crowse, or bitter root. Camas is a root in appearance like a small onion. It is sweet and glutinous and quite palatable, and may be eaten raw or cooked. The squaws prepare it by digging a hole in the ground in which they build a fire and heat the surrounding earth, after which they sweep it out and putting in the camas they place over the roots the inverted turf and covering the whole with heated flat stones on which they keep a fire until the camas is cooked. In this condition it may be eaten, or when pounded up, it may be baked into bread, or if desired it will dry and keep for a long time. Crowse is similar to the camas and is plentiful in countries west of the Rocky Mountains. These esculent roots are flour and potatoes to the Indians.[21] The Flatheads took us across their great river in a pine bark canoe, and although [they are] Mission Indians, we have to keep a sharp lookout for little things about camp, and notwithstanding all our care, we missed a handy little knife which we had used about camp. The river is so wide and deep that Mr. McLaren did not think it safe to have some of the weaker horses swim it, and a few of those driven in came near drowning. We followed up the Flathead about twelve miles to the Jocko [River], where we bade farewell to Captain McLaren and his men who have been very kind to us. Following up the Jocko and crossing a divide we came to St. Ignatius Mission. Here we found extensive buildings, a church, saw and grist mills, and many other evidences of civilization, and the mission Fathers very hospitable.[22] They invited us to supper and furnished us with provisions for the continuance of our journey. There were about eight hundred Pend-Orielle and Flathead Indians here, and we much

St. Ignatius Mission, *by Peter Tofft (watercolor on paper, circa 1865).*
Thompson left San Francisco in March 1863 to return to Montana goldfields
as a general store proprietor. On the journey his party visited St. Ignatius
Mission, where they enjoyed the hospitality of the priests and witnessed
the Pend d'Oreilles and Flatheads racing horses.

Montana Historical Society Museum, Helena

enjoyed witnessing their horse-racing. It is very pretty here and
everything shows the careful work of the faithful priests. Two
Indian boys came into camp bringing with them a horse in exchange for one of ours which was unfit for duty, which was very
kind and thoughtful of Mr. McLaren. We sent the boys away
happy. Later we went on about ten miles to the government
agency for the Flatheads.[23] Here we met one of the fathers, who
warned us against war parties of Snake and Bannack Indians
who infested the country, and would rob us, if they thought that
they would not suffer in the attack. We three kept on alone and
crossing some mountains came out upon the Bitter Root river,
which we had traveled the fall before, and going up that stream

came to Worden & Co.'s store.[24] Frank L. Worden came to this country in 1860, in company with C. P. Higgins and others and was in trade at Missoula for many years. He was a man of strict integrity with a high sense of honor. He represented this region in the first Legislative Council of Montana "and occupied many positions of honor and trust and was always faithful in the discharge of every public duty confided to his hands." He died Feb. 5, 1887.[25]

Being now upon the Mullan road, traveled on my journey to the Pacific, which has been described, I shall only mention some incidents which happened to us on our journey to Fort Benton, where I go expecting to receive goods upon the arrival of steamers from St. Louis. Our party of three are a little nervous for fear of meeting hostile Indians, as we were told at Worden's that the Blackfeet stole one hundred and twenty-five horses at Deer Lodge the week before. [The stolen horses] Being pursued, all but seven which were ridden by the thieves, were recovered. Coming to Flint creek we were much relieved to find a wagon train on their way to Fort Benton to get freight from the steamers which were expected there. We made a short visit at our old deserted home on the Deer Lodge, and rode up to Johnny Grant's to obtain supplies. Here we found a large number of teams assembled to travel in company to Fort Benton. Several disappointed men from the Bannack mines were loud in their curses of the country, and a few lucky ones who had "made their pile" were very jubilant. One poor fellow who had hoped to take his small fortune home by the steamer, had been robbed of all his treasure on his way from the mines, and was sadly debating whether to go home or return to the mines and try to retrieve his losses. Our faithful man Cook left us here to try his luck in the mines. We arranged to have our baggage taken in the wagons, and sold our extra horses, and purchased of Johnny Grant five pounds of sugar for five dollars and two of salt for another dollar. May 19, 1863, we left Deer Lodge in company with white men, white women, squaws, half breeds, and Indian herdsmen, twenty in number, and two hundred head of stock, making a motley crew indeed.

Our first camp was made just west of the summit at Mullan's pass, in a cold driving storm of snow and rain. The loose stock was badly scattered by the storm and a late start was the result. I found ten feet of snow, hard and icy, at the summit, on this my eighth time of crossing the Rocky's. Mr. Boltee, the manager of the train overtook us at Little Prickly Pear, having rode from Gold Creek, seventy-five miles in one day, on one mule. As we passed the lonely grave of young Lyon who was accidentally shot on Medicine Rock hill, we were reminded of his pleasant companionship on the trip up the Missouri. The next day Mr. Boltee and I rode ahead, forty-six miles to the government farm on Sun river. Here we found our old friends and companions Mr. and Mrs. Vail, Miss Bryan and young Swift, who seemed very glad to see me, and urged me to stop with them until the arrival of the boats, which I am very glad to do. The season has been very dry and the Sun river valley is all parched and burned up, and the stock has been driven up into the mountains. Mr. Boltee and Mr. Wheeler left the farm for Fort Benton and Mr. Crump of St. Louis, Judge Barry, and Mr. Williamson from Walla Walla, came in ahead of the train and stopped at the farm. Many trains are crossing Sun river on the Benton road, among others Johnny Grant's [train] with twenty two wagons. We, at the farm are mourning the death of Iron, our Indian hunter. He was the best Indian I ever knew, and was killed by Bannacks near Crown Butte while on a hunting excursion. The murderers left signs that Bannacks did the deed, and captured two horses and saddles, gun and blankets which belonged to the farm equipment.

One day we came near having a tragedy in our midst. An Indian and his squaw came to the farm seeking his other squaw who had left his bed and board in company with another young buck. He declared that if he could find her he would kill her, or else cut off her nose and ears and let her go, punishment which Indian law permitted. We truthfully told him that we had seen no strange squaw, and he kept on his search, but had not been gone an hour before the missing squaw came in alone. When told that she was pursued, she only remained to take a little food and Mrs. Vail loaded her with a blanket and provisions, and she struck out for the mountains. We had determined that no murder or maiming should be done in our midst and hoped that she would reach some Flathead camp. Mr. Vail and I hunt enough to furnish meat for the farm and the many visitors, and sometimes get out the government ambulance and escort the women and children as they drive over the plains. Some of the train men brought me eleven long lost letters, some being dated ten months previously, but none the less welcome.

June 1st, 1863, one of the fathers from the Mission of St. Peters, located a few miles away, in attempting to ford Sun river, came near being drowned. He finally reached our side of the river and came to the fort, but his horse returned to the opposite shore. I swam my horse over and after a long search recovered his horse and brought him to the farm. The next day there came to the fort Henry Plummer, sheriff of Bannack city. He is expected to marry Miss Bryan when the Indian agent, Rev. Mr. Reed comes to the fort upon the arrival of the steamers. Just as a party of us were about to start for Fort Benton the Walla Walla expressman came in from there, and reported that nothing had been heard from the boats, so we delayed our journey. We pass away considerable time and expend a good deal of ammunition in shooting at prairie dogs, which are pretty hard to hit and not very excellent food when secured.

Mr. and Mrs. Vail, Messrs. Plummer, Wheeler, Swift and I with the two Vail children, make up a party to visit the Great

Great Falls of the Missouri, *by A. E. Mathews. In June 1863 a party from Sun River visited the Great Falls of the Missouri River, where Thompson noted an "eagle's nest (perhaps the same) written of by Lewis & Clark."*

From A. E. Mathews, *Pencil Sketches of Montana* (New York, 1868), plate 24

Falls of the Missouri, distant about thirty miles from the farm. Mr. Vail drives the ambulance and the other men are mounted. We leave the fort in the care of one man with directions not to admit any Indians within the gates. We reached the Horseshoe falls before dark and built our campfires in a deep-ravine so as not to attract the sharp eyes of any roving Indians, as many of them are very saucy and "clean out" small parties when they run but little risk of getting hurt. The succeeding day we visited all the falls, saw the eagle's nest (perhaps the same) written of by Lewis & Clark, and were impressed by the lower, or "Great" falls, but the others are only pretty and interesting. On our return Plummer, Swift and Wheeler riding ahead, suddenly turned on the top of a hill and rode toward us who were with the ambulance. We supposed they had discovered Indians, and made ready for defending our women and children; but it proved to be a herd of antelope, which they wished me to stalk. When we came in sight of the fort we saw a lot of horses on the plains, and wondered whether they belonged to enemies or friends. Carefully approaching I recognized a dudish young buck who a few weeks before had helped us across the Flathead river, and at that time I had joked him as being a masher among the young squaws, winking at him with one eye, which seemed to tickle his fancy very much. When he saw me he came in front and made the most amusing and ridiculous attempt to wink one eye, imaginable. He was the most dudish young buck that I ever saw. We could talk a little Chinook jargon, and I impressed upon him the enormity of his offence in taking possession of the fort, as it appeared that they came to the fort and the keeper discovering them in season, shut and locked both gates, but while parleying with those at the front some young fellows went to the rear of the palisade and climbing over let the others in. They then compelled the keeper to get them some dinner, and were having things their own way when we appeared. There were ten Flatheads going to the Snake country on a horse stealing expedition. While there they discovered my telescopic rifle which much excited their curiosity. One old fellow who had in some way become possessed of an old silk hat over which he had slipped a bottomless tin pail which he kept highly polished, came up and examining the rifle said "puff!" "puff!" to ascertain if it was a double barreled gun. I shook my head and drew his attention to the telescope, and seeing a man on horseback a long distance away I rested the gun on the corral fence and getting it in range let him look through the glass. He soon caught the object, and shouting "Ugh!" drew his scalping knife and made motions as if he were scalping an enemy whose hair he held in his hand, intimating that it brought the object so near that he could grab it. Then every man in the party had to take a look through the wonderful glass. Old tin kettle offered me three horses for the gun.

We have St. Louis papers saying that the *Shreveport* left that port April 19th, and nothing has been heard from her here, this 8th day of June. Plummer and Swift just returned from Benton report that all there have given up expectation of seeing boats, and the wagon trains have started for the mouth of the Milk river, three hundred miles below.

June 20th, 1863, all the inmates of the fort assembled in the best room to witness the marriage by Father Minatre of the St. Peter's mission, of Miss Electa Bryan to Mr. Henry Plummer. The pretty bride was neatly gowned in a brown calico dress, and was modest and unassuming in appearance. The dapper groom wore a blue business suit, neatly foxed with buckskin wherever needed, a checked cotton shirt and blue necktie. The best man was the tall and graceful Joseph Swift, Jr., who wore sheep's gray pants foxed and patched with buckskin, a pretty red and white sash and a grey flannel shirt, and was under the necessity of wearing moccasins both of which were made for one foot. Being a leader in Blackfoot fashions he wore no coat. Want of more modest and better material is presumably the reason that the Reverend father suggested that I act as a substitute for bride's maid, but I meekly obeyed his order, and my moleskin trousers, neatly foxed in places which came to wear, a black cloth coat and vest and buffalo skin shoes made up my wedding gear. The ceremony was long and formal. Immediately after the wedding breakfast, of buffalo hump and bread made of corn meal ground in a hand mill, the happy couple left in the government ambulance drawn by four wild Indian ponies, for Banack city, the new metropolis. The poor sister, Mrs. Vail, was almost heartbroken. Leaving the antecedent and subsequent career of Mr. Plummer for after-consideration, we continue our relation of events. Hardly had the wedding ceremony been concluded, when Bulls Horn, messenger from Benton, arrived with intelligence that the *Shreveport* would probably reach Benton the next day. Mr. Vail immediately started for Benton, intending to ride through the night, it being cooler and the danger from Indians being lessened. Report came to us that all the horses at St. Peter's mission had been stolen, and we suspect that three half breeds who camped at the farm the night before are the thieves. Some travelers report the finding of clothing and papers on the Little Prickly Pear trail, which would indicate a murder or other tragedy. Two letters were dated at Wasiago, Dodge County, Wis., one Feb. 5 and the other Dec. 25, 1860, addressed to John Little, and signed by Mary Harding. The writer was attending school at Wasiago. Upon Mr. Vail's return from Benton he reported that the *Shreveport* had reached a point about two hundred miles below Benton, (Cow Island) and had unloaded her freight on the river bank, and returned to St. Louis. The Missouri showed the effect of there being no rain in the country since September of the previous year. Nick Wall who had come from St. Louis by way of Salt Lake, arrived on his way to Benton, and informed me that he had left several letters for me at Bannack city. Mr. Wheeler returned from Benton and took his way to Salt Lake on his journey to St. Louis overland, being discouraged by reports of Indian atrocities from descending the Missouri by Mackinaw boat. The passengers put on shore by the *Shreveport* were coming into Benton on foot, many used up by their experiences. Provisions were very scarce at Benton, and none could be supplied until the teams came in from Cow Island. July 3rd, the first of the *Shreveport* tenderfeet, reached the farm and were loud in curses for the captain of that boat. I am very busy in the construction of what Mr. Vail calls a "go-devil." I found at the fort a pair of wheels to which I fitted an axle, and upon the thills attached thereto, I erected a frame upon which I stretched two rawhide thorough-braces like those of a chaise.[26] On these I fastened a dry goods box to which I built a seat and a dasher, all the joints being tightly laced with buffalo rawhide which when dry made them very strong indeed. I cannot conscientiously say that the vehicle was handsome, but it was most useful. It saved the trouble and expense of a pack horse, and was much easier than riding a horse. When finished Mr. Vail drove my horse "Colonel" in it, sixty miles to Fort Benton, stopped there twelve hours and returned the third day.

July 4th Mr. Vail and I got out the fort cannon and fired a national salute, but we had no fire-works. All expectation of the arrival of the Indian agent having been given up, and Mr. Vail having no funds to pay Mr. Swift for his year's services, they agree that he [Swift] shall take from the farm stock at an appraisal for, the amount due him. It seemed necessary that I should go to Bannack for my letters and find out whether I had a stock of goods on the *Shreveport* or not. Mr. Swift entered my employ, and just as we were to start for Bannack with the intention of driving his cattle with us, the expressman from there came in on his way to Benton, and informed me that he left all my letters at the new mines on the Stinking water [Ruby River]. July 17th we got off, I driving Colonel in my "go-devil" with a spare horse hitched behind, and Swift riding a horse and driving six oxen. The first night out we made camp on the Dearborn [River], and as he sat with his back against a tree on one side and I on the other both engaged in writing up our diaries, it may have struck some stray Blackfoot as a literary institution. At Deer Lodge, Swift was enabled to turn his stock into money and at Johnny Grant's I found a number of letters including one from my brother in St. Louis, informing me that he had sent me six tons of goods by the *Shreveport*. We continued on our way to Bannack to find a location for business there, or at the newly discovered mines. At

Cariboo's we camped and fed on beaver tail, and with that delicacy and some bread for food we rode the next day to Fred Burr's
camp on the Big Hole river, I having crossed the main range for
the tenth time.[27] The next day we reached Bannack, and found
letters containing bills of lading for goods, key to safe, etc., and
within two hours were on our way to the new mines on Alder
gulch. Having camped on the Rattlesnake, and at Beaverhead rock,
we rode into the new mines the third day, where we found about
two thousand people in three embryo towns.[28] Retaining one horse
we exchanged the most of our earthly possession for three yoke of
cattle and a wagon, and boldly struck out for Milk river for our
goods, by [a] way over which no wagon had ever been taken,
keeping on the east side of the mountains all the way to Benton.
From the bridge over the Stinking water we followed down the
river and fording the Jefferson [River] struck up a creek which I
soon recognized as one we had prospected upon, when we discovered the Boulder mines. At the head of this creek we ran our wagon
up into a canyon so narrow that we were forced to unyoke our
cattle and drive them out by the side of the wagon, and then draw
it out backward. I finally found a very steep hill over which we
took our wagon, but had to attach two pairs of cattle behind the
wagon to hold it back as we descended it on the other side. We
were glad enough to make camp when following down a little
stream we came out on a rich bottom, up which we had followed
when we made our discovery the fall before. At the crossing of
this stream we met four men from the steamer bound for Alder
gulch. Our trail led us to the top of a divide which we crossed and
soon following down on the little creek, ran into a nest of beaver
dams. The sides of the mountain were so steep that we saw no
way of taking a wagon along them, and the bottom land was overflowed by reason of the succession of dams made by the beaver.
Finally we were compelled to cut a long pole and fastening it

across the wagon, one of us holding on the end of it, kept the wagon from overturning, while the other drove the patient oxen. A hard day's work brought us to Prickley Pear creek. In the morning we found the camp of some miners whom we knew, with whom we stopped three days. The boys were meeting with very good success with their sluicing.[29] Late in the evening after leaving our friends we came to Silver creek and the Mullan road. In the night, Warren Witcher came into our camp and the next day he and I pushed on with his mule team, toward Benton. We hear that some of the teams have reached Benton with goods. [After] camping at Bird Tail rock we reached the farm where I was warmly welcomed by the Vails. I was glad to be where I could feel at home, for I was completely used up. The next day Swift came in with our team, and pushed on for Benton. Although unfit for the effort, I started for Benton, all alone, sleeping on the bank of the Missouri at the mouth of Big Coulee. The next morning I rode into Benton, but there was not a spear of grass within miles of the camp, the country being so dry. I paid at the rate of eight dollars a bushel for corn to feed my pony, and the poor suffering beast did not know enough to eat it. Provisions had become very scarce both here and at the farm, because of the drought and the failure of the boat in reaching Benton. Mr. Vail and I had, since Iron was murdered, been able to furnish all the meat needed, but we had no flour and for weeks we were compelled to depend upon what corn meal we could grind out in a hand mill; coarse, but wholesome food. All the cows had gone dry for want of food, and our coffee without milk or sugar was not like nectar, and butter was but a sweet remembrance.

"'Tis an art that needs practice, of that there's no doubt,
But 'tis worth it—this fine art, of doing without."

The next day Swift started his team toward Cow Island, and I, toward Bannack city, alone. Was at the farm August 22nd, and taking my "Go-devil" from there, was at Dearborn [River] the 23rd, Morgan's ranch the 24th, Little Blackfoot [River] the 25th, having crossed the Rockies the eleventh time, and at "Yankee's" cabin in Deer Lodge the 26th, having been entirely alone on the trip.

From the door of the cabin I shot enough grouse for my needs, and leaving a note of thanks for the proprietor, who was absent, I drove to the Cottonwood "Store" to obtain supplies. The store-keeper asked where I was going, and I replied to Bannack. He says, "Alone?" "Yes." "I wouldn't do it, it's not safe." "Well, I have to go, should like company, but must go, alone if necessary." He then informed me that there was quite a party in camp a mile or so below, who were waiting to find a guide to take them to Bannack. He said that they seemed to be nice fellows and were from Lewiston, or some place on the west side. I drove down to their camp and told them I was going to Bannack and would like company, as the Indians were very ugly on the route. One Dr. Howard seemed to be the spokesman, and informed me that one of their men had a lame back and could not ride. I offered to exchange with the party and let him ride in my "go-devil" and I would ride his horse. They, after a short conference fell in with my proposition, and they invited me to stay with them until the next morning and then make a start, which I was glad to do. The party seemed well organized, and consisted of twelve men. They had a good cook called "Red," and I was not permitted to even take care of my horse, but was their guest. Dr. Howard claimed to be a Yale man, and he and James Romaine seemed to be educated men of agreeable manners.[30] On the fourth day we came after dark to a ranch just out of Bannack, and took up our lodgings in a haystack.

As I walked into town in the morning, almost the first person that I met was Henry Plummer, the sheriff of the mining region. I told him that I came in with a party, some of whom were old

friends of his and spoke very highly of him. He asked their
names and when I told him, he seemed surprised, and finally said,
"Thompson, those men are cut throats and robbers! Hell will be to
pay now! You need not associate with them any more than you
choose." I was thunder-struck, but afterward wondered how he
knew so much about these people. In the mean time Mr. and
Mrs. Vail had abandoned the government farm and removed to
Bannack city, and the Plummers were boarding with them. I was
invited to remain with them also, and gladly accepted their terms.
I find this entry in my diary. "Sept. 2nd, 1863, Mrs. Plummer left
by overland stage for the States." This was the last time I ever
saw her.

My faithful young helper, Joseph Swift, went down to Milk
river where he met William Vantelberg whom Carroll & Steell
had contracted with to deliver my goods in Bannack, for which
I was to pay him ten cents per pound.[31] On his way back to
Bannack Mr. Swift had his horse stolen by Indians, which he
never recovered. He sold our team for fifty-five dollars more
than it cost us. Mr. Swift remained with the train which did not
arrive at Bannack until November 9th. The cost of the goods in
St. Louis was $4,012.43 and Mr. Vantelberg's freight bill amounted
to $4,762.32 and I had yet to fight out with the *Shreveport* its
charges for transportation, and my bill for damages for abandoning my goods upon the back of the Missouri, several hundred miles below Fort Benton where they had contracted to
deliver them.

The report of the discovery by William Fairweather and his
companions in the spring of 1863, at Alder gulch, of the rich
placer mines, spread through the country like wildfire. It brought
into this vicinity thousands of adventurers, and hundreds of gamblers, cut-throats, and robbers followed their wake. The most
desperate and reckless men from all the old mining camps rushed

to this new Eldorado. "Holdups" of travellers on horseback and in public and private conveyances, became of daily occurrence. Every mining camp supported its saloon and gambling hell, and fracases and shooting matches in them were of common occurrence. Almost a reign of terror existed. On the 17th of September there arrived at Bannack, Sidney Edgerton with his wife and several children, and his nephew Wilbur F. Sanders with his wife and two boys. Mr. Edgerton, has been appointed by Abraham Lincoln chief Justice of the new territory of Idaho. Coming on their long and weary journey across the plains, to the crossing of Snake river, they had been directed to East Bannack instead of the town of the name of Bannack on the west side of the Rocky mountains, which was then the capitol of Idaho. Idaho had recently been erected from Washington territory and then included the Beaverhead country. Communication over the mountains was thought almost impossible during the winter months, and the new comers were compelled to remain at East Bannack. The prominence of these two men in the affairs of this region will develop as the story proceeds.[32]

Will the reader now go back with me to the time of my arrival at the government farm on my return from the Pacific coast? The train men whom I overtook on the road told me of there being at Bannack a young desperado named Henry Plummer. I was told that he had killed a man in San Francisco and had escaped from the California state prison, and had run such a pace at Lewiston and Oro Fino, that he and Jack Cleveland had fled and crossed the mountains late in the fall, with the intention of going down the Missouri in a Mackinaw boat.[33] Upon reaching Benton the fear of Indians was so great that they could find no person willing to undertake to run the river. Just at this time, Mr. Vail at the government farm feared an attack by Indians, and went to Fort Benton to find help to protect his family.

Plummer and Cleveland were engaged to return to the farm for the winter. Here Plummer first met Electa Bryan, the young sister of Mrs. Vail, a pure and beautiful young woman. Mr. Plummer was a good looking young man of twenty-seven, polite, and of good address, and the unsophisticated young lady, isolated in a palisaded log house with no companion of her own sex, excepting her married sister, was easily led by the pleasing manners and quiet assurances of Mr. Plummer to believe that he was the victim of circumstances which for his own preservation compelled him to commit the deeds which gave him a bad name. The Indian scare calmed down when the snows came, and Plummer and Cleveland, his chum, went to the new mines on Grasshopper [Creek]. From being friends the two became enemies, and Plummer let fall some expression which indicated that he was fearful that Cleveland in his oft repeated drinking bouts, would disclose some secret concerning him, and during a melee in Goodrich's saloon in Bannack, Plummer shot Cleveland, inflicting wounds from which he died soon after. When Cleveland lay wounded upon the floor of the saloon, Hank Crawford and Harry Phleger, two good men, took him to Crawford's cabin and cared for him until he died and saw his body decently buried. Plummer anxiously inquired of Crawford what Cleveland, as he lay wounded, said of him. Crawford repeatedly told him, "Nothing." Plummer answered, "'Tis well he did not, for if he had I would kill him in his bed." In answer to Crawford's inquiries Cleveland only said, "Poor Jack has got no friends; he has got it (his death wounds) and I guess he can stand it." In answer to Phleger's questions as to their differences, he said, "It makes no difference to you," and died with the secret, if secret there was.[34] For the present the miners did not trouble themselves about the shooting, so long as it was confined to the members of the gambling fraternity. For weeks Plummer sought every opportunity to engage

Crawford in a fight so that he might have a shadow of an excuse for his murder. At last some of his friends saw Plummer standing behind a wagon resting a rifle across its wheel, evidently waiting for Crawford's appearance from his cabin across the street and fairly driven by his friends to improve the opportunity to save his own life by taking that of his persecutor, Crawford from the corner of his cabin shot at Plummer, the bullet entering at his right elbow and stopping at the wrist. Crawford fled to Fort Benton where he was protected by Major Dawson until he was enabled to make his way down the Missouri, in the spring.[35]

When the true character of the man, Plummer, became known to the Vails and Miss Bryan, she was implored not to unite her destiny with such a character.

It was at this time that I reached the farm upon my return from the Pacific Coast. Sun river, upon my arrival was not in condition to be forded and [hearing my] hailing from the opposite bank Mr. Vail recognized me, and returning to the fort announced my arrival. Immediately Miss Bryan informed her sister that she would follow my advice in the matter of her marriage to Mr. Plummer. In a day or two I was enabled to cross the river and was warmly welcomed by my friends. Hardly an hour had elapsed before Mrs. Vail besought me to plead with her sister to give up her infatuation for her lover. She was a most devoted Christian woman, and loved her sister most tenderly and felt that she was responsible for her future, as would a mother for her daughter. I calmed her as best I could and soon Miss Bryan sought an opportunity to rehearse her love for her persecuted and maligned lover. To her unsophisticated soul, he was a pure, good man, persecuted beyond all endurance, and the fatalities which had surrounded him were such that in no instance was he to be blamed. The little blind god had taken complete possession of her soul. She said that she loved Mr. Plummer, that she knew that he loved her, that she had the utmost faith in him, that the terrible stories of him were told by men not worthy of belief; that she could never be happy unless she married him. I asked her if she did not know that he had killed Jack Cleveland whom she knew, and that even if the taking of his life was for just cause or not, whether she did not also know that in this country it was generally the case that a man who had killed another, died a like death? Whether she could afford to rush into such trouble which could well be avoided. I counseled her not to rashly make a change which was of so much importance in her life, and urged the distress of her sister and her other friends, and advised her to await the arrival of the boats and then go home to the states and in the fall if she and Mr. Plummer remained of the same mind, he could then go and meet her. After a long time she gave her assent to the plan I had suggested and made some preparation for her journey. Her sister seemed much relieved at her decision. But a few days elapsed when Mr. Plummer made his appearance at the farm, to fulfil his promise to marry Miss Bryan. Rev. Mr. Reed, the Indian agent and the Vails' pastor at their Iowa home, was hourly expected.

I had never before met Plummer. I knew that he had won the affection of my young friend Swift, during his stay at the farm, and when I saw him I could but wonder if this could be the young desperado whom people so much feared. He was about five feet ten inches in height, weighed perhaps one hundred and fifty pounds, and was, as Langford well says, "In demeanor quiet and modest, free from swagger and bluster, dignified and graceful. He was intelligent and brilliant in conversation, a good judge of men, and his manners were those of a polished gentleman."[36] He seemed devoted to Miss Bryan, and I could not much wonder at her happiness when all my well intended advice was thrown to the wind and it was announced that the marriage would take place upon the arrival of Mr. Reed. From June 2nd to the 20th we all awaited the arrival of the boats which would bring Mr. Reed. Finally all hope of seeing the Methodist Elder was given up, and, as I have already written, Father Minatre from St. Peter's Catholic Mission was called in and the marriage was duly celebrated.

FIVE

The Vigilantes and
the Road Agents

I HAVE ALREADY WRITTEN that about the last of August, 1863, I innocently piloted into Bannack a considerable party of road agents. While on our journey I learned that the men were named Doctor Howard, Chris Lowry, James Romaine, Robert Zachery [Zachary], William Page, Erastus Yager, (called "Red") John Wagner and Steve Marshland. They treated me with much consideration, not allowing me to furnish any supplies, but Dr. Howard, who seemed to be the leader of the party and claimed to be a graduate of the Yale Medical school, was very inquisitive in relation to my affairs. I frankly informed him that I had an assorted stock of goods on the way from Milk river, and that I did not have any money to pay the freight bills, and would not be in funds until I realized [a profit] from the goods. He claimed to be well acquainted with Mr. Plummer of whom he spoke in the highest terms, and claimed that he [Plummer] was an honorable man, and that his shootings had always been in self defence. His defence of Plummer gave me much pleasure, which was abruptly ended when Plummer himself told me, "They speak well of me for they don't dare do otherwise." I supposed that this referred to his office of sheriff and thought no more of it. When he told me that there were likely to be rough times ahead, he warned me never to open my store doors after retiring, (for I slept in my store) without first finding out who desired admittance. He also assisted in piling up in front of my bunks packages of goods as a barricade, and in arranging a port hole through them to be convenient in case of attack. The Vails having taken up their residence at Bannack, they pressed me to make my home with them, and Mr. Swift and I consented to take our meals with them. Mr. and Mrs. Plummer also boarded there. Mrs. Plummer told me that Mr. Plummer was away from home so much attending to his duties as sheriff, that she with his consent had concluded to go to her home in Iowa, and he was to meet her there in the fall. The second day after my arrival she took the overland stage for Salt Lake on her way east.[1] While on our way from Deer Lodge with Dr. Howard and party we overtook the extensive pack train of Lloyd Magruder, a wealthy trader from Elk City, Idaho; who was taking his goods for sale to Bannack City. At the crossing of the Big Hole river he heard of the wonderful discoveries at Alder gulch, and decided to go with the crowd to the new mines. My late comrade only made a short stop in Bannack and went into Virginia City with the Magruder train. There he took a store and for six weeks was busily engaged in disposing of his stock of goods. Dr. Howard, Lowry, Romaine and Page assisted him in making sales, and made the store their headquarters and knew as well as did Magruder, of his accumulation of gold dust, greenbacks, and coin. He had a train of seventy good mules with their necessary outfit, and when he had sold out his goods had in his possession about twenty-four thousand dollars. When Magruder was ready to return to Elk City he engaged the quartette to assist him on his western journey. Besides Howard and his men, Charley Allen, who had been successful in mining operations, the brothers Horace and Robert Chalmers, who were new comers to the mountains, and William Phillips, an old mountain man, accompanied the Magruder train for companionship on their journey west.

For some reason known only to himself, perhaps a touch of pity, Romaine tried to persuade Phillips not to make the trip. Not until well on their way did Dr. Howard make known to Lowry and Romaine the whole of his murderous scheme, but they needed little persuasion to become partners in the crime. Meeting Bob Zachery in Bannack, Dr. Howard broached the matter to him, but as the murder of the five men was intended he refused to join the expedition. Crossing the Bitter Root valley, one October night the train wound its way near the summit of a pass through the mountains, a hundred miles away from any white settlement. The air was cold and the keen wind was the excuse for a bright fire when camp was made. When the pack animals were relieved from their burdens, and Page came to drive them away from the camp, Dr. Howard hissed to him, "Drive the animals a half mile from camp and don't come back 'till supper time, for we are going to kill Magruder and his four friends, and if you value your life don't you breathe a word to any living being." Lowry killed Magruder with an axe as he was stooping toward the fire to take a coal in his pipe. It is unnecessary to detail the horrid particulars of the awful tragedy then and there enacted; suffice it to say that the heartless wretches completed with axe, pistol and knife the murders they had planned. When the infamous Romaine came to Phillips as he lay in his blanket, he said as he stabbed him, "I have to kill you, you old fool; I told you at Virginia city not to come." Page who had no hand in the actual murders, was found wrapped up in his blanket and was ordered by Howard to assist in concealing the evidences of the great crime. Reserving for their own use the few personal belongings of their victims, they burned the rest and cast the remains of the saddles and indestructible property over a bluff into a deep canyon, together with the bodies of the five murdered men, hoping that wild beasts would soon make them beyond recognition. The murderers attempted to ride away and leave the animals with the exception of seven horses and one mule reserved for their own use, but the herd persisted in following the old bell mare, and they finally drove them into the canyon and shot them.

Having as they thought concealed all traces of their awful deed, and being short of provisions, the robbers hastened toward Lewiston, and leaving their horses at a ranch outside the town, one of the party purchased tickets to Walla Walla. Hill Beachy, the stage agent at Lewiston recognized Dr. Howard, Lowry, and Romaine, as three of the roughs whom he had assisted in running out of Idaho a few months before. He at once suspected that his friend Magruder had been murdered, and a boy who was then in his employ, but who had formerly been with Magruder, recognized a saddle left with the horses at the ranch, as one which was owned by Magruder.

Another person was sure that one of the horses was the same that Magruder had when he left for Beaverhead. Hill Beachy determined to follow and arrest the men whom he believed had murdered his friends. One Tom Farrell volunteered to keep him company. When they arrived at Walla Walla they learned that their quarry had left for Portland four days previously. At Portland they found that the robbers had sailed for San Francisco the day before. Beachy pushed on overland to Yreka where he was able to telegraph to the authorities at 'Frisco asking for the arrest of the murderers, and the next day at Shasta [he] received word that the whole party were safely in prison. For four weeks Beachy fought for the extradition of his malefactors to Idaho, and having plenty of money Dr. Howard exhausted every means to prevent his success. At last Beachy had his prisoners on board the steamer bound for Portland, and upon their arrival at that place, Gen. Wright then in command, detailed a military escort to guard them to Lewiston. A great concourse of people met them at the wharf at that place, and shouts went up, "Hang 'em! Hang 'em! string 'em up!" but protected by the military, Beachy succeeded in getting his prisoners to the hotel.

He soon after appeared on the balcony and announced to the people that one of the conditions upon which the California authorities surrendered the prisoners to him was, that they should have a fair trial under the law of Idaho. He asked that all who would uphold his pledged word, should stand upon the other side of the street, and they all passed over to the side of law and order. After many delays a trial was had; Page was allowed to turn state's evidence, and Dr. Howard, Lowry and Romaine were found guilty of murder, and sentenced to be hung on the 4th day of March, 1864. A gallows was erected in a circular valley near the town and on the fatal day, in presence of a great crowd, including the most of the Nez Pierce Indians, the three murderers met their just doom.

A few weeks after Hill Beachy had witnesssed the culmination of his efforts for justice, he and a few of Magruder's friends taking with them Page as guide, visited the place of the massacre, and tenderly gathering up the remains of the murdered men they returned with them to Lewiston where they were decently interred. Page remained for a season in Beachy's employ, shunned and detested by the people, but within a year was killed in a drunken row. Thus ended the lives of four of that pleasant party with whom a few months before I journeyed from Deer Lodge to Bannack.[2]

Beachy received from the United States mint seventeen thousand dollars, the value of the gold deposited by the robbers for coinage, and turned it over to Mrs. Magruder. After some years the Idaho legislature made an appropriation for the payment of the expense attending the capture and conviction of the murderers. Mr. Beachy died in San Francisco in 1875, leaving many loyal friends.

Beachy, in relating to Gov. N. P. Langford the story of the Magruder murder and its avenging, said that when he made up his mind to bring the murderers to justice, "I then felt that the time had come when I needed more than human help, and I went out to the barn and got down on my knees and prayed to the Old Father—and that's something I haven't been much in the habit of doing in this hard country—and I prayed for a half an hour; and I prayed hard; and I promised that if He'd only help me catch these villians, I'd never ask another favor of Him as long as I lived! *and I never have!*"

Langford in his *Vigilante Days and Ways*, a work of great merit giving a true history of organization and work of the "Vigilance Committee" says that Lloyd Magruder was a wealthy merchant of Elk city, Idaho, and that he fitted out his Beaverhead pack train at Lewiston and boarded at the "Luna House" which was kept by Hill Beachy, who was also agent of the stage and express line. They were boon companions and the day before Magruder set out with his rich stock of goods, Beachy had told his wife that he had dreamed that he had seen Chris Lowry dash out Magruder's brains with an axe. His wife wished to tell Magruder, but her husband forbade her; but so impressed was Beachy that he felt great relief when he learned that his friend had safely arrived at Bannack. The next day after Magruder left Lewiston, Dr. Howard, Lowry, Romaine, Zachery and some other gamblers left that place bound, as they announced, for Oregon, but after travelling about 50 miles in a direction that would allay any suspicion, they then turned and followed Magruder's trail toward the Beaver head mines. Page joined them later on in their journey. These were the men I found camped on the Deer Lodge and piloted into Bannack.

In the marvelously rich placer mines at Alder gulch, many experienced miners soon accumulated sufficient means to satisfy their longings either by taking from the earth the shining scales of gold, or by selling their ground rights to greedy purchasers. With the prospect of a long winter before them during which enforced idleness must be the rule, many longed to return to the states, or to return to their old stamping grounds where the winter expenses would be much less. Inquiries in later days, made by friends of men who had been traced to these new mines, and were known to have been there, but who had suddenly disappeared, made it evident that many fell victims to the road agents who had established themselves along the route which travellers were compelled to take. Fear of robbery had become so great that persons who had determined to leave the country often secretly left without informing their nearest friends. At the head of a dry gulch between Bannack and Horse Prairie I discovered the remains of burned clothing, the jaws of a carpet sack, buttons and other debris which convinced me that a murder had been committed near that place.

Henry Plummer had been elected by miner's meetings sheriff of all the different mining camps, many being convinced that his killings had been done in self defence, and all knowing that he had qualities which peculiarly fitted him for the duties of the office.[3] He resided in Bannack and named deputies in the different mining camps. The men selected as deputies were acquiesced in rather than approved, but consideration was had that good law abiding citizens were scarce who would take their chances with the desperadoes and gamblers with whom they would be compelled to deal. Plummer's office was sufficient excuse for his frequent absence from Bannack, but after a few months the feeling grew, but could not be safely expressed, that our sheriff knew more concerning the frequent hold-ups and robberies than he saw fit to confide to those he called his friends. He was somewhat hampered by the presence and anxious inquiries of his loving wife, and she was sent to her old home in Iowa. After her departure robberies became more and more frequent. [Plummer] being my fellow boarder at Mrs. Vail's, I knew of all his absences and noticed, as my suspicions arose, that all the big hold-ups and robberies happened when he was away from home. I recalled his warning when I told him of Dr. Howard's arrival, and with what certainty he spoke of the future operations of the roughs. I became certain that he knew of the plans of the road agents before they were carried into execution. He was also the acknowledged owner of the Rattlesnake ranch located about fifteen miles from Bannack, which harbored a notorious lot of scoundrels.[4] I could not breathe a word of my suspicions to my clerk and fellow boarder, young Swift, who loved Plummer like a brother, and indeed he was a loveable man.[5]

At last the climax came, and as usual, in an unexpected manner. Judge Edgerton and his nephew Wilbur F Sanders had become my intimate friends. I was almost daily at the Edgertons and he as frequently at my den. One of the last days of October the stage coach from Virginia city came into Bannack with the story of its having been robbed a few miles out of Bannack. Among those [aboard the stage coach] relieved by the road agents was Frank R. Madison (a member of our company), Dan McFarden [McFadden] (known as "Bummer Dan"), Percy and Wilkinson. "Dan" had just sold out his claim and had $2,000 in a belt upon his rotund person. Bill Bunto[n] the stage agent at Plummer's ranch had detained the coach over night, his excuse

Wilbur Fisk Sanders. Thompson, who became a lifelong friend of Sanders, named him as "the acknowledged leader" in the vigilante movement, writing that "in constant peril of his life he led the way to the establishment of law and order." Sanders later represented Montana in the U.S. Senate.

R. A. Lewis, photographer, Montana Historical Society Photograph Archives, Helena being that he could not find the change of horses. In the morning he took his seat on the coach with the driver and when the road agents covered the passengers with double barreled shot guns and shouted "Hold up your hands" he went through that ceremony with the others, and cursed his luck with the stoutest.

There was much excitement when the robbery was noised about in Bannack and Judge Edgerton being in my store when no one but us was present, I turned the key in the door and asked, "Judge, who is doing all this business?" He waited a moment, looked around the room, and said, "I think I know!" I exclaimed, "HENRY PLUMMER!" We then compared notes.[6] He told me of the robbery of his ward Henry Tilden a young man living in his family. I knew of the robbery but not that Tilden had recognized Plummer as one of the robbers. A cow belonging to the judge had strayed and Tilden in his search for her had ridden to Horse Prairie ranch located about twelve miles out on the Salt Lake road. Returning toward Bannack soon after dusk he was held up by three highway men who ordered him to dismount and throw up his hands. Looking down the muzzles of three revolvers he found not pleasant and quickly obeyed the command given him. Finding only a dollar or two on his person, the robbers cursed him roundly and in their gentle manner told him that if they ever caught him in that condition again they would blow the top of his head off. They then permitted him to mount and Tilden rode toward Bannack with such reckless speed that his horse fell into a prospect hole, and his screams brought him help.

Reaching home he excitedly declared that he had been robbed "and I know one of the robbers! It was Henry Plummer!" Immediately the Judge cautioned him and all the household never to tell of Tilden's suspicions as it might cost them their lives. The effect of Crawford's bullet in his arm had caused Plummer to draw his pistol in a peculiar manner, and Tilden had recognized him, although they were all masked. Mr. Sanders was called in and Tilden told his story in full, and no doubt was left in the minds of these men but that Plummer was the leader of the gang.

The presence of the robbers at that place at that time is accounted for by another story. My friends, Nathaniel P. Langford from St. Paul and Samuel T. Hauser from St. Louis (a fellow passenger on the *Emilie*), two as brave men as ever served Montana, had determined to visit the states.[7] Langford was a man peculiarly obnoxious to gamblers and men of that ilk, and had been shot at by one Ed French at Virginia city the day before that fixed for his departure. The bullet slightly abraised one eye, which had from riding in the alkali dust become so much inflamed by the time he reached Bannack, that he was detained there several days. His companion was to come to Bannack as soon as Langford had completed arrangements for their journey to Salt Lake. They had agreed to take to St. Louis for Dance & Stuart, merchants at Virginia city, $14,000 in gold dust. Clubfoot George was a clerk in Dance & Stuart's employ, and what *he* knew the road agent gang knew. Langford, at Bannack completed arrangements with eight Salt Lake freighters traveling together and they set Nov. 14th at noon as the time to leave Bannack. When Hauser left Virginia city with his gold he found as his fellow passenger in the coach, Sheriff Plummer. The trip over the intervening seventy-five miles was a very pleasant one, and as usual when the stage arrived at Bannack the citizens gathered at Goodrich's to get the news and welcome any friend who might be a passenger. Judge Edgerton, myself and others were present when Hauser undid from his blankets the buckskin bag of gold and handing it to the sheriff, said, "Plummer, I hear that any man who has money isn't safe in this town, over-night. I've got fourteen thousand dollars in that bag which I'm goin to take to the states with me when I go, and I want you as sheriff to keep it for me 'till I start!" Plummer said, "That's all right, I'll take the gold and return it to you," a promise which he faithfully performed. He kept the money in George Chrisman's store overnight. The Mormon train agreed to wait at Horse Prairie for Langford and Hauser until five o'clock P. M. and then push on if they did not appear. Before noon a rumor arose in Bannack that rich silver veins had been discovered near the Rattlesnake (in the opposite direction from Horse Prairie) and among other men riding in that direction were Buck Stinson, Ned Ray and George Ives, who said that Plummer had been seen going that way and that he was the only person who knew the location of the discovery. Even so keen an observer as W. F. Sanders tried to find the trail of Plummer and spent the night at Rattlesnake ranch in the vain hope that Plummer would come there before he returned to Bannack. It was afterward proved that Plummer, Stinson, Ray and Ives crossed the Grasshopper above Bannack, and riding toward Horse Prairie were concealed by the roadside awaiting the arrival of Langford and Hauser when Tilden met with his experiences. While riding from Virginia city Plummer had presented to Hauser a large red woolen scarf, remarking that it would be a nice thing to have these cold days and nights on his long journey; probably with thought that it might serve to identify the man who had charge of the bag of gold. After the little comedy with Tilden, thinking that Langford and his comrade had passed before their arrival, the quartette made a diversion around the Horse Prairie station and came out on the Salt Lake road beyond the camping place of the Mormon train.

It happened that Langford and Hauser did not leave Bannack until seven in the evening and thus escaped meeting the party who intended to welcome them on the heights between Bannack and Horse Prairie. At night, the wagons being overcrowded,

Langford took a buffalo robe and lay down under a wagon. Awaking before daylight and thinking he would get no more sleep, he took his rifle and went down to the creek to gather sticks to lay a fire. Wandering some distance below the camp, he thought he heard voices, and listening, his suspicions were confirmed, and creeping through the brush he caught sight of three masked men. A slight noise aroused the suspicions of the trio, or for some other reason they disappeared down a bank. Brave man as he was, his first impulse was to alarm his companions, but the first flurry over, he determined to examine farther. Creeping to the bank he discovered four men, one of whom was holding four horses, in a former bed of the stream. Evidently the masked men feared that they had been discovered, for after a whispered conversation they led their horses away, and were seen no more. The train and with it our friends and the bag of gold all reached Salt Lake in safety. When a few months later, Langford and Hauser returned to the mountains, there had ceased to be any danger from road agents.

I have already stated that Mr. Sanders was compelled to remain at the Rattlesnake ranch (owned by Plummer) after his vain search for the silver mine. Bill Bunton was the chief at the ranch and his aids were Frank Parish and Erastus Yager, or the man "Red" who was the cook when he accompanied me from Deer Lodge to Bannack. Parish, who was at this time keeping a Bannack squaw, was very sick and seemed likely not to live many days. When at last Sanders found Plummer he denied that he knew of any discovery of a silver mine, but said that he had learned that if Parish died, the squaw was to gather up all the horses and drive them to her tribe who were camped near Fort Lemhi, and he started that story to cover his intention to drive the horses to some safe place. After an exciting day Dr. Palmer, in attendance upon Parish, Yager, Bunton and Sanders spread their blankets upon the floor of the living room and were soon in dream-land. About midnight a terrible pounding upon the door brought Yager armed with a double-barreled gun to his feet and a shout "Who's there!" A voice answered "Jack!" and in stalked Jack Galligher [Gallagher]. His temper had been badly warped by a long search for the cabin in a driving snowstorm. He demanded something to eat and drink which necessaries Yager furnished, trying all the time to keep him quiet on account of Parish's condition. During Galligher's swagger, Sanders raised his head and inquired if he know where Plummer was. Instantly Galligher covered Sanders with his revolver and swore that he would "shoot the top of his head off." But he had waked up the wrong passenger; before Galligher knew it, Sanders jumped up and seizing Yager's gun which lay on the bar, he covered Galligher, who threw his pistol on a table and tearing open his shirt told Sanders to shoot. He told him he had no desire to shoot anybody, but that if there was shooting to be done he intended to have the first chance. Things quieted down and Galligher, determined to do the handsome thing, would not be comforted until he had treated the crowd. Silence came at last to the occupants of Rattlesnake ranch, but toward morning another alarm roused the sleepers. This time it proved to be caused by two sterling men of Bannack who were at the behest of his distressed wife hunting W. F. Sanders.

Only a few days subsequent to these occurrences, three wagons owned by Milton S. Moody left Virginia City for Salt Lake, via the Red Rock cut-off a few miles below Bannack. Seven well-known business men of Virginia City improved this opportunity to take with them about $80,000 in dust for transmission from Salt Lake to their eastern creditors. The road agents were fully informed of this arrangement and John Wagner (Dutch John) and Steve Marshland, (both members of my Deer Lodge party) were selected to rob the train. One of the merchants, John McCormick, had at one time, befriended George Ives, and in a moment of confidence he had warned McCormick to be always on his guard and not to sleep until the train had crossed the divide north of Snake river. It was afterward known that when the train was in camp in Blacktail Deer canyon, the two robbers crept up when the men were scattered in groups around the fire, eating their supper, and afterward retired a short distance for conference, that Dutch John tried to induce Marshland to attack at once, claiming that they could kill four at the first fire and by rapid firing and shouting give the impression that they [the campers] were surrounded by a large party, and in their fright they would run and leave the train. Marshland thought it too risky and would not consent.

While the campers were at breakfast next morning, hidden by a sharp point of rocks which caused a turn in the road, they heard a voice in a nearby thicket say, "You take my revolver and give me your gun, and you come right after me." In an instant every man made ready, and the click of the gun locks gave notice to the robbers that the game was against them and they drew off. A few hours later these two men rode into the noon camp with their guns ready for instant use, and making some conversation, made particular inquiry about some lost horses, and then rode on down the Salt Lake road.

Two days later the train approached the divide, and the horsemen of the party rode ahead as was their custom, to select a spot for the night camp. Only three or four men remained with the train. Suddenly out from the brush close beside the way, rode two disguised men with double barrelled shot guns in hand, who shouted, "Hold up your hands every one of you or we will blow the tops of your heads off!" Instinctively up went every hand in sight, no one thought of resistance. While Marshland searched the men Dutch John covered first one and then another of the victims. Marshland was nervous and did not discover a revolver in Moody's boot-leg or $100 in his shirt pocket. In the first wagon he secured a satchel containing $1,500 in greenbacks. As he climbed into the third wagon he was shot by Melancton Forbes who was inside, caring for a sick man, the charge entering his breast. Forbes had watched the robbers through a hole in the wagon cover and was prepared for them. Marshland jumped from the wagon and gained cover. As Dutch John fired at the driver the act caused his horse to rear which probably saved the driver's life. Then Moody made use of his revolver wounding Dutch John in the shoulder, but before pursuit could be organized he was able to gain cover in the thick brush. Marshland's horse and twenty pounds of tea which he had stolen from a Mormon train were confiscated, but both robbers escaped. After overtaking those of their party who had chosen the camp a delegation returned to the place where the robbery took place, and followed the trail of Marshland. They found the missing greenbacks but they did not find either robber. Marshland afterward informed the vigilance committee, that at one time the men were within fifteen feet of him. Leaving this train to make its way to Salt Lake, we will now turn to another section of the country.

Near where the road from Bannack to Alder gulch strikes the Stinking Water [Ruby River] stood at this time Robert Dempsey's ranch. Situated in a beautiful valley with unlimited range of good pasturage, it became the place where nearly all those people on Alder gulch (a branch of the Stinking Water) kept their stock. A German by the name of Nicholas Tiebalt placed his fine pair of mules on this ranch for safe keeping. He afterward sold them to Burtchy & Clark for whom he worked. Having occasion to use them, they sent Tiebalt down to the ranch to bring the mules to Virginia City. Several days elapsed and Burtchy & Clark heard nothing of Tiebalt or the mules, and concluded that he had sold the mules and gone to the states. Nine days after Tiebalt disappeared, one William Palmer shot a grouse as he was travelling toward Virginia City, and it fluttered into the air for awhile and fell among some bushes in a little ravine. Searching for his bird he found it lying upon the frozen corpse of a man. He went to the wickiup of John Frank (Long John) and George Hilderman not far away, and asked them to assist in putting the body into his wagon, so that he could take it to Nevada City (just below Virginia City) but they both refused to have anything to do about it. Palmer, however, without assistance loaded the body into his wagon and took it to his home in Nevada City. Here, when viewed by the public it became evident that the man had been dragged while still alive by a rope placed around his neck, through sage brush to the place of concealment, for his hands still contained pieces of the brush which he had clutched as he was dragged along. The discovery of this murder sealed the doom of the road agents. Before dark twenty-five brave and determined men had signed a written obligation that they would not disband until the country was free from the control of the desperate gang who were terrorizing the people. At ten o'clock at night, well armed, they took up their march for Dempsey's ranch. At break of day having arrived near Long John's wickiup, a barking dog gave an alarm, but the scouts putting their horses into a run had surrounded the shack before its occupants were aroused. The leader, putting his head inside shouted, "The first man who rises will get a quart of buck shot in him before he can say 'Jack Robinson!'" With guns covering the prostrate men who could be seen through the entrance, the leader called out "Long John!" "I'm here," said that individual. "Come out!" Under the escort of four men Long John was taken to the spot where Tiebalt's body was found and he was charged with his murder. This he stoutly denied, but after long

questioning he admitted that George Ives, then in the wickiup
killed Tiebalt. The men arrested at the wickiup were, besides
Long John and Ives, Alex Carter, Bob Zachery, Whisky Bill
[Graves], Old Texas [Jim Crow], and Johnny Cooper. At
Dempsey's they captured George Hilderman and closely guarding them all they reached Nevada about sundown. The members
of the gang not yet captured, some of whom were not even under
suspicion, immediately dispatched Club-foot George to Bannack
to beseech Plummer to come to the rescue and demand that the
prisoners be tried by a jury, well knowing that the sheriff by miners law would have the selection of such jury. But the assembled
people had become the governing power at this time, and it was
determined that the trial should proceed before all the people,
but under the direction of twelve men appointed from each mining district, but the verdict should be by the people. Wilbur F.
Sanders and Charles S. Bagg were chosen to prosecute, and
Alexander Davis and J. M. Thurmond had been secured by friends
of the accused to defend the prisoners. All four were skilled attorneys and each exerted all his talents in conducting the case.
Two days were spent in unprofitable wrangling and little advance had been made toward a decision, when a spokesman for
the people assembled, announced that the trial must end by three
o'clock in the afternoon. Long John had turned state's evidence,
each prisoner being tried separately, and George Ives being then
on trial for killing Nicholas Tiebalt. In his testimony Long John
said that Ives had told him the following words, "When I told
the Dutchman I was going to kill him, he asked time to pray, and
I told him to kneel down then. He did so and I shot him through
the head just as he commenced his prayer." The scene of the trial
was described by one who was present as something awful to
behold. The swaying multitude; the deep silence which would
fall upon the crowd when some witness told of the terrible deed

of some member of the murderous gang; the intense interest of the few sympathizers with the accused; the citizen guard with loaded guns stationed to prevent any attempt at rescue; the murmerings of the large majority of the people who were impatient and disgusted at the long delay in arriving at judgment, made the whole wild scene a most impressive exhibition of the fearful passions inherent in humanity.

It was nightfall before the special jury took the case under consideration. The great crowd seemed stifled as they waited for their report. After what seemed an age to the anxious people, a verdict of "guilty" was announced with only one dissenting voice, this being a man who believed that George Ives was a member of the road agent band, but that he did not actually kill Nicholas Tiebalt. A brave, honest man. The attorneys for the accused put in a plea for adjournment, but the assembled people voted instead [on the motion of Wilbur Sanders] "that the report of the special jury be received and that the jury be discharged." Wrangling again commenced, but a motion [also offered by Wilbur Sanders] "that the assembly adopt as their verdict the report of the committee" was put and carried.

The counsel for Ives had vehemently opposed this, but the almost unanimous action of the people was an assertion that delay would no longer be tolerated. The leaders for good government now saw that there was necessity for immediate action, and W. F. Sanders made a motion "that George Ives having been proved guilty of the murder of Nicholas Tiebalt, he be immediately hanged by the neck until he is dead." Ives then realized his deadly peril and begged for delay until morning; he wished to write to his mother and sister. Some person in the crowd who knew that Ives had caused a letter to be written them some months before that he had been killed by Indians, caught Sanders by the hand and said, "Ask him how much time he gave the Dutchman?" Notwithstanding all this, ample time was given for his counsel to write several letters for him, and to execute a will by which he gave to counsel and some boon companions, all the property that he had, excluding his mother and sister. A hundred men with leveled guns surrounded the hastily erected gallows as Ives was placed upon the box below the fatal cord. When all was ready he was asked if he had anything to say, he replied in a firm voice, "I am innocent of the crime charged against me; Alex Carter killed the Dutchman!" At the word of command, "Men, do your duty!" the box flew from under the feet of George Ives and his soul went to a tribunal which could not err. In some never explained manner the fact of the arrest of Ives and the other road agents reached Plummer before the arrival at Bannack of Club-foot George, the special messenger sent to him. He found the people wild with a story, started by Plummer, that a vigilance committee had been formed at Virginia City, that they had already hanged several of the best citizens of the district, and that a very large party were on their way to Bannack to hang him, Ned Ray, Buck Stinson and several of the most prominent and worthy men of the place, some of whom, he named. The dragging in of the names of respectable people with those belonging to the gang, failed of the desired effect. The brave and determined stand of Wilbur F. Sanders at the Ives trial put him in the position of leader in this revolution for good government. George Hilderman was next placed on trial. It was proved that he was knowing to Tiebalt's murder and kept silence; that he knew of the murder of a man at Cold Spring ranch; that he kept the Tiebalt mules after they were stolen; that he knew and associated with all the men who had taken part in the stage robberies and was a member of the gang; yet he was recommended to mercy by the jury who convicted him, and when told that he was given ten days in which to leave the country forever, he fell on his knees exclaiming "My God! Is it so?" He then made full confession and fully confirmed all of Long John's testimony given at the Ives trial. Plummer assisted in getting him out of the country. Long John was permitted to go free because of his evidence at the Ives trial. The people were fully convinced that the safety of the community depended upon the extreme punishment of the gang of desperadoes, who were largely composed of men appointed as conservators of the public peace by the chosen executive officer of the several mining districts; the sheriff and his deputies. In the midst of this excitement came the appalling story of the murder of Lloyd Magruder and his companions by Dr. Howard and his pals. Magruder had made many good friends at Virginia city and his murder gave great impetus to the efforts of the Vigilance committee.

An executive committee of twenty-four men, selected for their sterling character and known bravery, well armed and fully equipped for long, cold riding, immediately set out for the capture of Alex Carter. As soon as Ives was executed, Carter, Bill Bunton, William Graves and some other suspects found that they had important business which required their prompt attention upon the west side of the Bitter Root mountains, and in their sudden departure did not fully discriminate in the ownership of the horses they rode. The Vigilante scouts after crossing the Big Hole river in pursuit, while riding down Deer Lodge met Erastus Yager, my old companion, "Red." He was very communicative and informed them that Carter was just below at Cottonwood, drinking, and boasting that it would take thirty men to take him and his crowd. When the scouts reached Cottonwood they learned that the gang had received a letter from George Brown warning them that the Vigilantes were in pursuit, and the road agents had hastily fled into the mountains. Suspecting that "Red" had been the messenger, they decided to return to the Beaver Head ranch, and arrest "Red" and Brown for interfering with the administration of justice. Terrible weather set in and the party were compelled to make a camp near the divide in which they were storm bound for two days, suffering intensely. Inquiry at the ranch established the fact that "Red" had gone to Rattlesnake and that Brown was at Dempsey's. A detachment volunteered to go after "Red" and the main party agreed to wait for them at Dempsey's. At Plummer's ranch on the Rattlesnake they found Buck Stinson and Ned Ray, who informed them that "Red" was at a wickiup a short distance up the creek. "Red" surrendered without resistance and was taken to the ranch where the party remained over night.

They then took "Red" to Dempsey's where the united party remained for the night, having Brown for their host. When ready to ride in the morning the captain took Brown to one side for a private interview, and accused him of being a member of the gang and giving information to Carter. He admitted that he sent word to Carter, but declared that he was not a member of the gang. He was placed under arrest, and "Red" was privately interviewed, and then both were examined by the whole squad. Leaving the prisoners under guard, the rest of the squad rode to the bridge over the Stinking water, where they went over the whole evidence, and the men who were for conviction were asked to step across the bridge. Every man voted "Guilty." Taking up their march toward Virginia City at Lorain's ranch other members of the Vigilance committee were met, a conference was held, and immediate action was decided upon. By the dim light of lantern, ropes were thrown over a limb of a large cottonwood tree, and with little ceremony the souls of Erastus Yager and George Brown were launched into eternity. From the time of his capture to the final scene, "Red" had shown most wonderful nerve. He asked no stay of punishment, said that he deserved it all and had for years, and that he would die content if he could see those far more deserving than he, hanged, or knew that they would soon suffer the same death. He acknowledged that he was a member of the gang, and thanked God that he had never taken a human life. He gave the names and offices of the men in the gang; Henry Plummer, chief; Bill Bunton, roadster; (he escaped to Salt Lake and was executed by the Utah government); Cyrus Skinner, horse thief and roadster; George Shears, the same; Frank Parish, the same; Hayes Lyons, telegraph man and roadster; Bill Hunter, the same; Ned Ray, keeper of the council room at Bannack; George Ives, Steve Marshland, William Graves ("Whiskey Bill"), John Wagner (Dutch John), Johnny Cooper, Buck Stinson, Frank Pizanthia (Mexican), Bob Zachery, Boone Helm, Billy Terwilliger, Gad Moore and Club-foot George Lane, were spies and roadsters. Their oath bound them to follow and shoot at sight any other member of the organization who divulged any secret relating to their affairs, or who proved unfaithful to orders of the chief. They were to take life only when plunder could not otherwise be secured. Their pass-word was "Innocent" and they wore their neckties in sailors' knots, mustaches and chin whiskers. Yager said that Bill Hunter led him out of the path of rectitude years before. He gave the names of those who had been engaged in the most startling robberies, and told of the commission of many unknown crimes by members of the gang, against persons who had secretly departed for the states. As he stood on the block beneath the gallows, he said, "Brown, if you had thought of this three years ago, you would not be here now and give the boys all this trouble." Thus passed out of life another of the party which I piloted into Bannack.

Brown was a coward. He begged piteously for his life, and bemoaned the helpless condition of his Indian wife and his children in Minnesota. The Virginia City committee immediately equipped three of their number bearing a copy of "Red's" confession and sent them post haste to Bannack urging the formation of a Vigilance committee. The messengers arrived Sunday morning before day break and found that the leading citizens of the settlement were already in session deliberating what action it was best to take in regard to other members of the gang, present in the settlement.

While the trial was in progress at Alder gulch, the robbery of the Moody train on the Salt Lake road took place. As the train moved on toward its destination it was met by Neil Howie and John Fetherstun who were bound for Bannack. Two braver men never lived than these.[8] The train men thoroughly described the robbers and at the ranch at Horse Prairie they immediately recognized Dutch John, who in his wanderings in the mountains had frozen his fingers so badly that his sufferings drove him to risk appearance at the ranch. He had picked up a stray Indian who had helped him saddle and care for his horse. Howie and Featherstun took Dutch John with them to Bannack and placing him in a room at Sear's hotel, Fetherstun stood guard while Howie sought some one with whom to counsel. He met Plummer, and told him that he had Dutch John who was charged with robbing Moody's train. Plummer offered to relieve him of the care of his prisoner and said he would have him tried by a miners' jury. Howie told him that he would first see a few friends about the matter. The people were then, and had for most of the night been in session, and just before Howie made his appearance, the three men from Virginia City had been admitted to the conference and were rehearsing "Red's" confession. An examination of Dutch John was decided upon, and a squad sent to the hotel to bring him in. John Fetherstun was a brave man, but a stranger in Bannack, and when fifteen [men] came into the room where he held his prisoner, and one who seemed in authority laid his hand on Dutch John's shoulder and said "You are my prisoner!" visions of a rescue arose and covering his prisoner he determined to die rather than let his prisoner escape. His fears were, however, soon quieted and falling in with the squad he was taken with his prisoner to a large rear room of a store, where he not only found his chief, Neil Howie, but a large gathering of the leading men of Bannack. In the presence of this assembly, John Wagner was examined, and then sent away under guard to another place. Plummer, Ned Ray, Buck Stinson, and the Mexican, Pizanthia, were known to be in Bannack at this time. Men were placed to watch the corrals where the robbers kept their horses. An executive committee of picked men organized under a chief that knew no such word as fear, and the execution of these robbers was determined upon. In the early hours of morning all but the executive committee sought needed rest.

Sunday morning came, and an unusual silence seemed to brood over the little settlement at Bannack. Untold secrets were locked in many breasts which seemed suffocating to the owners. At the Vail house breakfast table, gathered Mrs. Vail and her two children, Sheriff Plummer, my clerk Swift, and myself. Mr. Vail, if I remember correctly was absent from Bannack. Only one of that party possessed the terrible secret, and love for an individual and stern duty to a whole community struggled for the mastery, in the bosom of that person. Patriotism, or prudence, I never knew which, gained the mastery and the sealed lips sounded no alarm. Judge Edgerton was early at my store and sat by the fire and talked, Buck Stinson's head suddenly appeared at the door, but he said nothing and did not come in. Few people seemed moving in the village street, but again the store door opened and Ned Ray stepped in and made some casual remark. It was very evident that these men were very nervous and anxious to know what was taking place. Plummer had been ailing for several days and had been at home much more than usual. At dinner he ate but little and soon laid down upon the lounge in the living room.

Joseph Swift. Thompson's clerk Joseph Swift, who served as best man at Henry Plummer's wedding, believed in Plummer to the end and begged for Plummer's life at his hanging.

Wenderoth & Taylor Late Broadbent & Co., photographer,
Montana Historical Society Photograph Archives, Helena

A few of us had established a Sunday service and for that purpose had attractively arranged a small log cabin situated in the rear of Oliver's stage office, now known as "Hang-mans gulch." A. W. Hall from St. Paul, Mrs. W. F. Sanders, Miss Lucia Darling, (a ni[e]ce of Judge Edgerton) and his daughter Martha, (now Mrs. Plassman) and myself constituted the choir. We were in the habit of gathering each Sunday evening at the Sander's cabin for rehearsal, and being at the Edgerton's when evening spread over the valley the young ladies made preparation to go to the Sanders home, as usual. Soon Mrs. Edgerton said, "Girls, you will not go to Yankee Flats this evening!" Murmurings were hushed by the heavy tread of many men on the footbridge over the creek, close by the Edgerton house.[9] In the dusk fifty or seventy-five armed men were dimly seen to be crossing to Yankee Flats. Seemingly without command, the men divided into two parties after crossing the bridge, and one squad silently surrounded the Vail cabin. A well known citizen rapped on the door, and when Mrs. Vail opened, he asked if Mr. Plummer was in. Plummer, who was lying on the lounge came to the door and the strong man threw his arms around him, pinioning his arms to his body. Not feeling well he had taken off his belt containing his pistol and heavy knife and laid them beside him on a chair, a most unusual thing for him to do. He always went armed even in the house. He was allowed to put on his coat, and quietly exerted himself to calm Mrs. Vail's excited condition, telling her he was needed to do something about Dutch John. The armed men closed in around the prisoner and at the bridge were met by the other squad, who had been equally successful in arresting Ned Ray at the cabin of a Mr. Tolland, where he boarded. Stinson was afterward found asleep on a billiard table in one of the saloons. No attempt was made that night to find the Mexican.

The prisoners were taken to a gallows which Plummer had erected as sheriff, for the execution of one John Horan, convicted by the Miner's court of the murder of Lawrence Keeley in 1862, which stood near our little log meeting house. Hardly had the party passed the Edgerton house than in came Mrs. Vail hysterically calling for me. Mrs. Edgerton was a most motherly woman and calmed her as best she could, and then I took her home. I told her that Mr. Plummer's being taken, had some connection with Dutch John's arrest, as indeed it had; in fact, I told her anything which I thought would allay her excitement, and awaited events with nervous apprehension. After a long time I saw a man standing before the cabin. I went to the door and spoke to him. He simply said "It is all over!" Then came the hardest trial of my life, to tell this woman the true life and of the death of Henry Plummer. She dropped to the floor in a swoon, and I called Mrs. Sanders and returned to the Edgertons. At the gallows a most pitiful scene was enacted. Plummer begged in abject misery for his life—for the sake of his young wife—for the sake of Mrs. Vail—for time to pray. He was too wicked to be rushed into eternity without preparation—they might maim him in any manner, only spare his life and he would leave the country forever. The Vigilante chief told him that he had a duty to perform which was as hard as death itself, but that there would be no change in the decree; that they all must hang. A young man who had been won by Plummer's loveable qualities and had just learned of his danger [Joseph Swift Jr.], now rushed in and embracing Plummer begged for his life, and had to be forcibly removed from the scene. When everything was ready and the command "Bring up Ned Ray" rang out from the chief, the committee lost no time in placing that individual on a box beneath the halter, for both he and Stinson, ever since their arrest, had spent their breath in cursing and swearing, using the most provoking and vile epithets toward the Vigilantes, and the public, that their unlimited command of villainous language enabled them to do. Soon the body of Ned Ray was dangling at one end of the beam. Plummer had become calm and as Stinson stood under the noose and offered to confess, Plummer told him, "We've done enough already to send us all to hell!" There was no hesitation on the part of the committee in disposing of two such bloody rascals as Ray and Stinson.

But now came a moment of suspense. Under the gallows which he had erected and used as an officer of the law in sustaining good government, stood a nice clean looking young man, only twenty-seven years of age, of pleasing and affable manners and of good ability, who had attracted many friends. The ardent affection exhibited by his impulsive young friend who was a general favorite with the public, also created a certain sympathy with the assembled crowd. Plummer no longer begged for his life, but only that he be given a good drop. He took his scarf from his neck and casting it to his young friend, said, "Keep that to remember me by." When all was ready and the order came, no man stirred. A moment, and then came the stern command, "Men! do your duty!" and several strong men lifted the body of the robber chief as high as they could reach, and dropping it, he died almost without a struggle.

Heredity had nothing whatever to do with the terrible criminality of Henry Plummer, who gained such notoriety as chief of "The Road Agents of Montana." He was a native of Connecticut [Maine], born of respectable parents, and his deviation from the path of rectitude resulted from leaving home influences while yet a youth into bad company. He became a gambler, a seducer, a murderer, an escaped convict, and was charged with killing a pursuing officer at the time of his escape from the California penitentiary. He was a leader in many crimes which are rampant in most mining towns in their early days, and his career in Lewiston, Oro-Fino, and other camps upon the west side of the mountains made it necessary for him to seek some country where he was not so well known.

For a few months we were by chance thrown into close companionship and our personal relations were pleasant and agreeable, except upon one occasion. January 1, 1864, Judge Edgerton's daughter Mattie, Misses Amoret Geer and Emma Zoller, came into my store and I was busy weighing the young ladies, when the door opened and Plummer came in. We were all talking and laughing, when a young man whose name has escaped my memory, but who was in some way connected with Oliver & Co's express walked in. Immediately both men began to fumble for their arms, and I saw that there was to be trouble. As they approached each other both began cursing and the young ladies fled shrieking to the street. I ran between the two men facing Plummer and put my two hands against his shoulders which hindered him from quickly getting at his heavy sheath knife. His opponent was unable to release his pistol in time to shoot, as I had crowded Plummer to the rear door of the store where he made a lunge by my face with his knife, but was unable to reach his victim. I threw open the rear door and pushed Plummer out and his opponent vanished by the front door and was hustled out of town by Oliver & Co. If I ever understood the quarrel between the two men I do not recall it, but Plummer afterward apologized for beginning a quarrel in my store, and more especially when ladies were present, but said that I saved the rascal's life. His own career ended ten days later. This was the only time that I ever saw Plummer otherwise than gentlemanly and polite. He was ever so at our meals with the Vail family and Mr. Swift.

After the execution, Dutch John remained in the hands of his keepers and on Monday morning a few of the principal men of Bannack met to consider his case. He was brought in for examination, and as he recognized me, he held up his frozen hands and said, "Dr., see those hands." His condition was sad enough to excite pity in a savage. Further action in his case was delayed by excitement on the street. A large armed party were engaged in a search for the Mexican, Jo Pizanthia, who was a member of the gang. When in his cups he had often boasted of having been a member of the celebrated Waukeen's band of robbers in California.[10] Many knew that he had recently been shot through his chest in a drunken brawl and that he was concealed in some cabin or prospect hole in the gulch.

Just down the creek bank at the rear end of my store was a little miner's cabin, and as a party of which Smith Ball, the only honest deputy of Sheriff Plummer, was leader, pushed open the door of his hut, Ball received a bullet in his leg, and George Copley, who was next to him was shot in the breast and immediately expired. The citizens were wild with fury at Copley's death, and opened fire on the cabin, Ball having tied a handkerchief over his wound and continuing in the attack. No person was so rash as to approach the cabin and learn the effect of their fusillade. In the excitement some wild shooting was done, and several bullets came through the door and window of my store. I noticed the chief justice of Idaho among the gathered citizens, armed with a Henry rifle, and as soon as decency would permit, betook myself inside my log walls. Pretty soon a party appeared dragging by a long lariat, a small brass cannon belonging to Judge Edgerton. They took a large packing box from my store and mounting the gun upon it bombarded the cabin with explosive shells. The enemy making no reply some bold man pushed open the cabin door, and discovered the Mexican lying upon the dirt floor, partially protected by a spare door. The lariat which had been used on the gun was slipped upon the Mexican's neck and some small lad shinned up a tall pole standing by a prospect hole, and the body was jerked to the top in a very short time. As the body swung in the air it was filled with bullets, and a hundred hands made short work of pulling down the cabin, and piling up the debris to which they set fire after putting the Mexican's body upon the funeral pile. I could not but moralize upon the sudden change in human feelings and conditions, as I saw a man the next morning panning out the ashes of the Mexican, hoping to find that he had gold dust upon his person when he was killed! Yesterday the people were excited with the most extreme passions of vengeance and destruction; today returned to the practical things of life!

After hearing the final confessions of Dutch John, the citizens meeting unanimously decided that he must die. His statement tallied with that of "Red," and that was the only trial these remaining road agents ever had. The decision was reduced to writing and a messenger read it to the miserable man. He was informed that he had but an hour to live, and that no change would be made in the decree. At first he begged for life, but soon became calm and asked that some German write to his mother at his dictation. When this letter was prepared and read to him, he was not satisfied with it, and unbound his frozen fingers and wrote himself. He informed her that he was to die at once, that he had been led into bad company, that he had helped rob a train, that his companion was shot, that his punishment was extreme, but that it was just. Many of the spectators deeply sympathized with poor John, and he seemed too

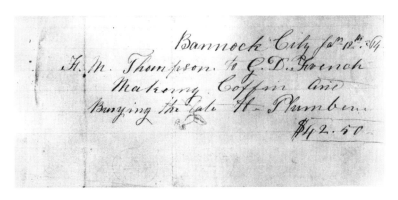

Bill for the coffin and burial of Henry Plummer. Thompson paid $42.50 on January 12, 1864, for Plummer's coffin and burial with money that Plummer had deposited with him. He sent the remainder to Plummer's widow.

Montana Historical Society Archives, Helena

Henry Plummer's grave. Plummer was buried in Hangman's Gulch within sight of Bannack.

E. C. Schoettner, photographer, Montana Historical Society
Photograph Archives, Helena

manly and inoffensive to have his life snuffed out in such cruel manner. On a bench in the unfinished store where he was taken for execution, lay the dead body of his leader, dressed for burial! On the floor near at hand lay the ghastly remains of Buck Stinson who had often been his companion in wicked transactions. Amid these surroundings the young desperado knelt down and asked the Father of all to forgive his great iniquities. As he mounted to the top of the barrel which had been placed under the beam, he was the calmest person in the building. "How long will it take me to die?" "I never saw a man hanged!" "It will be very short, John." "You won't suffer much pain." Suddenly by an attached cord the barrel was jerked away, and John Wagner had paid the penalty of his crimes. So passed from life another of the party whom I piloted into Bannack!

Mr. Plummer, sometime before his death had deposited with me quite a little sum of money. After consulting with Judge Edgerton, Mr. Sanders and some others, I paid from this fund for a coffin and the expenses of a decent burial, and the remainder I sent by draft to Mrs. Plummer in Iowa. I never received any reply to my letter telling her of Mr. Plummer's death or whether she ever received the remittance, I do not know.[11]

It was carefully concealed from me at the time, but I afterward learned that a physician in Bannack, robbed Plummer's grave, and took therefrom his skull and his forearm which carried the bullet lodged in it by Hank Crawford's shot, and that the bullet was worn smooth and polished by the bones turning upon it.

Plummer was executed Jan. 10, 1864, and three days later the Vigilantes surrounded Virginia City at night fall, as it was known that George Lane, Frank Parish, Jack Galligher [Gallagher], Hayes Lyons, Boone Helm and Bill Hunter were hidden in town.[12] As they drew in their lines all these men were secured but Bill Hunter, who crawled by the picket in a mining ditch and escaped for the present, but was afterward captured. No delay occurred in completing arrangements for the execution of these desperadoes, and they were all placed upon the same scaffold and swung off consecutively. The victims were placed on boxes about three feet high, to each of which a cord was attached, and the fall was sufficient to break the necks of the condemned men. Club Foot George was the first to suffer, and as he caught the eye of an acquaintance he exclaimed, "Well good bye old fellow, I'm off" and leaped from the stool and died with hardly a struggle. He had tried to get Judge Dance to intercede for him, and when he told him he could do nothing for him, he said "You'll pray for me, won't you?"

"Most willingly, George" and kneeling down with George on one side and Gallagher on the other he put up a fervid petition for the doomed men.[13] The committee had assured the sufferers that any requests they wished to make should be complied with so far as was possible, and Gallagher standing with the halter about his neck called for one more drink of whiskey. The committee and the people were astounded, but soon a miner called out, "You promised! Let him have the whiskey." The bravado's wishes were complied with, but the rope being too taut for him to drink with ease, he shouted "Slack that rope and let a man take a parting drink, won't you?" He cried and swore by turns. As he exclaimed "I hope forked lightning will strike every strangling villain of you," the box flew from under his feet and his effort to close with an oath was forever cut short. Seeing the contortions of Gallagher's body, Boone Helm exclaimed, "Kick away old fellow; my turn comes next. I'll be in hell with you in a minute." "Every man for his principles; Hurrah for Jeff Davis! Let her rip!" The twang of the fatal cord was the signal of almost instant death. Frank Parish had been completely subdued ever since his arrest, and at his request his face was covered with his black neck-tie as he speechlessly ended his career. Hayes Lyons had steadily hoped that he might at last be saved from the fatal knot, but when he found this would not be allowed, he requested that his body might be given to his mistress, and said that the watch he wore belonged to her. He was especially charged with the murder of W. S. Dillingham who had been appointed a deputy by Plummer, but had proved to be an honest and worthy young man, who had imparted information to a person who was likely to be robbed by some members of the gang. For this he was killed by Stinson, Lyons, and Charley Forbes, the latter being killed on the Big Hole, by Augustus Moore, who was also a member of the gang. The execution of Lyons, ended the active labors of the committee for that time at Virginia City. The remaining members of the road agent band had made every effort to escape from the country, but fate was against them. The great depth of snow on the Bitter Root range became an effectual barrier to their escape from the little mining towns to which they scattered.

It is due to the reader and to my own feelings that I express my horror and disgust at having felt compelled to put down so fully the bloody transactions which took place, at this period of the history of this section. But in no other way could I express with fidelity the actual condition of affairs in this community at this time. Far from the control of any organized government, the people felt compelled in their might to rise and show the gamblers, robbers, and murderers, that they could no longer terrorize the people. I have only particularized in my relation except in cases of members of the gang with whom by peculiar circumstances I had been more or less intimately associated.

After this terrible period had fully passed and some new comer came into Bannack, and made inquiry concerning the times and the road agents Judge Edgerton was wont to clap me on the shoulder and say, "Thompson is the only one left of his gang!" His vivid explanation of the meaning of his words, always gave me a feeling of relief and of re-established respectability. Of Dr. Howard's party, referred to by Judge Edgerton as my party, only the fate of Steve Marshland and Bob Zachery remain untold. Marshland was the man who at Deer Lodge was unable to ride his horse, and lending the animal to me, rode in my "go-devil." His "sickness" was the result of a gun shot received while stealing horses near Lewiston. He was gentlemanly in his manners and used good language.

Twenty-one brave and determined men left Virginia City, January 21, to find and execute Steve Marshland, Cyrus Skinner, Alex Carter, Johnny Cooper, George Shears and Bob Zachery.

These members of the road agent gang had fled to Deer Lodge with the expectation of escaping over the mountains to Lewiston, which the deep snows prevented them from doing. A detachment from the Vigilantes found Marshland at Clark's ranch on the Big Hole river. He was the only person at the ranch and was in bed suffering from the wound which he had received when he robbed Moody's train on the Salt Lake road, and from his frozen feet while wandering in the mountains. It is unnecessary to give the particulars of his execution by hanging, the gibbet being a pole projecting from the corral fence. His taking off, disposed of one more of my summer party on the Bannack road. When the Vigilantes approached Cottonwood, their scout reported that all the birds had flown, but Bunton and "Texas." Riding up to the door of the cabin at night, Bunton refused them admission, and when compelled to admit them he blew the light out. He was ordered to light up again and at length complied with the command, though grumblingly. Bunton was immediately grappled by a lusty Vigilante, but he was unable to secure him, without the aid of others, who bound his wrists with cords. When he became convinced that nothing would change the intention of the squad to hang him, he declared to the captain that he had no fear of death: "I care no more for hanging than I do for taking a drink; but I should like a good drop. I wish I had a mountain three hundred feet high to jump from! May I jump?" Being assured that he might, the noose was adjusted, and when he was placed upon a box under the cross-beam of the corral gate, he said, "I'll give the word, one-two-three!" and at the last word he jumped into eternity. Texas being tried and no evidence of actual murder having appeared, but only that he had acted as a stool pigeon, he was set at liberty, and he pushed out at once for the Kootnai mines.

It was mid-winter and the cold was bitter indeed, there were no bridges in the country and every icy stream had to be forded,

on every elevation the snow lay at great depth; but notwithstanding all these difficulties, these intrepid men kept on down
the valley of the Hell Gate, and found in the Bitter Root valley,
Alex Carter, Cyrus Skinner and Johnny Cooper, whom they executed. Thomas D. Pitt, captain of the squad, learned that a
stranger was stopping with "Baron" C. C. O'Keefe, of O'Keefe
Castle, at Korakin Defile, and sent a detachment of eight men to
learn whether or not the stranger was one whose presence was
desirable at headquarters.[14] He proved to be Bob Zachery. While
taking the prisoner to the home camp, Baron O'Keefe, who was
riding with them, incidentally mentioned that another unknown
man was stopping at Van Doorn's cabin, in the Bitter Root valley. Three men rode to the place, and at the door of the shack,
inquired if George Shears was in. Van Doorn answered that he
was, and Pitt asked if he could come in. Upon the door being
opened Shears was discovered, knife in hand, but he offered no
resistance, but said, "I knew I should come to this some time,
but did not think it would be so soon." As he walked to the
corral he pointed out to Pitt, horses that he said he had stolen,
and then was taken to the barn, where the men had already attached a rope to a high beam. Shears was good natured, and in
order to save the men the trouble of arranging a drop, he cheer-
fully complied with their request that he climb up a ladder and
jump from it. When he had climbed a sufficient height he said,
"I never was hung before and am not much used to this business; shall I jump or slide off?" The answer came, "Why jump,
of course." "All right! good bye!" So was snuffed out the life of
another of those red handed wretches whose lives had been for-
feited by their crimes.

The squad who had Zachery in custody, overtook the main
party, and a conference was had at which the execution of that
robber was decided upon. When his fate was made known to him

he dictated a letter to his mother in which he warned his brothers to avoid bad company, declaring that drinking, gambling, and bad company had brought him to the gallows. When the fatal cord was adjusted he broke forth in prayer "that God would forgive the Vigilance committee for what they were doing, as it was the only way to clear the country of road agents." Zachery died without exhibiting any fear, and apparently with little suffering. He was a member of that party which I escorted from Deer Lodge to Bannack, and of whom I was now the only survivor in the country. Having as they thought, finished the business which had brought them to Hell Gate, the party made preparations to start for Nevada City, when intelligence arrived that William Graves (Whiskey Bill) was at Fort Owen, some distance up the Bitter Root valley. He was said to be fully armed and thirsting for the life of the first Vigilante who should make his appearance. A party of three were sent to capture him. In mountain parlance, the Vigilantes "got the drop on him," and he surrendered without resistance, but refused to make any confession. A rope was thrown over the limb of a tree, and Graves being properly bound was forcibly mounted behind a Vigilante upon a horse, and when the noose was adjusted he exclaimed, "Good-by, Bill!" and put spur to the animal, and poor Bill was left dangling with a broken neck. The Vigilantes then took up their return ride to Alder Gulch, well satisfied that they had performed their duty as God fearing men, and thankful that in executing their mission, no member of the party had received any injury.

So far as known only one person remained who was suspected as being an active member of Plummer's gang of road agents. The missing man was Bill Hunter, who had by the aid of some guard, who did not believe in his extreme guilt, been allowed to escape through the picket line at Virginia City. It came to the leader of the Vigilantes that he was in hiding far up the

Gallatin valley. A party of volunteers, although it was mid winter and very cold, rode over the Madison divide, forded the Madison river, and coming to his place of hiding, allayed his suspicions by claiming to be on a stampede to find Barney Hughes new discovery, they returned to Virginia and made their report. Four Vigilantes were selected to pursue, capture, and execute the robber. The party were caught in a blizzard in the mountains, and one of the men came near drowning while crossing the Madison, but they succeeded in their mission, and Hunter admitted the justice of their action in his case.[15]

For the present the great work of the Vigilance Committee was finished. Its reorganization and its activities in subsequent years occurred after I had left the country, and of those events I am not qualified to write. No person whose life has been passed under the protection of civil law, administered by just and upright judges can ever fully realize the chaotic condition of affairs as they existed in the territory in question, before the organization of the Vigilance Committee. No man's property was for a moment safe, and no person's life was weighed when the robbers thought it necessary to take it, in order to get possession of his property. No prophet could foretell what a day would bring forth. Had I not frankly—perhaps foolishly, it might have been thought—told Dr. Howard, Lowry and Romaine, the exact condition of my finances as I rode with them to Bannack there is no doubt in my mind but that my bones would now be mouldering on the banks of the Deer Lodge or Big Hole. At the time the Vigilantes were organized, the country was terrorized beyond all conception. The remedy for this state of affairs was terrible and bloody, but it was most effectual, and in no other way could the incubus be removed. It seemed almost providential that the punishment dealt out by the committee should have been fully carried out without the loss of any life but that of George Copley, and the wounding of Smith Ball by the Mexican, Jo Pizanthia. Mr. Copley was a native of Vermont, of pleasing and gentle manners, faithful to every duty and an excellent citizen. His sudden death was greatly lamented and quickly avenged. He was the only deputy sheriff holding [office] under Plummer who was not a member of his gang.

Chief Justice H. L. Hosmer in his charge to the first grand jury organized in Montana, Dec. 5, 1864, said:—

"Gentlemen of the Jury: The assemblage of a grand jury in this new Territory affords an opportunity for a casual survey of the interests committed to its charge. The cause of justice hitherto deprived of the intervention of regularly organized courts, has been temporarily subserved by voluntary tribunals of the people, partaking more of the nature of self-defense than the comprehensive principles of the common law. It is no part of the business of this court to find fault with what has been done, but rather in common with all good citizens to laud the transactions of an organization which in the absence of law, assumed the delicate and responsible office of purging society of all offenders against its peace, happiness, and safety.

"Such societies originating in necessity have been in communities without law, and in which the penalties of the laws were not in proportion to the criminality of the offence. Their adaption to the necessities of new settlements has obtained for them an approbation so universal that they are the first measures resorted to by well intentioned men to free themselves of that vile class of adventurers, which infest all unorganized communities, for the purpose of fraud, robbery, and murder. In no part of our country have they labored more efficiently than here. Nowhere else did they enter upon their duties amid greater embarrassments. It was questionable even, when they commenced, whether they were numerically equal to the task. The sources of official power had been monopolized by the very class which preyed upon society. The greatest villain of them all, with hands reeking with the blood of numerous victims was the principal ministerial officer of the territory and had at his beck a band of wretches who had become hardened in the bloody trade, years before they came here to practice it.

"In this condition of affairs there could be but one of two courses to pursue; to hang the offenders or submit to their authority and give the territory over to misrule and murder. Happily the former course prevailed and the summary punishment visited upon the few, frightened the survivors from the territory and restored order and safety."

SIX

The Beginning of a New State

AFTER THE TERMINATION of the reign of terror, white winged peace settled upon the gulches, mining camps and settlements of the territory, and busy men began to think of other things than robbery and murder and the terrible work done by the Vigilance committee. When I had decided to take my goods to Bannack and had made ready a store for their reception, I received an invitation from Col. Darius H. Hunkins to build him a three room log house, at Marysville. Col. Hunkins had formerly been a railroad contractor, his home being in Galena, Ill. He came up the Missouri on the *Emilie* with the avowed purpose of getting as far as possible from the seat of war, and shipped up a large stock of clothing that he might have some business. He never opened a store, and I purchased his goods. He paid me five dollars per day while building his house, the timber for which was hauled from the mountains some fourteen miles up the Grasshopper [Creek]. He was much pleased with his house when it was finished.

Once more the Miner's court, accountable to none but the people, resumed jurisdiction of all matters in dispute, and if its business was not accomplished with all the dignity and formality of courts of justice in the eastern states, the decision of its judges was nearly always popular, and satisfied the people for whose benefit the court was established.[1]

One day when on the street in Bannack, to my surprise I heard my name called three times by an officer, and answering the summons I entered a cabin in which I found Judge Burchett holding a session of the Miners' court.[2] I was called to act as a juryman on a civil action. For some reason only known to the others on the panel I was chosen foreman. After hearing the evidence, the common sense rulings of the judge on law points, and the arguments of the learned counsel, the judge gave the jury a laconic charge and was about to submit the case, when one of the jury, more used to the local practice than the foreman, suggested to the court that the case had been a peculiarly dry one, and that to relieve the monotony each of the litigants be ordered to pay one-half the cost of liquid refreshments for the court, officers, lawyers and jury. The suggestion met the hearty approval of the court and in due time the jury retired, refreshed, and took up the consideration of the case. After a short conference it appeared that the jury were agreed in finding for the plaintiff, and I said, "Then gentlemen, I understand that we find for the plaintiff, Richard Joy." "What's that?" cried one. "Is Joy the plaintiff? Hell, no! I don't find for Joy! I'm for Peters! He's my friend!" and for Peters he remained and after four hours without more refreshments that jury was discharged, not being able to agree with Peter's friend.

A half century ago, the courts of Ohio did not compare in dignity and formality with those of Massachusetts, and yet chief justice Edgerton, an old practitioner in the Ohio courts was somewhat astonished at what occurred in the Miners' court of Bannack. His daughter, Mrs. Plassman, writes, "Shortly after arriving at Bannack my father strolled up Main street [to] see the town, and coming to a building where a Miners' court was in session he went in. The judge seeing that he was a stranger, (and suspecting that he was the new chief justice of Idaho) invited him to the bench. The trial of the case proceeded, but not for long, it being interrupted by the suggestion by some of the parties that it was time for liquid refreshments. The court and every one present approving the suggestion an old darky (Frank Pope) was dispatched to a neighboring saloon for whiskey. On his return the court took a recess and a drink—several of them, in fact. When the supply was exhausted and the court and those in attendance upon it were sufficiently stimulated, the trial went on, only to meet with a similar interruption in the course of a half hour or so."[3]

This was the initiation of the new chief justice into the far western methods of legal procedure.

Judge Edgerton had not been in Idaho territory more than three months before a suggestion was made that a new territory be organized from portions of eastern Idaho and western Dakota. Meetings were held at Virginia City and at Bannack, two thousand dollars was raised by subscription, and Judge Edgerton who had recently been a member of Congress, was induced to go to Washington and secure if possible the legislation necessary to work out this new scheme. The matter had been delayed by the operations for the extinction of Plummer's band of road agents. It was the middle of January, 1864, before the Judge was able to start for Washington, and the prospect of a winter trip to Salt Lake and overland, was not to be anticipated with pleasure. Every respectable man in the territory possessed more or less influence with the member of Congress from his old home district, and nearly every one used all the means at his command to promote the scheme which Judge Edgerton represented. Langford and Hauser and some others were already in Washington, and worked with good effect with the judge, when he arrived.[4] Large quantities of gold in dust, ingots and nuggets, was exhibited in the halls of Congress, and then turned over to various banks to be placed to the credit of the business men of the mountains who owned it. Thanks to the Vigilantes, there was no fear of the road agents during its transportation. By a previous arrangement with the Judge, I left Bannack on the 22nd of February for Salt Lake and the east, in company with Judge W. B. Dance and others. It happened that a few days before starting, in retorting a lot of gold which had been gathered by quicksilver, over a blacksmith's fire, that the crucible broke and the gold ran down into the cinders, making when congealed, a most beautiful spangle of the value of $1,500. This wonderful specimen Col. Hunkins purchased of me and requested that after I had exhibited it at Washington and at my home in Massachusetts, that I should send it to his daughter in Galena, Ill., for her to use as a mantel ornament.

Our journey to Salt Lake was made on horseback, and we drove some pack animals and spare horses. We slept in a cabin the first night out on our four hundred-mile trip, but not again until we reached Salt Lake city. If the night was very cold and windy, we built some little protection of brush to cover our heads as an ostrich is said to run his head in the sand, but otherwise our bodies were wrapped in our blankets and we lay on the ground with our feet converging toward the camp fire. We were fortunate enough to be able to cross the Snake river on the ice, the ludicrous thing being the fact that the pack mules would make no effort to stand upon the glare ice, and we had to attach lariats to them and snake them over like a sled. Two other large fast flowing streams we were obliged to cross by swimming. Stripping, and swimming an icy stream in mid-winter cannot be recommended as an agreeable diversion at the best, but what made our passage much worse was, the streams were frozen out to the swift water which ran like a mill race in the centre of the river. One of our bravest fellows swam over taking with him a long lariat. Others followed, using the lariat for safety. After gathering wood and building a large fire, we attached our end of the lariat to a pack mule, and pushing him to the edge of the ice he was plumped in and the men helped him upon the ice on the opposite side, when he was towed to it. In this manner each animal was towed over, and our bedding was rolled in an elk skin and was taken over without getting wet to any extent. It is candidly admitted that these proceedings were a little trying to both man and beast. Even the animals were willing to stand upon the smoky side of a big camp fire. Two nights of this journey we were compelled to camp in deep snow in the mountains, with no feed for the horses. I remember waking one morning with a feeling of unusual comfort and warmth, to find that the whole camp was buried under about eighteen inches of fresh snow. We were all glad to see the glistening waters of the great Salt Lake, and took up our quarters at the Salt Lake House, one of whose landladies was a daughter of Brigham Young. The long drawn out trip from Salt Lake to Atchison, [Kansas,] by the Overland stage was vexatious and trying. We awoke one morning to find that we had been sleeping in a coach since midnight, in front of the home station, because the driver who had brought us there, had neglected to fully awake the driver who was to take us forward. Although the morning was cold and frosty, there was one driver on the old Overland [stage line] who was made warm, for I never heard Judge Dance wax more eloquent than on this occasion. The Indians were reported wicked all along the Platte, and we rode with heavy dragoon pistols lying in our laps ready for instant use. Hundreds of horses had been stolen along the line, and transportation was badly demoralized, but it was this or none, and we did the best we could.

When we arrived at St. Louis, dressed in moccasins and all our mountain toggery, we created quite a sensation at the Leland [Hotel] and the next morning the papers announced the arrival of a distinguished party from the mountains, loaded with gold. Three of our party pushed on immediately to Washington, where we at once commenced lobbying for the passage of the bill for the organization of Montana Territory. Being with Judge Edgerton, admitted to the floor of the House, we, or at least our gold nugget, became the center of attraction to scores of the members and officials of the House, and several senators came over to see the remarkable specimen, which all thought was as nature had made it. We improved our opportunity to impress upon the members the necessity of the immediate organization of the new Territory. I was much aided by Hon. William B. Washburn, member from my home district in Massachusetts, and Mr. [Charles] Upson from Michigan, a valued friend.[5] In the discussion of the bill a question arose whether Idaho should retain the Flathead Lake and Bitter Root country, or that it should be included in the new territory. Governor [William H.] Wallace of Idaho was a broad minded man and gave his assent that the territory in question be included in the new Territory of Montana.[6] When assured that the bill would pass, I signed a petition for the appointment of Sidney Edgerton as governor of the new territory, and went to New York, and my old home in Massachusetts. It was almost unanimously the desire of the Union men of the mountains, that Mr. Edgerton should receive the appointment as governor, and all [of us] then in the east worked together for that purpose.[7]

Mrs. Plassman writing of this time says, "Whether my father's ultimate appointment to the position was the result of his last visit to Mr. Lincoln, will never be known, but this is his account of the visit he made and the story he told."

"When the division bill passed, I went to the White House to make my farewell visit, as I had been in Washington for some time and was anxious to get home. On my way there, a gentleman told me that a senator had filed a protest against my appointment as governor. On meeting the President I asked him if this report was true, and he said that it was. I inquired if any charges had been made against me. He said, none, but that I had called the senator a liar. He insisted that it was the truth, and if he (Mr. Lincoln) chose to appoint some one of the other applicants, it would be satisfactory. As for me, [I said,] I should return home and go mining, as Dorsheimer kept tavern. 'Dorsheimer!' exclaimed Mr. Lincoln. 'Why I knew Dorsheimer! What was the story?' Why Dorsheimer attended a convention at Utica hoping to obtain the nomination as Canal Commissioner. He was defeated, and rising in his seat, said, 'Shentlemen, I goes back to Buffalo and keeps tavern, like hell.' I left Mr. Lincoln laughing heartily at the story, and it was the last time I ever saw him. I did not hear of my appointment until I reached Salt Lake city."

During Mr. Edgerton's absence in the east, the historic stork alighted at the gubernatorial log cabin upon the banks of the Grasshopper, and left a little blue eyed baby girl, who was named Idaho, and became the idol of the capital town of Montana.

I spent a few happy weeks with my friends in old Massachusetts, but was unable to persuade the lady who afterward became my wife, to return with me to the wilds of the Rocky Mountains. But her parents intrusted to my care her young brother, Lucius Nims, Jr., and when I again departed for the mountains I also took with me my brother, John W. Thompson, and Newcomb Warner of Charlemont, Mass. At St. Louis I purchased a steam saw mill, a small stock of general merchandise and a large supply of Ynkee notions.

I shipped my goods by the steamer *Shreveport* and Mr. Warner and my brother took passage on the same boat. Needing a little more time in St. Louis young Nims and I overtook the boat at Kansas City, and continued with her to Sioux City, but the river was low and progress so slow, that I thought it best to leave the steamer and take the overland stage, as I had been from my business for a long time.

Finding a transport about to leave for Omaha, Nims and I took passage and were soon trundling rapidly down the Missouri. All went well until we were about opposite the mouth of the Little Sioux river when the boat ran on a sawyer (submerged log) and in less than twenty minutes the rear part of the cabin was under water, while the nose of the boat was high and dry. [After] putting two life preservers on Nims, who could not swim, we secured our baggage and getting upon the dry part of the boat, thought we were having pretty fair luck. As the boat was liable to slip into deep water, the captain hurried the passengers to the Nebraska shore, but at our request he took us to the Iowa side of the river. Loaded down with our baggage, we bravely struck out through the brush, snags and slough holes of the river bottom, to find a stage road which I knew ran along the river bottoms. When nearly exhausted, we reached a clearing and the good motherly woman who presided over the little log cabin we found there gave us a good breakfast.

We learned from her that it was but two miles to Little Sioux, that the mail boat went up the river one day and down the next, and that she thought it went up that day, but that we could find out at the "Pike." While negotiating at the "Pike" for a team to take us to Council Bluffs, a farmer appeared driving in that direction, and we soon closed with him for transportation in his farm wagon. We finally reached Omaha and took passage on the Overland coach for Kearney Junction, distant one hundred and eighty miles. Through the Loup Fork country the Indians were very ugly, and we rode fully prepared for defence a good share of the way. Opposite Kearney we made preparations to cross the Platte river, which is made a hazardous undertaking by reason of the constant shifting of the quick sands in its bed. Where it is safe fording today, it may be frought with much danger on the morrow. The coach was abandoned and the baggage and mail transferred to a long wagon with body set high up above wheels at least six feet in diameter, and with felloes and tires about a foot in width. Into this we climbed, and to it were attached nine pair of cattle. Everything being ready, we rolled forward into the river. Where the sand was hard packed the wagon jarred as though upon a street paved with cobble stones. When we came to the main current one after another of the pairs of oxen were swimming, but as the last yoke began to swim the forward ones struck bottom and the train was straightened out. Water came into the wagon body at the deepest portion of the stream.

At Kearney junction we were compelled to wait a day for the western coach, and were a little dismayed to find upon comparing notes that we had not enough money with us to pay our fares to Salt Lake city. The change in our plans had not received that attention which was demanded; but I had the overland agent telegraph to Oliver & Co., at Salt Lake, who paid our fares there. When the coach arrived from the east, and we informed the passengers of our situation several entire strangers offered us funds for our journey. The long journey in the alkaline dust was most trying and tedious. The coach was full, and Nims and I, had to pile the baggage around the edges of the deck of the coach, and make our bed there. We had a rubber blanket with us which we spread over us at night, but unfortunately lost it before we reached Denver junction, and missed it very much during the rest of our journey. At Salt Lake we made only sufficient stop to gather provisions for our four hundred mile drive over the Oliver line to Bannack. This apology for a stage line was simply a box wagon without springs of any kind, drawn by two mules. The company had no ranches upon the route, but every thirty or forty miles some man was stationed who put up a little wickiup and guarded a few animals, if the Indians kindly left any, so that the change might possibly be made if the team could go no further. Passengers had to furnish their own provisions and do their own cooking.[8]

The season was usually dry, feed for stock very scarce, and all the animals were weak and scrawny. Our principal reliance for food was a boiled ham, and wrap it as we would, we were always compelled to scrape off a covering of alkili [alkali] dust before we could slice off our meal. It [the alkali dust] found its way into everything, baggage, clothing, ears, eyes and nostrils. When possible we drove in the night, and it often became necessary for me to grope around on the ground to find the trail, which a stupid driver had strayed from, while asleep. All roads have an ending, and so did the one from Salt Lake to Bannack, and when greeted by friends at the end of our journey, all the little discomforts of a tedious overland trip were forgotten. Reviewing that trip after more than forty years have elapsed, the principal things fixed in my memory are the picturesque view of the great Salt Lake and the Mormon city; the beautiful temple and Brigham Young's house; the clear water flowing in the streets; the great hot spring near by the city; the sublime scenery of the Portneauf canon; the fording of Snake river above old Fort Hall; the magnificent grandeur of the Three Tetons; Market Lake; and the Red Rock canon. Then the country was a wilderness; now, cities, villages, mines, ranches, dominate the scene, and instead of the expected Snake [Shoshone Indian] war-whoop at every turn, the shrill steam whistle resounds from bluff to bluff.

During the summer of 1864 nothing more exciting than stampedes to newly discovered "diggins" disturbed the quiet of the

people. Immigration was large, and Alder Gulch was being torn
up by ten thousand people. Money was plenty, prices were high,
and every willing worker seemed prosperous. The steamer
Shreveport found it impossible to reach Fort Benton, and for the
second time my freight was put off near Cow Island, hundreds of
miles below the point named in the bill of lading. It was October
before my messenger met "Baron O'Keefe, of O'Keefe Castle,"
at Big Hole river, with directions to take the saw mill to Alder
gulch and the store goods to Bannack.[9] I had decided to locate
my mill at Brown's Gulch, some nine miles from Virginia City,
and at the nearest point where I found fine timber. I was compelled to build quite a bit of road in order to get my machinery
into Uncle Sam's timber, but I only made the way passable, and
awaited the advent of lumber to make bridges and sluices for a
road which could be used for hauling lumber. My brother and
Mr. Warner were men of much experience in lumbering and they
contrived by attaching levers to the truck which carried the engine and boiler to keep it right side up as the cattle snaked it
along the side of the gulch. We soon had the mill upon the ground
in the midst of an immense pine forest, and digging a ditch along
the hill-side we conducted a little stream of water to a sufficient
elevation above the boiler for our use. It was a sweet sound as
the saw cut its way through the first log we rolled upon the mill
carriage. The finest trees were larger than our saw would reach
through, and we would run the saw through, and then turn the
big log over on the carriage, and running through again the log
would be split in halves, and then could be managed. We had a
crew of five Yankees, and ran the mill night and day. Lumber
delivered at Virginia City or the mines found ready sale at $150.
per thousand, and every slab was worth twenty-five cents. I opened
a lumber yard at Virginia City, and soon after, the Methodists
began the erection of a chapel near the foot of Jackson street,

the first Protestant church erected in Montana. I furnished the most of the lumber for the building and they paid what they could, and the balance I felt went toward a good cause. The building was dedicated November 6, 1864 by Rev. A. M. Hough, acting pastor.

Upon his return from Washington in the early spring of 1864, Governor Edgerton was enthusiastically welcomed by the people, and he proceeded as best he could to organize a civil government, according to the organic act establishing Montana Territory. Communication with the east was at best very slow, and at times suspended almost completely. Nothing had been heard from the person appointed secretary of the new territory.[10] As the time approached which was named in the proclamation, for the assembling of the first legislature and no secretary having put in an appearance, Governor Edgerton asked me to allow him to ask the president to appoint me to that position. A petition was drawn and signed by Governor Edgerton and another signed by prominent citizens, and sent to Governor [James] Doty of Utah [Territory] for him to endorse and forward to Washington.[11] If this petition ever reached the president, no notice was ever taken of it and the territory had no secretary until the arrival of Thomas Francis Meagher in the summer of 1865.[12] Having traveled in almost every part of the territory I was able to be of assistance to the governor in apportioning the council and representative districts for the election of members to the first legislature. Judge James Tufts was also sent into some parts of the territory to make estimates of the population.[13] In the fall of 1864 the governor issued his proclamation for the election of seven members of the Council and thirteen members of the House of Representatives, and the persons elected were to meet at Bannack early in December. Our county of Beaver Head elected Dr. Erasmus D. Leavitt, a native of Berkshire, Mass., and myself to the Council.

The war of the Rebellion was at its height and party feeling was rampant. The iron clad oath required of the members, excluded all who had served in the confederate armies. It was well known that John H. Rogers, elected to the house from Madison county had been an officer in that service, and that being a man of honor he could not take the prescribed oath. Efforts were made to have the governor omit a portion of the prescribed form, but without avail. When the members met for organization the lines between Southern sympathizers and Union men were tightly drawn. The governor refused to administer the oath until Mr. Rogers had withdrawn, and the excitement was intense.[14] When the members elect of the Council were drawn up to take the oath, Charles S. Bagg a member from Madison county, an intense Southern sympathizer, happened to stand at one end of the line and I at the other. As the governor repeated the solemn words of the prescribed oath, Major Bagg interspersed words of contempt, "That means obey Abe Lincoln!" "I guess not!" Keeping silence as long as I could at last I said, "Governor, I move that we proceed to take the oath prescribed by law without further interference." Major Bagg immediately stepped over and stood close to me, and the governor again read the oath with no more interruptions. I expected that at its close the Major would attack me, but he said, "Dr. Thompson, I'll make you the best friend I have before the winter is over!" I retorted, "I am your friend now; when you are sober, Major Bagg, you are a gentleman; when you are drunk you are an infernal nuisance!" Ever after, we were good friends. He was a good citizen, and an able man and good lawyer, and I hope overcame his great failing.

Creating a whole code of laws for a new state without the aid of a library or a printing press was not a task of easy performance, and it has always been a wonder to me that we made as much of a success of our work as we did.[15] My associate, Dr. Leavitt, was nominated by the democrats as president of the Council, and I was named by the republicans. It soon became evident that neither of us could be elected unless we voted for ourselves, and a chance occurring, I led our side to the election of Robert Lawrence, of Virginia City, a good War democrat and a fine man and good presiding officer.[16] The three republicans in the Council got satisfactory places on the committees.

Upon reviewing my work in the Council I take most pride and satisfaction in having been chairman of the committee to report upon a design for a territorial seal. Accompanying my report I made a sketch of the proposed seal, from which has come the coat of arms of the great state of Montana, and the original sketch is preserved in the archives of the Historical Society of Montana.[17] I also made the report of the committee appointed to divide the territory into counties, and feel that in making the summits of the mountains dividing lines rather than rivers, we did a good thing for the territory.

There was no suitable place in Bannack for the use of the Legislature, but the governor rented a large room over a log store for the use of the representatives, and in order to accommodate the council, I went to Virginia City and purchased a partly built two story log building which a party [had] commenced to build for a hotel, but abandoned to go on the Alder Gulch stampede. This I cut down to one story and made convenient for our use as a legislative hall. The main room was quite large and when anything of unusual interest was being transacted, the space between the rail and the entrance was often filled with spectators. Thomas D. Pitt, a wealthy and prominent citizen, of English birth, often maltreated the letter "H." When feeling jovial he had a habit of singing with great gusto, the popular ditty, "John Brown's body, &c." When he came to the words, "John Brown's knapsack was number *highty-four*," he always roared it out strenuously, and every one was ready to cheer

Original sketch of the proposed seal for the Territory of Montana. On May 26, 1864, President Abraham Lincoln signed an enabling act creating Montana Territory. As a member of the first territorial legislature, Thompson chaired the committee that designed the territorial seal, drawing this original sketch of the committee's proposal.

Montana Historical Society Archives, Helena

him, which he took to be an encore, and would repeat. The legislature was at this time granting to stock and ranchmen, the exclusive right to use certain figures and devices as brands for their stock. Thinking to have a little fun, I introduced a bill granting to Tom Pitt the exclusive right to use "No. 84" as his brand, and a certain hour the next day was fixed for its consideration. When the bill came up, many witty remarks were made, which might have been more proper in a mock session than one for regular business. The Council chamber was filled to overflowing, and when finally passed, up jumped Tom Pitt and shouted, "Come boys, adjourn! Come let's liquor!" The motion was put and declared carried, the whole crowd voting "Aye."

I doubt if any other state or territory in the Union in its first legislative session passed an act for the organization of an Historical Society. I think that I may justly claim the credit of initiating and putting through the bill granting a charter for the

First Legislative Hall, Bannack, Montana Territory. Two branches comprised the new territorial legislature, the Council and the House of Representatives. As a member of the Council, which had no suitable place to meet, Thompson purchased an unfinished building in Virginia City, cut it down, and reconstructed it in Bannack for the Council's legislative hall.

Montana Historical Society Photograph Archives, Helena

Historical Society of Montana, and I attended a meeting of the corporators at Virginia City February 25, 1865, held for the organization of the society.[18]

By reason of the limitation fixed in the Organic Act, the legislative session closed February 9, 1865. The mock session in the Council and House was supremely ridiculous. Before the day closed it seemed as if nine-tenths of the men in Bannack were drunk. I had become somewhat conspicuous by never lowering my standard as a temperance man, which was something very unusual in this country. The members and clerks of the two houses concocted a scheme to get me drunk. I eluded them for some time, but was at last captured and taken by superior force to a saloon opposite my store where pandemonium reigned. On one side [of] the long room stood the bar, against which leaned a lot of men, the clerk of the council with glass in hand singing in a loud voice, "The Star Spangled Banner," &c. I was lead up to the bar, a lusty fellow holding on to my coat collar on each side. Along the dead wall of the room were piled beer casks, some with spigots in them ready for use. As I stood there, all at once I ducked my head, turning my coat wrong side out and in turning to run, hit a spigot in a beer barrel, the contents spirting clear across the room. All attention was at once given to stopping the flow of the precious beer, and I had no difficulty in reaching that seclusion that I so highly desired. I never was aware that I lost any popularity for standing firmly by my avowed principles. Late in the fall of 1864 rich discoveries were made at Last Chance gulch, where now stands the city of Helena. Stampedes took place from all the mining camps in the territory, and the discovery showing every sign of proving rich and permanent, and having accumulated a large stock of lumber at Virginia City, I sold to W. F. Sanders a half interest in my mill and we decided to remove it to the new mines. This was safely accomplished while I was attending the legislature, and at its close having met with moderate success, and having large interests in partnership with Gov. Edgerton, A. W. Hall, and Leonard A. Gridley in numerous quartz veins I determined to forego further experience of mountain life, and return to my old home in Massachusetts. Nims and I decided to go to Fort Benton and await the first boat and descend the Missouri to St. Louis, while my brother and Mr. Warner remained to manage the mill. Mr. Sanders finally purchased the remaining half of the mill and his brother became its manager.

Among the other mining interests which we had obtained was No. 6 north of the discovery, on the "Dakotah," above the

gulch at Marysville. No. 4 had been found to be very rich in
pockets, and it was right near town. From the discovery claim
two miners by most primitive methods took out over six thousand dollars during the winter months. They dragged the quartz
in rawhides to their cabin, where they pulverized it in a mortar,
and washed the crushed quartz in a pan and secured the gold.
One day some miners at work on No. 4 broke through into a
cavern of considerable extent which they asserted was of great
beauty. When they had arranged their machinery so as to be able
to lower people into their mine, they extended an invitation to
the governor and the members of the legislature to visit the new
discovery. We were all lowered safely into the cavern, which was
indeed a wonderful sight. While not of great size the walls of the
room and the stalactites suspended from the roof were beautiful, and the stalagmites in rare and picturesque form covered the
floor of the cave. Before the crib containing the governor and
some of the council was raised to the surface, the occupants were
made to pledge themselves to pass a bill pending in the legislature in which the miners were interested, which trick they con-
sidered a huge joke upon the members.

When the time came for severing the intimate relations which
had for so long existed between us and the Edgerton and Sanders
families, it was much harder than I had anticipated. It was particularly trying to leave the sweet babe, Idaho, who had been a
pet, and for whom I made from a shoe box the cradle in which she
slept. When grieved, she would come to me even from her
mother's arms. And the little five year old Pauline, whom I called
"my little wife" was very dear to me. One day when she and her
mother were alone Mrs. Edgerton said, "Pauline," receiving no
answer she again spoke, "Pauline." No answer. "Why Pauline
Edgerton! why don't you answer when I speak to you?" The
little minx looked up and said, "I'm not Pauline Edgerton; I'm

Mrs. Thompson!" I am informed that among the treasures hoarded by the Historical Society of Montana are to be found a barrel chair which I constructed from a ten gallon molasses keg for my "little wife," and the cradle made for little Idaho.[19] Young Nims who was the post master of Bannack, resigned his office, and securing a light wagon and span of horses with Henry Tilden for driver, we set out for the head waters of the Missouri at Fort Benton. On the journey I crossed the Rocky Mountains for the eleventh time into Deer Lodge prairie, and the twelfth time as we went out at Mullen's pass. We stopped at the ranch of Malcolm Clark on the Little Prickley Pear, little thinking that our friend would be murdered within a few years by the same dirty Indians who were hanging about his ranch at that time.[20] I had purchased a Mexican bridle, the most beautiful piece of leather work which I ever saw, [in]tending to present it to a lady in Massachusetts, but Mr. Clark having caught sight of it, frankly told me that it could not go out of the country, and that if I would not sell it to him, one of his Indians would steal it. Under the circumstances, I felt *compelled* to exchange it for a fine bead pouch, the work of his Blackfoot wife. I possess it yet, together with the lady to whom I presented it. In the Prickly Pear canon we secured a fine set of deers horns and the head of a large Big horn [ram], which we took to Massachusetts. At Sun river we found the government farm abandoned, and there met a messenger sent out by Carroll & Steell to warn people on their way to Fort Benton to travel only in large parties, and to keep a sharp lookout as all the Indians were very ugly, and that a large war party of Bloods were out and would be likely to attack any small party. There was no other way for us to do, but cross the high prairie for sixty miles which lay between us and Benton. We drove on forty-five miles and camped at the "Springs," and before noon next day arrived safely at Benton, and committed ourselves to the kindly care of Carroll & Steell. These progressive men, formerly clerks of the American Fur Co. had built a convenient store house and other buildings a mile or more above Fort Benton and entered into the Indian trade upon their own account. Here we remained several weeks waiting with all the patience we possessed, for some intelligence from the Missouri river boats. The ugly attitude of the Indians prevented any white man from hunting, and the poor horses and cattle suffered severely from want of feed, for that near, or within safe distance of the fort, had been gnawed to its roots. Mountain Chief, a Blackfoot and a few other of his tribe, relatives of the squaws of some of the half breeds and white men had wickiups near at hand, and hunted enough to keep us supplied with meat.[21]

Henry Bostwick, who at one time had been our teamster, whose squaw was Mountain Chief's relative, was taken suddenly sick and sent for me to come and see him.[22] I found him at his wickiup near that of the Mountain Chief and evidently very sick. There was no more shape to his head than to a pumpkin, both eyes being closed and his head a mass of sores. I went down to Fort Benton and tried to find some remedy which I thought might relieve him, as I had no idea that he could recover. I found nothing but a few packages of pressed hops. The squaw and I made of these a compress and applied it as hot as the patient could bear, to his head and face, which we often renewed. The patient soon slept and the next day seemed improved. He said that before I came, he made up his mind that he must die, and said he, "I prayed." "Well, Bostwick; what did you pray for?" "Well, I'll tell you; I prayed that these d—d Indians might have the same disease!" It was not many days before Bostwick appeared at Carroll & Steel's store, but such a looking specimen of humanity was never before seen; there was not a hair on his head, not even an eye-lash or eye-brow! The Mountain Chief came down with the same disease, and his squaw sent down for me, but luckily for me, and probably for him, a regular physician strayed into the Fort, and I gladly retired from practice. There were about fifteen men waiting at Benton, and our entertainers ran out of both sugar and salt. A few weeks previously, ten men had laid out a town at the junction of the Marias and Missouri rivers, about fifteen miles by land below Fort Benton, and some thirty miles by the big river. They were cutting timber and building cabins expecting the town to rival Fort Benton.

Volunteers were called for to go down to "Ophir" and procure the need[ed] supplies. Being cooped up as we were was pretty dull business for me, and I told Carroll that if he would find me a companion and let us have the two best buffalo horses there were in the herd, that I would make the trip. This was agreed to, and soon my companion and I were journeying toward "Ophir." We kept upon the highest land—the ridge lying between the Teton and the Missouri—known as the "Cracon-du-Nez" intending to make a run for safety should we discover any Indians. We reached the camp without incident, had a good visit with the boys, (one of whom, Frank Angevine, had been a clerk in the legislature) purchased our sugar and salt, warned the party of hostile Indians, and safely returned to Benton without any Indian scare.

Twenty-four hours later the bodies of these ten men lay naked, stiff, and stark, in their blood, scalped, maimed, and mangled, in the most fiendish and inhuman manner which can be imagined. They had been surprised by one hundred and fifty Blood Indians, who immediately after the massacre fled toward the British line. Only Little Joe Kipp, a half breed who had been employed as a herder, was left to tell the story. On his arrival at the fort a party was made up to pursue the murderers, who followed the trail for a day, only finding a white man's scalp, and the first camping place, where ten fires had been built. At Ophir they found the remains of Frank Angevine, George Allen, James Andrews, N. W. Burris, Franklin Friend, George Friend, Abraham Low, James H. Lyons, Henry Martin and James Perie. The bodies of the murdered men were buried in one grave and the settlement was blotted out. A friendly Blackfoot reported that the Bloods said that the whites fought like devils; that one man had got his back against a tree and killed three Indians before he died. The body of Frank Angevine was found terribly mutilated at the foot of a large cottonwood tree. We subscribed quite a sum of money to induce Joe Kipp to go out on the Deer Lodge road and warn travelers of the danger of venturing out in small parties.[23]

We were so hemmed in that our food supplies were getting pretty short. One day the squaw cook served a most savory soup, and we all ate heartily; but when upon inquiry, it was learned that the basis of the feast was a buffalo calf taken from its slain mother, it caused some of the tender-feet to feel a little gruesome. There were a few buffalo cows running with the herd of cattle, which had been captured when calves, but they were only killed for food supply, when hunger made it necessary.

Late in May the long waited for boat arrived, and we took ourselves, baggage, and trophies, on board for our three thousand mile voyage.

I had, by the kindness of Carroll & Steell, who had no goods for trade, been permitted to trade all those things which I did not care to take to the states, with a large party of Crows, for robes and furs. One morning we discovered upon the opposite side of the Missouri, perhaps two hundred lodges of these Indians, who had noiselessly come in and made camp since the preceding day. A boat was sent over from the Fort and two or three chiefs came over, and after a palaver, although neither Fort Benton or Carroll & Steell had any goods to exchange, they decided to cross and go down to Fort Union, by way of Milk river. In a few minutes after the boat returned to the Crow camp, the wickiups were all down, and each boss squaw had her household goods securely rolled up in the tent skins, making a large, round bundle. The river was now running high from melting snows in the mountains, and was very swift, but before long five hundred ponies were in the river, and attached to the tail of each was the family tent skin, and clinging to the huge ball and partially supported by it were the more mature members of the family, while the papooses were perched on top. The bucks swam along side the ponies, holding to their manes, and keeping them guided against the current of the stream. The young girls and maidens modestly unloosed some article of clothing as their feet touched our shore, but the old squaws were not in the least abashed to land quite in the costume of the original inhabitants of Paradise. A few weaklings floated a long way down the river and we assisted the men at the fort in launching a large flatboat and picking up the stragglers. The whole affair did not occupy an hour's time, and was a very interesting exhibition of native courage and capacity. A bevy of young girls came up in the vicinity of Carroll & Steell's store, and Nims, Tilden and another young man went out to make their acquaintance. Perhaps too abrupt in their missionary work of civilization, it was not long before we saw the three gallants hoofing it for the home station, closely followed by about a dozen handsome young squaws who were very fleet of foot. They could not be induced to enter the trading post. We dickered with the old squaws, and instead of taking home old clothes, jack-knives, fish-hooks, percussion caps, and other knick-knacks, we carried some fine robes—whole skins—deerskin hunting shirts, leggings, bows and arrows, lariats, moccasins, and skins and small furs. In fact I took home a whole bale of selected robes, and from Carroll & Steell's warehouse containing many thousand beaver pelts I selected twelve which I had made into a coat, which after more than forty years service is still a very comfortable garment.

The boat brought report of many Indian murders along the river, and we went prepared for trouble. At a bend of the river just below the mouth of the Musselshell, where the channel which the boat must follow ran close under the curving bank, the pilot discovered about three hundred warriors who were evidently intending to attack the boat. The alarm was given just as we had sat down to breakfast, and as I rushed to my stateroom to get my rifle, right before the door lay a big colored waiter evidently hoping to escape any stray bullet. A full head of steam was applied, and as the boat rushed past the Indians they poured in a fire of bullets and arrows, but luckily without damage to any person. I secured for my collection an arrow which penetrated the smoke stack. As we passed, our two field pieces loaded with grape were let go, and then a second time, as the red-skins skedaddled over the hills. I saw a big rascal in a clump of brush about six rods from the river bank, and fired both barrels of my rifle at him, but with what effect I do not know. I anxiously watched the clump of brush as long as possible, but saw nothing of him. This attack was made in the Crow country, but was probably the work of some other tribe.

When we reached Fort Union we found near by, a large Indian village fully occupied by the Gros Ventres, who were then deeply engaged in a devout religious ceremony.[24] A very large booth had been constructed of poles covered with green branches, and in the center stood a high pole from which the roof sloped to the leafy screen of the sides. This green tent was surrounded by hundreds of Indians of all ages and sexes, peering curiously through the foliage. From the inside issued the tum-tum of the skin drums, the singing of the excited inmates and the tootings of innumerable whistles. Pressing among the crowd who fell away when they discovered a white man, I soon had a peep-hole and obtained a good view of the performances going on within. On the ground surrounding a dry hide tightly stretched over a hole in the earth, sat a half dozen Indians solemnly pounding in unison upon its surface. Near by were others beating upon skin heads tightly drawn over the ends of sections of hollow logs, something like an ordinary drum. Every man taking active part in the ceremonies was stripped to the skin, with the exception of a breech-cloth. Some were entirely covered with white clay, some streaked with vermillion, some with yellow ochre, and others daubed with black and other colors. The big medicine man, master of ceremonies, was clothed in the most fantastic manner, with his medicine bag and his potent charms displayed in the most attractive manner. He was the chief manager of the concern and conducted himself with the greatest dignity, and with a haughtiness which seemed to indicate his assurance that he had all the gods under his direct command. It seemed as though a hundred men had either long or short whistles in constant use, emitting ear piercing toots, keeping time with the singers and the drums. The singing seemed mostly "Hi-ya! Hi-ya!" repeated over and over, now soft and low, then swelling to the fullest volume, as the occasion seemed to demand. From the center pole extended several long ropes of rawhide, ending in loops, four or five feet from the ground. In the middle of the ring stood a number of young bucks, their legs and arms lacerated and bleeding, and having in their breasts two parallel cuts perhaps three inches in length and an inch and a half apart. The skin between the cuts was raised and beneath were thrust on each breast, a wooden peg perhaps three inches in length. Soon a young fellow slipped a loop over each button and ran settling back upon the throngs, swiftly around the pole. As the throngs wound up the unearthly music rose to its highest pitch, and the bleeding victim threw himself back upon the ropes and slowly unwound, the whole weight of his body borne by the throngs. At the climax the excitement is most intense. The singers yell their loudest; the drummers pound most furiously, and the whistlers cheeks swell with their efforts to make more noise.

The antics of the medicine man reach the highest flights of the grotesque. While I was an observer one of the victims passed into a swoon. Whether he would again have to make the crucial test, or whether he would be in disgrace, and fail of becoming a warrior, I was unable to learn.

Then followed an impassioned address by a battle scarred old warrior, and at his telling points, the other old men would grunt assent. The whole scene was one long to be remembered, and was worthy the pencil of Frederick Remington. No murmur of pain came from any actor while I watched the scene, and the countenances of some seemed to indicate that their bodies were entirely under the control of their fanatic spirits. I was told that these ceremonies continue for three days and that during that time the chief actors take no food.

Governor Stevens tells this story of these Indians. A Gros Ventre brave was married to a woman of the Blackfeet tribe, and while they were traveling he was killed and his fleet horse was stolen. The assassin proposed that she marry him and go northward, and the Gros Ventres would never learn of the death of their fellow tribesman. She assented, and he gave her the slow animal which he had ridden and took the better one himself. They came to water on their journey, and leaving her horse with him she went for some, and returning, pressed him to go for some also. He consented, and leaving his horse with her, she mounted the fast horse and fled to her own people, who soon took revenge for the murdered man.

Our trip down the Missouri was without special interest excepting as related, and in due time we arrived at the end of our journey and were warmly welcomed. After spending a short time in Massachusetts I took an office at the corner of Broadway and

F. M. THOMPSON,
Commissioner of Emigration
FOR
MONTANA,
AND
Agent for the Sale of MINING PROPERTY therein.
Office 171 BROADWAY,
ROOM 7, NEW YORK.

Frank Thompson's New York business card. When he returned to the states, Thompson rented an office at the corner of Broadway and Courtland streets in New York City, where he eventually sold the Montana mining property he owned jointly with Sidney Edgerton and others.

Montana Historical Society Archives, Helena

Courtland streets, New York City, for the purpose of disposing of the mining property owned jointly by myself and others.[25] My desk overlooked Courtland street, up which came marching at the close of the civil war, regiment after regiment of ragged and dirty heroes, keeping step to patriotic music, and as they turned the corner into Broadway, they were greeted by thousands of cheers and the shouts of an enthusiastic populace. Base indeed must have been the man who witnessed these events, without feeling his heart stirred to the depths with patriotic fervor.

I took the precaution before leaving Montana, of having taken from each mine owned by our company, a generous sample of the ore, having the same sealed in a rawhide case, and annexed to each package a statement signed by the miner who took it out as to its genuineness, and the date of said transaction. This was sworn to before a magistrate, and then the parcels put into large raw-hide packages of convenient size, and sewed up.

I brought with me about a ton of these samples, of course at quite a large expense, but this extra caution paid us well, for of all the men from Montana during that season trying to interest eastern people in mining property, I think I was the only one who met with much success.

After having several assays made at the mint, I arranged with the superintendent of the School of Mines of Columbia College, whereby in consideration of my furnishing them with gold bearing Montana quartz, they would make assays and report to me the result of each separate original package. In this way I obtained accurate knowledge of the value of the mining property which I offered for sale. I also had about a pound of selected nuggets of gulch gold, which I exhibited, to show the richness of the country. Somehow these nuggets disappeared like melting snow, but I have no doubt but the missing gold helped to make advantageous sales of our mining property.

I was successful in disposing of mines to the value of upwards of one hundred thousand dollars, principally to merchants in the leather trade, in the district known as "The Swamp." When the option which I first negotiated matured, and the parties accepted the properties, my partners Edgerton, Hall, and Gridley came on from Montana, and we executed the formal conveyances, to the purchasers.

Having disposed of all my mining interests in Montana, I gave up my office in New York and my wife and I returned to our old New England home, where we are content to spend the fast fleeing years, in leading a "simple life."

I have kept touch with many old friends all these years, and my interest in them, as well as in the great Commonwealth which has arisen from the small beginnings which I helped to foster, is keen and loyal. Occasionally we receive ever-welcome visits from some of my mountain friends, but many have passed over that great divide which separates us from the undiscovered country.

BEING NOTES ON MEN AND THINGS

in Judge Thompson's Montana Reminiscences

JAMES AND GRANVILLE STUART, the first gold miners of Montana, then located at Gold Creek, came into this region in 1857. They were natives of Virginia, their father being a pioneer in California in 1849, and taking his two sons with him to that country in 1852. When the young men were on their way home in 1857, upon nearing Salt Lake, they found their way blocked by the Mormons, who were preparing to resist the United States troops under Albert Sidney Johnston.

Together with Reece Anderson they turned north and made their way into the Beaver Head and Deer Lodge valleys. James was an associate of mine in the first legislature of Montana, and a charter member of the Historical Society. He possessed a most adventurous spirit and was the bravest and coolest man, when in a tight place, that I ever knew. He was the leader in the celebrated Yellowstone expedition of 1863, and the survivors of that party all agree that it was only by his coolness, sagacity, and knowledge of Indian character that any of the party escaped. He and fourteen others, among whom were H. A. Bell of our original party, Samuel T. Hauser, and others mentioned in my sketches, left Bannack April 9, 1863, for an exploration of the then little known Yellowstone country. Six others had agreed to meet them at a certain point, but they were stopped and turned back by a large party of Crow Indians. This disappointed party were the lucky discoverers of the mines at Alder Gulch, while on their escape from the Crows.

About two weeks after setting out on their expedition the party under Stuart crossed the divide into the Yellowstone valley, having been detained by meeting Winnemucca and a large party of Bannacks returning from a buffalo hunt. Two days after they were surprised by thirty Crow warriors, who came in their camp. After the men had stood all the provocation they could, and Stuart gave no orders to attack, they made preparations to commence the fracas without orders. Stuart then commanded the chief to call his men off and make them behave themselves, which he did. Placing double guards, they got but little sleep, as thieving Indians were busy all night stealing from the camp. They intended to start at daybreak, and try and escape toward Fort Benton. Before they could get away in the morning they were again surrounded by the Indians, who began to forcibly exchange their poor horses for the best of Stuart's. Seeing that it was time to die or do something, Stuart took his hands full of cartridges and his rifle and told the Indians to mount their horses and leave or he would kill the last one of them, his men all being ready to open fire upon them upon signal from Stuart. The Indians finally weakened and drew off, two chiefs and six others saying they would go with them and get breakfast. After getting their stomachs filled they offered Stuart their robes as a peace offering, but he declined; having, as he told them, nothing to give in return.

Getting rid of their tormentors they followed down the Yellowstone and then up the Big Horn, and upon the night of

May 13th, while Stuart and another were on guard, their tents were fired into by a large party of Crows. Ordering the tents pulled down and the men who were able, to crawl out from them and lie close to the ground, they awaited the coming of the morn. In the morning they found that two of the party were fatally wounded, three more severely, and two others wounded, but able to care for themselves. Five horses were killed and several had arrows sticking in their bodies. The Indians could be seen in the hills and ravines near the camp. C. D. Watkins died of his wounds, and E. Bostwick urged his companions to not delay their escape on his account, but to give him his revolver and he would get even with the crew when they came. H. A. Bell was so badly wounded that no one thought he could travel, but upon placing him upon a horse he pluckily held out and made his escape. Throwing away all their provisions but for a few days supply, after making a fire and drinking coffee, the stricken party mounted their horses, and bore off southeast toward the overland route. As they left, poor Bostwick, placed his pistol to his ear and ended his life. At the supper camp H. T. Geery, who had received an arrow wound, in taking up his rifle from the ground fatally wounded himself in his left breast. Thoughtful to the last of his comrades, he told them they must not remain to wait for his death, and asking them to bury him in his army overcoat, he bade them all good bye, and placing his revolver to his temple he put himself out of misery.

After fifteen days of travel, up pathless canyons and over rocky mountains, the party came upon telegraph poles and rejoiced in civilization.

James Stuart became post trader among the Sioux, and died at Fort Peck, Sept. 30, 1873, aged forty-two years.

Granville Stuart, also a charter member of the Historical Society of Montana, was for many years associated with Judge W. B. Dance in mercantile business, and was, by President Cleveland appointed minister to Uruguay and Paraguay, in 1895.

Fort Pierre, was at the time of my visit one of the principal posts of the American Fur Company. It took its name from Pierre Choteau, Jr., a prominent member of the company. It was of the same general character of the other trading posts, a palisaded headquarters. It was built in 1831, the timber for its construction being floated from sixty miles above. This post was the home of Dorian, a famous interpreter and trader. About 1855 the government purchased it for a military post.

Fort Be[r]thold was built in 1845 by the [American] Fur company and in its day was an important trading post. In 1865 when I knew it several companies of Iowa cavalry were garrisoned there, but soon after Fort Stevenson was erected as a military post and it was abandoned. Nothing remains of it now.

Louis Dauphin was for a long time a most skillful and fearless hunter on the Missouri. "He seemed to have no fear of Indians and delighted in danger, but his lack of prudence cost him his life, for he was killed by the Sioux near the mouth of Milk river in 1865."

Mackinaw boats were built primarily to go *down* the river, and were flat bottomed and sometimes fifty to seventy-five feet in length and ten or more feet in width, and could carry quite a large amount of freight, even on shoal water. Originally goods were taken up the river in keel boats built in St. Louis and other towns. Sometimes sails were used on these boats, but they were generally cordelled against the current by men tracking along the shore, in the same manner that canal boats are drawn by horses. It was slow and heavy work.

Fort Union was in 1862 by far the best of the trading posts on the Missouri river. It was situated on the northerly side of the river about three miles above its junction with the Yellowstone, and was established in 1829. The buildings were enclosed in a high palisade of hewn logs made square and placed close together. The palisade was 220 x 240 feet, and at the southwest and northeast corners were built two story stone mounts or bastions, loopholed with cannon in place. The buildings were well constructed and admirably fitted for the Indian trade, and for many years this station was the general headquarters of the American Fur Company's posts.

In 1833 William Sublette, in the interests of Robert Campbell built Fort William, a few miles below, in opposition to Fort Union, but it went to decay, and the United States government took the site and built thereon Fort Buford, for military purposes. When I first saw Fort Union there were but few Indians there. The enclosed space had been used all winter as a corral for stock, and I thought it about the dirtiest place I ever saw used by white men as a residence.

CRACON DU NEZ. The Lewis and Clark party were here June 11th 1805. They called the Teton the Tansey river, which at this place frequently flows quite near the Missouri, before discharging into the Marias. The high clayey bluffs lying between the two rivers is known as "Cracon du Nez." From this elevation they first caught sight of the glistening snow on the Rocky mountains. Clark speaks of a fine spring where "we refreshed ourselves with a good drink of grog." Near here they killed two brown bears, and made a *cache* in which they deposited "corn, pork, flour, some powder and lead" relieving themselves of over one thousand pounds in weight. Capt. Lewis also killed several fine elk, and hung what they did not need on trees for the use of the men on the boats in the Missouri.

MALCOLM CLARKE. Perhaps the most picturesque character whom I met in my wanderings in the mountains, was Malcolm Clarke. He was the son of Nathan Clarke, an officer in the U.S.

army, and was born at Fort Wayne, in 1817. When yet a lad his father was stationed at Fort Snelling, then in a wilderness, and Malcolm became an expert hunter and trapper while yet in his teens. When seventeen years old he received appointment at West Point, but having cowhided a fellow cadet for some real or fancied wrong, he was court martialed, and dismissed [from] the service. He then sailed for Texas, determined to offer his services to Sam Houston, to aid in the liberation of that country.

On the voyage, the captain of the ship not living up to the agreement entered into for their passage, he excited and commanded a mutiny, and bound the captain and took him as a prisoner to Galveston, where he liberated him and reported to Houston as having been in mutiny on the high seas. After hearing the case, Houston dismissed him, and gave him a commission in the Texas army. When twenty-four years old, he met John [Albert?] Culbertson, in Cincinnati, and enlisted in the service of the American Fur Company for service at their forts upon the upper Missouri. By his dash and daring deeds he obtained a great renown among the Indians of the upper river, and took a chieftain's daughter of the Blackfeet tribe, for his wife. He remained in the Fur company's employ for many years, being often in charge of some of their trading posts. He sent his children to the states for education, generally visiting them once each year. He was a daring hunter and gained the name of Ne-so-ke-i-yu, (The Four Bears) from having killed four grizzlies in one day. At an encounter with a grizzley he ventured too much, and at one blow the bear took the scalp from the side of his head, and ever after he had great respect for that species of bear. He advised me never to attack one unless I was on horseback or where I could climb a tree. Retiring from the service of the company, he took up the Indian trade upon his own account, taking his goods into the villages and camps of his Indian friends. During this period he passed through marvelous experiences and wonderful escapes. Once while trading in Calf Shirt's village, he caught an Indian stealing, and knocked him down. The village was at once in an uproar and cries of vengeance filled the air. With a derringer in each hand he stood off the crowd until the older men came, when a council was held, and after the truth was known, Calf Shirt declared "This man shall live; he has a big heart!" At one time when in charge of Fort Benton, he gave shelter to a half dozen Blackfeet who were pursued by three hundred Arickarees. These Indians after spending nearly all their ammunition and arrows in an attack on the fort were obliged to draw off in defeat. He had long had a feud with McKinzie, an old mountain man, and by some chance they met in 1863, on the Fur company boat, below Fort Union. Frank Worden, an old friend of mine who was present informed me that McKinzie, who had been drinking, began the quarrel at this time, which ended in the shooting of McKinzie by Clarke, as he claimed, in self defense. By Worden's advice Clarke and his young son Nathan, left the boat at Fort Union and drove to Fort Benton by the Milk river route. No judicial notice was ever taken of this affray.

Retiring from the Indian trade, Mr. Clarke gathered his family together and established a ranch on the Prickley Pear in 1864, and it was here in the spring of 1865 that I was his guest. At that time many of his wife's Indian relatives were hanging about his premises, living upon his lavish generosity. Not long after I was there, his own and his Indian guest's horses were stolen. After examination, the Indians declared the thieves to have been white men. The visitors ill will was aroused when all the horses bearing Clarke's brand came straggling back into camp. They suspected that Clarke had played them falsely.

In revenge, the Indian relatives stole Clarke's field glass and enough horses to get away with and fled toward the north. Not long after, Clarke and his son Nathan, rode into the Blackfoot village, and almost immediately Nathan discovered his mother's cousin, Ne-tus-che-o, riding his (Nathan's) favorite horse. Nathan took his horse from his relative and gave him a cut across his face, calling him a "dog." Nathan was at once surrounded by twenty young bucks, when the old men came upon the scene. They prevented bloodshed, but Malcolm Clarke had called his wife's cousin "an old woman."

The difficulty was at length adjusted, and Mr. Clarke traded in Calf Shirt's camp the next two winters, when Ne-tus-che-o might have taken his revenge.

In 1869 the feeling between the Indians and whites had become so intense that Mountain Chief's brother and a young Blood Indian, sent on a mission to Major Culbertson, were killed by white men, who thought them enemies. Ne-tus-che-o saw that this was his chance to wipe out the stain he had received from Nathan and his father. He made up a party, and went to Clarke's ranch, where he was kindly entertained, but treacherously killed Mr. Clarke and his son Horace, Nathan being at this time absent from home.

"Big Gwynn" was killed by the Sioux while descending the Missouri in a mackinaw boat in the fall of 1863.

What was in the early days known as "The Beaver Head Country" was located near the junction of Red Rock and Beaver Head creeks, and made prominent by Beaver Head rock, frequently called "Point of Rocks," which was a noted locality in Vigilante days as being a resort of the "Road Agents."

John Owen was sutler to a regiment of United States troops called the Mounted Rifles, which left St. Joseph, Mo., for Oregon in 1849. The detachment was snowed in near Snake river, and built Cantonment Loring, where they wintered. In the spring Owen threw up his commission and spent the summer trading with emigrants on the old overland route. In the fall he made his way north to the Bitter Root valley where he found the priests at St. Mary's mission, which Father De Smet and others had founded in 1841.

The fathers had suffered so much from incursions of the thieving Snake Indians, that they sold their possessions to Major Owen and moved their station north among the Flatheads. Mr. Owen made great improvements, by erecting several adobe buildings for ranch purposes, and surrounding them by a palisade.

He entered into Indian trade, making yearly pilgrimages to Oregon to sell his furs and purchase supplies. Even his strong palisade did not always stop the rascally Snakes, for once they dug up some of the pickets and drove off every horse on the premises.

The life led by the occupants of these isolated posts may be inferred from the following incident. One John F. Dobson, from Buffalo Grove, Ill., worked for Owen and kept a diary from the time he left home until he made this last entry. "Sept. 14, 1852. I have been fixing ox yokes and hay rigging. Helped haul one load of hay. Weather fine."

The next entry was in Owen's writing and reads, "Sept. 15. The poor fellow was killed and scalped by the Blackfeet in sight of the fort." The Major obtained his military title by being government agent for the Flathead Indians. He was a most companionable man, exercising a prodigal generosity, and Fort Owen became noted among mountain men for the geniality of its host. Within his fenced farm he proved the abundant agricultural resources of the country. In carrying on the original surveys for a Pacific railroad, Governor Stevens caused Lt. Mullan to winter in this valley, and he erected buildings near Fort Owen which he named Cantonment Stevens, which were his headquarters during the winter of 1853-54. With Lt. Mullan there came to this region, W. W. Delacy, C. P. Higgins, Thomas Adams, Fred H. Burr and others. I acknowledge many favors received from Major Owen.

Sidney Edgerton, the first governor of Montana Territory, was born in Cazenovia, New York in 1818. His parents came from Connecticut, his mother being left a widow with six young children before Sidney was six months of age. Circumstances compelled his removal from the family home at the tender age of eight years. He made his own way in the world and with some assistance gained sufficient education to become a school teacher, studied law and was admitted to the Ohio bar in 1846. He began practice in Akron, Ohio, was married to a most excellent helpmate in 1849, and became prosecuting attorney for his county in 1852. He was elected to Congress from the 18th Ohio District in 1858, which position he retained until 1862. Mr. Lincoln appointed him chief justice of the newly formed Territory of Idaho in 1863, and in company with his nephew, Wilbur F. Sanders, they with their families crossed the plains in the summer and fall of that year.

When the party reached the Snake river, they found that there was no time to reach the capitol of Idaho, and turned their faces toward that Bannack on the east side of the Rocky mountains. The tired and dusty travelers unyoked their oxen for the last time, after three months and seventeen days travel, on the banks of the Grasshopper, Sept. 17th, 1863.

Judge Edgerton's winter journey to Washington, his successful labors in getting the new territory of Montana erected, and his return as its governor, were all very satisfactory to the people, and he took up the duties of his new position with zeal and good judgment.

Many men who had served in the Confederate army had taken refuge in Montana when Price's army was defeated in southwestern Missouri. Of these many who were well qualified in other respects were excluded from serving in official capacities, because of the iron clad oath which had been prescribed in the territories by the government. This made the organization of the new government in the territory peculiarly embarrassing to the chief magistrate.

The services of these men were needed and desirable, but Governor Edgerton was firm in the performance of the duty imposed upon him, and it became necessary to exclude a gentleman otherwise eminently qualified, who had been elected to the legislature, for the reason that he had served as an officer in the Confederate army. This naturally caused much excitement, although the parties immediately concerned admitted the justice of the Governor's position.

Having traveled in all inhabited portions of the new territory, I was enabled to give the governor considerable assistance in apportioning to the different sections their proper numbers of representatives and councilors, which should be chosen to make up the first legislature. Consequently my relations with the governor and his family became very intimate, and were most agreeable to me. He and his excellent wife were of the good old fashioned kind, who avoided all unnecessary formalities, and were most kind and cordial in all their ways.

Upon Andrew Johnson's accession to the presidency, Mr. Edgerton felt that his usefulness to Montana was over, and he began preparations to return with his family to his old home in Ohio. As soon as he conveniently could after the arrival of Gen. Thomas Francis Meagher, who had been appointed secretary of Montana, he took his family to Akron, and renewed his law practice, leaving Gen. Meagher as acting governor of the territory.

Mr. Edgerton was almost as fond of a joke as was his friend Lincoln. He could extract crumbs of comfort from the most adverse circumstances. He was full of the spirit of charity, and it was not an easy thing to persuade him that a well appearing person was not always worthy of trust. Himself the very soul of honor, he believed everybody else honest until convinced to the contrary. He loved fun and games, and his home was a most happy one.

Writing from Virginia City to a niece who was a member of his family, he says: "I am well and happy and having a good time. Everything is lovely and 'the goose hangs high.' Hoping that you are enjoying the same blessing, I am your loving uncle." He died July 1, 1900, aged eighty-eight.

Wilber F. Sanders. Mr. Sanders was a young man when he arrived at Bannack after his long journey by ox team across the plains, on the 17th of September, 1863. He had seen service in the civil war, and withdrew from ill health. He was a member of the Ohio bar, and practiced his profession during all his business life, excepting when a member of the United State Senate.

He was a man of intense action, aggressive, forceful, brilliant, brave and talented, good natured and always willing to aid in a "square deal," and an opponent must possess many of these qualities or he would be borne to the wall in a clash of arms.

Mr. Sanders was the acknowledged leader in the great struggle of the people against the oath bound band of robbers, who at one time in the history of the territory had the community at their mercy, and in constant peril of his life he led the way to the establishment of law and order.

He was the organizer of the Republican party in Montana, and in his spirited canvass with James M. Cavenaugh [Cavanaugh] for election as the first delegate from Montana territory to Congress, he established his reputation as a speaker of high order. He however had a forlorn hope, but he earned the name of "The War Horse of the Republican party," which he retained all his remaining days.

Ever ready to sacrifice himself in any cause which to him appeared for the advantage of the public, he was always active in helping forward all enterprises which were calculated to advance the interests of the people of Montana, his beloved home.

He was a charter member of the Historical Society of Montana, and for many years its president, and always deeply interested in making the society active and progressive in its noble work. As an orator he was second to none, and was often called upon to deliver addresses upon public occasions. He spoke with eloquence of "The Pioneers of Montana," upon the dedication of the Capitol, in 1902.

The real character of the man may perhaps be better shown by a letter addressed to me.

DEAR THOMPSON:

Contrasting recent winters with those you knew in the mountains, you would not know the country, for it is, and with the exception of less than a week, has been for eight months like summer; no snow, and only floods of golden sunshine with warm weather. Every one here is well excepting me. I harbor no illusions and feel that "sleep is beginning to lay me in the arms of her brother."

My trouble is of twenty-five years standing and is slowly culminating, and though I am well and work in the office every day, it is idle to say or hope it can long continue. A near denoument brings no terror. One hates to close the rhapsody of domestic life such as it has been my fortune to enjoy, and leave the relatives and friends which are mine.

And then this poor debouched state; it needs me, being wofully lacking in men of sensitive natures who resent civic treachery as a crime. What with the R. Roads and copper companies, and the millionaires, everything is pecuniarily appraised, except the scars on a soldier.

I have fought bribery and every form of civic corruption for forty years and now that it has become triumphant, I fight it still, and bear its contumely with becoming indignation.

I have led a strenuous life for forty years, and have lived for the state, and seeing my mistakes and omissions, know they cannot blot out my history, with which

I am reasonably content. I have never fawned to, or flattered the coarse, or condoned wickedness in high places.

But I drop this. Don't think I am to die soon. I tell you those boys of 1863-4, are missing, one of them being of rare occurrence. . . . No man ever came to Montana and staid so short a time, left so deep an impress on history as did you, and it is a pleasure to know, in a rude time, the influence was wholly wholesome. . . . Come and stay with us on your way to Portland.

Yours very sincerely,

W. F. SANDERS.

When, after a long and bitter struggle, Montana was admitted to representation in the United States senate, Col. Sanders drew the short term, and at its expiration he returned to Helena and resumed the practice of his profession, with his son. His long and faithful service ended in the fall of 1905, after years of suffering which he bore with fortitude and resignation. In his death, Montana lost a most honest, able, and faithful citizen.

On the first of March, 1906, the legislature of Montana having established the county of "Sanders" in honor of the man who had done so much for the commonwealth, the citizens met at Thompson, which was named as the county seat, and installed the county officers.

> "Fearless and firm, he never quailed,
> Nor turned aside for threats, nor failed
> To do the thing he undertook.
> How wise, how brave, how well,
> He bore himself, let history tell."

NATHANIEL PITT LANGFORD. I first met Mr. Langford at St. Paul, Minn., in the fall of 1859. He was then cashier in the banking house of his uncles, W. R. Marshall & Co., and I was in that city in the employ of Wall street parties who intended to start a bank of issue under the laws of Minnesota. The friendship then begun has since continued. Mr. Langford was associated with Captain

James L. Fisk in organizing a party of emigrants to cross the country from St. Paul to Fort Benton, practically upon the line of the present Northern Pacific Railroad, then an unoccupied wilderness.

The party left St. Paul, May 16th, 1862 and consisted of one hundred and thirty men, women and children, and arrived safely at Fort Benton Sept. 6th, and were soon scattered among the new mining camps in the mountains.

Mr. Langford was one of the first at Bannack, and being active and energetic, in company with others erected a saw mill some ten or twelve miles above Bannack, near to fine timber. These ingenious men manufactured most of their necessary iron work for the mill from old, worn out wagons which had crossed the plains.

In January, 1863, a party of gamblers and roughs from sheer wickedness fired into a wikiup of the Sheep Eater tribe of Bannacks, killing an old chief, a lame Indian, a papoose, and a Frenchman named Cazette. "Old Snagg," the chief, was afterward scalped by Buck Stinson.

The law abiding citizens arose to the occasion and determined that the roughs who had perpetrated this outrage should be tried, and if found guilty suffer punishment. J. F. Hoyt was elected judge, and twelve good men selected as a jury, among whom were Mr. Langford. W. C. Rheem, an able lawyer, was assigned as counsel for the accused and the trial proceeded.

Mr. Langford was a man of courage and solid worth, and became a marked man, when he voted "guilty" while all his comrades decided to clear the prisoners. The enmity of the road agents against him is easily accounted for, and he narrowly escaped death at their hands. He was the first post master of Bannack, but resigned in 1864 to become Collector of Internal Revenue of the new territory of Montana. He was succeeded as post master by Lucius Nims, Jr. Truman C. Everts was Assessor of Internal Revenue.

He occupied official positions in Montana until 1876, being appointed governor of the territory by Andy Johnson, but the strained relations then existing between the president and senate, prevented his confirmation to that office.

In August, 1870, he with other prominent citizens of the territory organized the Washburn Yellowstone expedition, and through the public press made known to the world the unparalleled phenomina of "Wonder Land."

He was the first superintendent of the National Park, and continued in that position for more than five years without compensation, and paying his own expenses. He is an honorary member of the Historical Society of Montana, to which association he has contributed many valuable books and papers. He is president of the Historical Society of Minnesota, and makes his residence at St. Paul.

SAMUEL T. HAUSER. Mr. Hauser was from St. Louis and was a passenger with me on the *Emilie* in 1862. He was a civil engineer, a strong man both physically and mentally, and became one of the leading men of the new territory. He organized the First National Bank of Helena, and served as governor of Montana by appointment of Grover Cleveland. He was brave and fearless, and was severely wounded by the Crow Indians in the fight on the Yellowstone in 1863, while a member of the James Stuart party.

In his interesting story of *The Life and Adventures of Captain Joseph La Barge*, (Francis P. Harper, N.Y., 1903) Hiram M. Chittenden, of the United States army, says, "The danger from snags was always present and sometimes very great, and passage of these obstructions was a matter of anxious solicitude on the part of both passengers and officers. Less dangerous, but not less annoying, was the passage of shallow bars where there was not sufficient depth to float the boat. This usually occurred at the 'crossings' or places where the channel, after having followed one side of the river-bed for a distance, crossed over to the other. In these places the channel generally split up into chutes, none of which might have the required depth of water. The pilot's first step would be to select the most promising channel. If this failed, he retreated and tried another."

If no channel could be found, some officer of the boat would go out in the yawl, and sound for the deepest water, and if only a few inches in depth was lacking, the steamer would try "walking." Huge spars would be planted each side of the bow, with the tops leaning up the river. By the use of tackle and the "nigger" engine, the boat would be partially lifted over the bar. At times when a depth of two or three inches more water would float the boat, the wheels were turned backward, thus damming up the water, while the spars and "nigger" engine would push her forward.

JOHN F. GRANT, popularly known as "Johnny" was son of Captain Richard Grant, who had been an officer of the Hudson Bay company, and was well known as a trader on the old emigrant road. C. P. Higgins, an able and worthy man, married one of Captain Grant's daughters. He and the Grant's settled in the Bitter Root Valley, near Fort Owen in 1857, and at the time of which I write, the Grants were rich in horses and cattle. "Johnny" was perhaps the earliest settler in the beautiful Deer Lodge Valley, and his herds swarmed therein when we first came to it. It was understood that he kept a squaw from each of the surrounding tribes of Indians, and when any approaching party of Indians were discovered, their tribal relations were early made out, and all the wives of other blood were carefully concealed, that no quarrel might result, during the entertainment of the uncles, aunts and cousins, of the wife of the blood of the visitors. Mr. Grant was a kind and generous friend to those whom he trusted, but was harsh with those he disliked.

One of the old pioneers was Louis R. Maillet who came into the country with the Stevens surveying party about 1855.[1] He tells the following story of an incident in the life of "Johnny" Grant. In the winter of 1855, Grant "whose camp was on Beaverhead creek, was in his lodge making pack saddles, when the brother of one of his Indian wives entered, and struck him on the head with a club, saying that his sister had been treated badly and that Grant loved his young Indian wife better than the old one. Grant threw the Indian down and held him, whereupon some squaws ran in armed with knives, and would certainly have killed him, had not Maillet interfered, knocking down two of them and threatening the others with his pistol if they did not leave. The trouble ended there, and Grant escaped. That night, another brother-in-law, his young wife's brother, arrived in camp. This was Tin-doy, who, Mr. Maillet says, was the bravest Indian he ever saw. Tin-doy rated the Indians roundly and told them that if they ever caused any more trouble he would take a club and knock their brains out. The Indians greatly feared him, and peace was restored in camp."

Once when taking four hundred head of cattle for "Johnny" Grant to California, Mr. Maillet, riding ahead discovered signs of Indians. Waiting for his train to come up, he formed the wagons into a corral, near a small creek, and awaited events. He told his men to load every gun, and await the attack behind the shelter of the wagons. As soon as the Indians fired, to make a rush before they could have time to load. They were attacked and the scheme worked admirably; the Indians took to their heels and escaped to the rocks. He further says; "Among our party was a young man who lived in California, and who had come east to get himself a wife. He had married a young lady in Philadelphia, a very pretty girl, who did not seem more than sixteen years old. When the attack began, the husband had made a place for her between sacks of flour and placed her therein. This same young man was one of the first to run after the Indians. After they were dislodged, we turned towards the wagons and there we met this dear little woman who had followed us. Her husband chided her for leaving her place of security. Her tearful reply was that she thought her husband would surely be killed, and if he was, that she wanted to die too. Every man in the outfit instantly fell in love with her and would have died for her. As for myself, I am sure I felt as the others did, for I love her still.

We had one man—a Mr. Hall, killed. One Indian was seen to fall, rise and fall again. I do not know if he has risen since or not."

BUFFALO. Persons who never saw a large herd of buffalo, can scarcely credit statements made concerning the unlimited number of these awkward, ungainly creatures which once roamed over the great plains. Captain Lewis of the Lewis & Clark expedition says of a herd which he saw on Sun river: "There were at least ten thousand of them within a circle of two miles."

Again, of a herd seen on Teton river, near the present town of Benton: "We continued through immense herds of buffalo for twenty miles." His associate, Capt. Clark, writing of buffalo seen on his trip down the Yellowstone: "The herd stretched as thick as they could swim from one side of the river to the other, and the party was obliged to stop for an hour."

While making their celebrated portage around the Great Falls of the Missouri, Lewis and Clark say; "They go in great herds to water about the falls, and as the passages to the river near that place are narrow and steep, the foremost are pressed into the river by the impatience of those behind. In this way we have seen ten or a dozen disappear over the falls in a few minutes."[2]

The herds were not perceptibly diminished at the time of our expedition. I have seen countless multitudes upon the rolling prairies bordering the Missouri River, between old Forts Pierre and Union. At times the wheels of the steamer were stopped for fear of injuring both the paddle wheels, and in consideration for the stupid, bull-headed beasts who blocked the way.

More than once when on a boat going down the river have I seen upon the bank below us a large herd grazing close to shore, and as the boat approached they would take fright and run down the stream, trampling down willows and brush as they ran, and coming to some turn in the river keep straight on, plunging over the bank and each other, hundreds upon hundreds, while the boat, unable to stop its progress in season, would strike many under its wheels.

When running free upon the prairie, its lumbering gait appears slow, and extremely awkward, leaning far over to one side, then changing and leaning to the other, like a sail boat in a vigorous breeze. In fact, their progress is rapid, and it takes the very fastest Indian pony to overtake and pass one.

In the old days when hunting them with bow and arrows, the pursuer would ride alongside and the beast of his selection, and let drive an arrow, and if placed in the right spot he paid no more attention to that particular animal but selected another for his victim. When hunting with the old Hudson Bay flint lock, the Indian carried his bullets in his mouth, and his powder in a horn. When loading he placed the horn in the muzzle of the gun, and let the powder run until he thought he had a charge, then dropped in a bullet which ran down to the powder, while he held the gun nearly perpendicular while riding at utmost speed. Coming along side his victim, he lowered the muzzle of his gun, and fired. If the bullet had not escaped from the gun before it went off, he was in luck. In this way many of the Indians' guns are shortened, which has often been the subject of remark by tenderfeet, the muzzles having been blown off while hunting buffalo.

Captain Chittenden in his *Early Steamboat Navigation on the Missouri River*, tells a funny story of a buffalo hunt in which

Captain Joseph La Barge took part. On one of his trips to the mountain, the men had got pretty tired of the regulation fare on the boat, and longed for fresh meat. His first mate was an Englishman who had never seen a wild buffalo. Soon after they saw four bulls swimming the river. Captain La Barge said, "Man the yawl, John, and I will go with you and we will have a buffalo before we get back." The Captain ordered the men on the steamer to shoot the animals, and he would lasso a wounded one and drag it to the boat. He placed the mate in the bow of the yawl with a line, while he took the rudder. The men fired and wounded two buffalos. To reach them the yawl had to pass close to the uninjured ones. To the consternation of the Captain, the mate slipped his noose over the horns of a big bull which had not been wounded. Too late, the Captain shouted that he did not wish to anchor to a live buffalo. "Oh," exclaimed the mate, "he's as good as any."

The crew backed the oars, but to no purpose; away went the bull with the boat, and when he struck the shore, they started across the prairie, but soon the stem of the yawl gave way, being wrenched entirely out of the boat and carried off by the beast in his flight.

PRICES OF PROVISIONS, &c. Upon my books I find charged out for Thanksgiving dinner, 1863

3	cans of peaches	$3.00
3	chickens	9.00
1	can of oysters	1.00
5½ lbs hominy		3.00

Sold A. J. Oliver & Co.

1	gal. molasses	$6.00
5	lbs. candles	5.00
5	boxes matches	1.00
1	tin bucket	1.00
23	lbs. butter	34.50
60	lbs. meal	18.00

Tobacco reached $15 per pound for a short time in 1863. In January, 1864, I find the following bill of goods credited to W. A. Clarke, since United States senator, and the celebrated multi-millionaire, then freighting and trading between the mines and Salt Lake City:

2 boxes of butter	299 lbs.	$299.00
3 sacks of flour	261 lbs.	208.80
5 sacks of peaches	201 lbs.	160.80
1 box of eggs	120 doz.	120.00
129 lbs. of oats		24.27
		$812.87

Staples, viz., coal oil and whiskey, were ten dollars per gallon.

MILK RIVER. On the 8th of May, 1805, Lewis and Clark came to a stream having "a peculiar whiteness, such as might be produced by a tablespoonful of milk in a dish of tea," which they named "Milk River." The stream has retained its name, and as in the early days of steamboat navigation, boats rarely ascended above this point, its valley became the great highway to Fort Benton and beyond. When the railroads were built, the engineers followed the broad trail in their course to the Pacific coast.

FIRST NEWSPAPER IN MONTANA. In Vol. III, page 300 of the publications of the Historical Society of Montana, N. H. Webster in writing of *the Montana Post*, which was the first regular newspaper printed in the Territory, says:

"This was an excellent paper, the first established in Virginia City, and with the exception of the 'News Letter' of Bannack, a small sheet of short life, the Post was really the first paper in the Territory."

The facts are, that I had a small hand press sent out in the spring of 1864 and with it the head lines for a news letter. Using this heading, I published a few numbers giving local news about Bannack, with no intention of making the publication a permanent affair. As this was the first attempt at a newspaper in Montana, I claim whatever credit there may be in the matter. I am informed that copies are on file in the archives of the Historical Society.

TRUMAN C. EVERTS came to Montana in 1864 bearing the appointment of Assessor of Internal Revenue. He made his headquarters at my store in Bannack, and was a cultured gentleman and proved an efficient officer. In 1870 he joined the Washburn expedition to the Yellowstone Lake country. Wholly devoid of skill in woodcraft, he managed to stray from his companions while in the wilderness, and for thirty-seven days wandered alone without blankets or arms, a portion of the time scarcely sane, living upon thistle roots, and dogged for hours by a mountain lion. He at length was found by a party which had been sent out for his rescue. He died at Hyattsville, Md., February 16th, 1901, aged 85 years. See his relation, *Scribner's Magazine*, November, 1871.

THE FIRST SCHOOL IN MONTANA. Miss Lucia Darling, niece of Governor Edgerton, taught the first school established in what is now Montana. It was opened in a room of the log cabin of her uncle, in the fall of 1863. When looking for a place in which to open her school, Miss Darling and her uncle called upon one patriotic citizen and explained their business. He said, "Yes, glad of it; d——d shame, children running around in the streets; ought to be in school; I'll do anything I can to help her, she can have this room; I'll give it to her cheap. She can have it for fifty dollars a month; it's dirt cheap!"

Miss Darling gathered about twenty pupils. She afterwards became Mrs. S. W. Park of Warren, Ohio. Mrs. Park died August 18th, 1905.

NOTES

EDITOR'S INTRODUCTION

1. Francis M. Thompson, "Reminiscences of Four-Score Years by Judge Francis M. Thompson," *Massachusetts Magazine*, 5 (1912), S133.

2. Ibid., S124.

3. Ibid., S125.

4. Ibid., S132.

5. Ibid., S134.

6. Ibid., S137. Other witnesses reported that it was Stephen A. Douglas who took charge of Lincoln's silk hat during the address. Allan Nevins, *The Emergence of Lincoln* (New York: Charles Scribner's Sons, 1950), 2:458.

7. Receipt dated January 12, 1864, Small Collection 297, George D. French Carpentry Receipt, 1864, Montana Historical Society Archives, Helena (hereafter MHSA).

8. The essential handbook of historical method, used by more than two generations of students, is Allan Nevins, *The Gateway to History* (1938; repr., New York: Anchor, 1962).

9. Thomas J. Dimsdale, *The Vigilantes of Montana; or, Popular Justice in the Rocky Mountains* (Virginia City, Montana Territory: Montana Post Press, D. W. Tilton, Book and Job Printers, 1866). Dimsdale's volume has been reprinted several times, and it remains in print.

10. Nathaniel Pitt Langford, *Vigilante Days and Ways: The Pioneers of the Rockies; The Makers and Making of Montana, Idaho, Oregon, Washington, and Wyoming*, 2 vols. (Boston: J. G. Cupples, 1890). This work has been reprinted several times since it was first published.

11. For the legal description of Idaho's borders, see the 1863 Idaho Organic Act, "An Act to Provide a Temporary Government for the Territory of Idaho," conveniently printed in Francis Newton Thorpe, comp., *The Federal and State Constitutions, Colonial Charters, and Other Organic Laws of the States, Territories, and Colonies Now or Heretofore Forming the United States of America* (Washington, D.C.: Government Printing Office, 1909), 2:905. Since Idaho kept these extensive boundaries only for one year,

until the formation of Montana Territory, followed in 1868 by the formation of Wyoming Territory, modern historical atlases commonly overlook or misrepresent the territorial boundary situation at the time of Edgerton's appointment. Regarding this appointment and his arrival at Bannack, see Edgerton to W. H. Hunt, May 23, 1892, in Anne McDonald, ed., "Edgerton and Lincoln," *Montana The Magazine of Western History*, 1 (Autumn 1951), 42–55; Wilbur Fisk Sanders, "The Story of George Ives," in X. *Biedler, Vigilante*, ed. Helen Fitzgerald Sanders and William H. Bertsche Jr. (Norman: University of Oklahoma Press, 1957), 40–79. See also the biographical sketches in Allen Johnson and Dumas Malone, eds., *Dictionary of American Biography*, vol. 6 (New York: Scribner, 1931), 20; and *Biographical Directory of the American Congress, 1774–1996* (Alexandria, Va.: CQ Staff Directories, 1997), 932. A personal account is Martha Edgerton Plassman, "Biographical Sketch of Hon. Sidney Edgerton, First Territorial Governor, by His Daughter," *Contributions to the Historical Society of Montana*, 3 (1900), 330–40.

12. Two different stories account for the decision of Edgerton and Sanders to come to Bannack in the upper Missouri country, rather than to make Lewiston or some other point in western Idaho their destination. One is that the chief justice's party was misdirected toward the newly established Bannack or East Bannack, when they really intended to head for Bannock or West Bannock in western Idaho. The other, more persuasive story is that by the time Edgerton and Sanders had reached Salt Lake City, traveling by ox-drawn wagons, it was so late in the season that Bannack was the only possible destination they could hope to reach in what was then Idaho Territory before winter blocked their way. At different places, Thompson relates both these stories, with no apparent concern for the contradiction.

13. For a summary of Sanders's career see *Biographical Directory of the American Congress, 1774–1996*, 1776. A detailed biographical tribute is A. C. McClure, "Wilbur Fisk Sanders," *Contributions to the Historical Society of Montana*, 8 (1917), 25–35.

14. Alexander Toponce, *Reminiscences of Alexander Toponce* (Norman: University of Oklahoma Press, 1971), 46.

15. Family history and biographical notes, folder 1, Manuscript Collection 37, Samuel Thomas Hauser Papers, 1864–1914, MHSA. Like Thompson, Hauser had long nurtured a romantic inclination to venture into the farthest west, an inclination in Hauser's case fed by the writings of Washington Irving.

16. Sidney Edgerton to W. H. Hunt, May 23, 1892, in Anne McDonnell, ed., "Edgerton and Lincoln," *Montana The Magazine of Western History*, 1 (Autumn 1951), 42–45.

17. On mining camp justice and miners' courts in California, the most recent reappraisal is Martin Ridge's essay, "Disorder, Crime, and Punishment in the California Gold Rush," which appears in Kenneth N. Owens,

ed., *Riches for All: The California Gold Rush and the World* (Lincoln: University of Nebraska Press, 2002), 176–201. The earliest scholarly consideration is Charles H. Shinn, *Mining Camps: A Study in Frontier Government* (1885; repr., New York: A. A. Knopf, 1948), a work that portrayed the miners' courts as a praiseworthy adaptation rooted in the supposed Anglo-Saxon genius for orderly government. At the other extreme, John W. Caughey's *Their Majesties, the Mob* (Chicago: University of Chicago Press, 1960) published a collection of documents that linked the most grievous miscarriages of justice by extralegal proceedings during the California gold rush to more contemporary violations of civil rights in quasi-judicial settings, particularly the anti-Communist scare promoted by Senator Joseph McCarthy during the Cold War era. For the records of the miners' courts on issues related to property, see especially Rodman Paul, *California Gold: The Beginning of Mining in the Far West* (Cambridge: Harvard University Press, 1947), 210–39; and Joseph Ellison, "The Mineral Land Question in California," in *The Public Lands: Studies in the History of the Public Domain*, ed. Vernon Carstensen (Madison: University of Wisconsin Press, 1963), 71–92.

18. See Kenneth N. Owens, "Pattern and Structure in Western Territorial Politics," *Western Historical Quarterly*, 1 (October 1970), 373–92.

19. S. T. Hauser to N. P. Langford, October 19, 1863, Virginia City, Small Collection 215, Nathaniel P. Langford Papers, 1863–1909, MHSA (hereafter SC 215).

20. Senator Morton Smith Wilkinson to President Abraham Lincoln, May 20, 1864, S. Edgerton Appointment file, Letters of Application and Recommendations, Appointments Division, General Records of the Department of State, 1756–1979, Record Group 59, National Archives, Washington, D.C. (hereafter Edgerton Appointment file, RG 59, NA). For Lincoln's response, see Lincoln to Wilkinson, June 20, 1864, Roy P. Basler, ed., *The Collected Works of Abraham Lincoln* (New Brunswick, Conn.: Archon Press, 1953), 7:403.

21. Frederick Allen, "Montana Vigilantes and the Origins of 3-7-77," *Montana The Magazine of Western History*, 51 (Spring 2001), 2–19, describes the appearance of this symbol in 1879 as a warning to suspected wrongdoers to go elsewhere. Although its meaning is a mystery, as Allen concludes, it is today incorporated both in the shoulder patch and car door insignia of the Montana Highway Patrol "as a benign message of law and order."

22. Recently reconditioned, the Sanders statue now stands on the second-floor landing of the Grand Stairway in the Montana state capitol, next to the statue of Jeannette Rankin.

23. Ruth E. Mather and Fred E. Boswell, *Vigilante Victims: Montana's 1864 Hanging Spree* (San Jose, Calif.: History West, 1991), 55. See also Ruth E. Mather and Fred E. Boswell, *Hanging the Sheriff: A Biography of Henry Plummer* (Salt Lake City: University of Utah Press, 1987); and Ruth

E. Mather, *Gold Camp Desperadoes: A Study of Violence, Crime, and Punishment on the Mining Frontier* (Norman: University of Oklahoma Press, 1993).

24. While making a final revision of this introduction before publication, I have had the opportunity to read in manuscript Frederick Allen's book-length work "The Montana Vigilantes." Scheduled for publication in autumn 2004 by the University of Oklahoma Press, this volume will prove to be the impartial, authoritative account that has long been needed both to describe the vigilante outbreak and to resolve, with superior research and good judgment, the lingering issues related to this controversial episode. Although Allen may differ with my characterization of Thompson in some details, he does give full credence to Thompson's statements and his conclusions are completely consistent with those advanced here.

AUTHOR'S PREFACE

1. For the history of the Oro Fino and Elk City mining areas in Idaho, a prime source is Merrill D. Beal and Merle W. Wells, *History of Idaho* (New York: Lewis Historical Publishing, 1959), 1:291–96. During the winter of 1861, according to the reminiscences of Edward H. Mead, the veteran Jesuit missionary Father Pierre-Jean De Smet arrived in St. Louis from the upper Missouri country. While he was there, Mead writes, "some chance remarks he made to the effect that the region in which he labored was rich in gold became generally known." But, Mead adds, Father De Smet refused to discuss the matter with the press, since he "naturally feared that a gold-seeking emigration would be dangerous to his Indian converts." Yet the news spread rapidly, and "the spring of 1862 witnessed the beginning of gold mining in the future Montana and Idaho. . . ." Early in May, Mead relates, several steamboats advertised trips from St. Louis to Fort Benton, the head of navigation on the Missouri River 2,100 miles above St. Louis. A member of Thompson's company, Mead also made the trip on the *Emilie*. His published account of the voyage titled "In the Footsteps of Lewis and Clark" appeared in a St. Louis newspaper May 12, 1914. A copy can be found in the holdings of the Missouri Historical Society Library, St. Louis. Apparently Father De Smet made his remarks during a brief visit while heading for Europe on a fund-raising tour. Robert C. Carriker, *Father Peter John De Smet, Jesuit in the West* (Norman: University of Oklahoma Press, 1995), 166–67.

2. Hiram Martin Chittenden's *History of Early Steamboat Navigation on the Missouri River: Life and Adventures of Joseph La Barge* (1903; repr., Minneapolis: Ross & Haines, 1962) provides a detailed description of the La Barge opposition enterprise, which challenged the dominance of Pierre Choteau Jr. & Co. in the upper Missouri trade. Chittenden inter-

viewed Joseph La Barge at length and supplied a full account of the 1862 voyage. It is highly likely that Thompson drew on Chittenden's volume in preparing his reminiscences, but he also had his own journal of the trip at hand. A more modern treatment of Joseph La Barge's career is T. S. Bowden, "Joseph LaBarge, Steamboat Captain," *Missouri Historical Review*, 62 (July 1968), 449–69, an account that relies heavily on Chittenden's work. Briefer treatment of these events appears in William E. Lass, *A History of Steamboating on the Upper Missouri River* (Lincoln: University of Nebraska Press, 1962), 32–35. The careers of captains Joseph and John La Barge, for many years the most esteemed of the American Fur Company's Missouri River pilots, can also be traced in John E. Sunder's excellent study, *The Fur Trade on the Upper Missouri, 1840–1865* (Norman: University of Oklahoma Press, 1965). A biographical sketch of Captain Joseph La Barge appears in Dan L. Thrapp, *Encyclopedia of Frontier Biography*, 3 vols. (Glendale, Calif.: Arthur H. Clark, 1988), 2:801.

CHAPTER ONE

1. Thompson provided in his original publication a biographical sketch of James and Granville Stuart, which appears here in his "Notes on Men and Things," at the end of this volume. The most complete account of the lives of these two Montana pioneers is in Paul C. Phillips's introduction to his edition of *Forty Years on the Frontier as Seen in the Journals and Reminiscences of Granville Stuart, Gold-Miner, Merchant, Rancher, and Politician*, 2 vols. (1925; repr., Glendale, Calif.: Arthur H. Clark, 1957). Phillips also describes the first Montana gold discovery by Benetsee. For recent biographical treatments of the Stuart brothers, see Thrapp, *Encyclopedia of Frontier Biography*, 3:1379–82; Howard R. Lamar, ed., *The New Encyclopedia of the American West* (New Haven, Conn.: Yale University Press, 1998), 1032.

2. At this point, readers should realize that Thompson inserts the journal account of a friend aboard the *Shreveport*, who is not otherwise identified. Thompson's own narrative resumes in the next chapter.

3. See Thompson's entry describing snags in "Notes on Men and Things."

4. This account of military action is misleading. Colonel Sterling Price and his Missouri Confederate troops occupied Lexington, Missouri, in the middle of September 1861, capturing a small Union garrison. General John C. Frémont, newly placed in command of the Missouri theater of war, marched with a superior force to surround the town, forcing Price and his men to retreat without a fight by the end of October. This was the sole military victory that Frémont could claim during his brief tenure in Missouri. Richard S. Brownlee, *Gray Ghosts of the Confederacy: Guerilla Warfare in the West, 1861–1865* (Baton Rouge: Louisiana State University Press, 1958), 17–18.

5. See Thompson's description of mackinaw boats in his "Notes on Men and Things."

6. For many years Charles E. Galpin was the American Fur Company's principal trader at Fort Pierre. According to historian John E. Sunder, Galpin arrived in the Dakota country in 1839, married a Sioux woman, and began a thirty-year career as a trader to the Sioux people. In 1862 he joined the La Barge brothers in opposition to the Choteau firm, investing ten thousand dollars as one of five partners in the new company. Sunder, *Fur Trade on the Upper Missouri*, 132–33, 230, 234, 237–38; Thrapp, *Encyclopedia of Frontier Biography*, 2:530–31.

7. Thompson included in his "Notes on Men and Things" a brief entry on Fort Berthold. See also 257 n. 8.

8. John Blair Smith Todd was a West Point graduate and a veteran of both the Second Seminole War in Florida and the Mexican-American War. After taking part in Major William Harney's 1855 campaign against the Sioux, Todd resigned and became an Indian trader at Fort Randall in the Dakota country. A Democrat, he was the cousin of Nancy Todd Lincoln, the President's wife. At this time he was serving as brigadier general of volunteers in the Union service. He soon resigned and waged a winning campaign to become Dakota Territory's first delegate in Congress. He remained active in frontier land promotion, townsite speculation, and political scheming in the Yankton area until his death in 1872. Norman Thomas, "John Blair Smith Todd, South Dakota [*sic*] Delegate," *South Dakota Historical Collections*, 24 (1949), 178–219; Thrapp, *Encyclopedia of Frontier Biography*, 3:1432.

9. William Jayne, Lincoln's appointee as Dakota's first territorial governor, was the former mayor of Springfield, Illinois, and the brother-in-law of U.S. senator Lyman Trumbull of Illinois. A Republican antislavery radical, he nonetheless cooperated with J. B. S. Todd during the first legislative session in making Yankton the territorial capital. This convivial gathering of territorial notables aboard the *Shreveport* came early in the legislative session. Subsequently Governor Jayne and Delegate Todd had a falling out, with Chief Justice Philemon Bliss also turning against the governor and his ambitions to take Todd's seat in Congress. Descriptions of this first political tempest in the Dakota teapot can be found in Moses K. Armstrong, *The Early Empire Builders of the Great West* (St. Paul: E. W. Porter, 1901), 61–66; and George K. Kingsbury, *History of Dakota Territory* (Chicago: S. J. Clarke, 1915), 1:207–32, 270–75. In *Dakota Territory, 1861–1889: A Study in Frontier Politics* (New Haven, Conn.: Yale University Press, 1956), 68, Howard R. Lamar characterizes Governor Jayne as man who possessed "a strong temper and . . . little political subtlety."

10. Dr. William Burleigh came to Dakota from Pennsylvania to direct the Yankton Indian Agency in 1860 with the apparent goal of enriching himself and his family by any means he could manage. His administration of Indian affairs is perhaps without equal for corruption during the nineteenth-century

history of this notoriously corrupt federal bureau. Later elected territorial delegate to succeed J. B. S. Todd, he engineered the appointment of his father-in-law, Andrew Jackson Faulk, as territorial governor to assist raids on the federal treasury. The activities of these two scoundrels are politely summarized in Kingsbury, *History of Dakota Territory*, 1:192–94, 438–52. Strike the Ree was a Yankton head chief, well along in his alcoholic dotage, who served as a willing tool of Burleigh's manipulations. Faulk's papers contain a rich exchange of correspondence between Burleigh and Faulk that reveals many facets of their plundering schemes. WA MSS 195, Andrew Jackson Faulk Papers, Collection of Western Americana, Beineke Rare Book and Manuscript Library, Yale University, New Haven, Connecticut. Additional information can be found in the investigative files in the National Archives records of the Bureau of Indian Affairs.

11. Thompson includes in his "Notes on Men and Things" an explanatory digression regarding the abundance of buffalo in the upper Missouri country from the time of the Lewis and Clark expedition until his own time.

12. Thompson describes Fort Pierre in "Notes on Men and Things." Although he did not make the distinction, the post Thompson saw in 1862 was actually the structure now called Fort Pierre II. Charles Galpin built it in 1859 for the American Fur Company. The original Fort Pierre, built in 1831–32, had once been the American Fur Company's main post in the Dakota country. In 1855 the Choteaus sold the post to the U.S. Army for a supply depot. The price was forty-five thousand dollars, an exorbitant sum for the fort, by then extremely dilapidated. Galpin sited the new fort along the Missouri about two miles upstream from the original post. The Choteau brothers intended to revive the Sioux trade at this establishment by vigorous competitive practices against rival traders. Sunder, *Fur Trade on the Upper Missouri*, 41, 168–72.

13. At this time Geminien Beauvais, a trapper and trader from St. Louis, was living with his Sioux wife among her people. He had first come upriver for the Choteaus in 1831, then engaged in the Indian trade with indifferent success over the next forty years. He served the U.S. government as an interpreter and intermediary with the Sioux in later years. He accompanied Red Cloud to Washington, D.C., in 1870, and he was a member of the Allison Commission during a badly bungled attempt to purchase the Black Hills from the Sioux in 1875. Three years later he died in St. Louis. Thrapp, *Encyclopedia of Frontier Biography*, 1:84.

14. Jefferson Smith, "an old trader" according to Charles Larpenteur, was briefly a partner in the upper Missouri fur trade at Fort Berthold with Larpenteur, Henry Boller, and Robert Lemon in a mismanaged, acrimonious attempt to oppose the American Fur Company. His trip downriver by mackinaw boat in the spring of 1862, coming from Fort Berthold rather than Fort Benton, marks his departure from the partnership and from the fur business. Louis Pfaller, "Charles Larpenteur," in *The Mountain Men*

and the Fur Trade of the Far West, ed. Le Roy Hafen, vol. 1 (Glendale, Calif.: Arthur H. Clark, 1965), 307–8; Ray H. Mattison, "Henry A. Boller," in *The Mountain Men and the Fur Trade of the Far West*, ed. Le Roy Hafen, vol. 3 (Glendale, Calif.: Arthur H. Clark, 1966), 51. More detailed accounts of Smith's role in this venture are in Charles Larpenteur, *Forty Years a Fur Trader on the Upper Missouri: The Personal Narrative of Charles Larpenteur, 1833–1872*, ed. Elliott Coues, 2 vols. in 1 (1898; repr., Minneapolis: Ross and Haines, 1962), 2:309–11, 321–27, 340–41; and Henry A. Boller, *Among the Indians: Four Years on the Upper Missouri, 1858–1862*, ed. Milo M. Quaife (Lincoln: University of Nebraska Press, 1972).

15. James P. Ronda, *Lewis and Clark among the Indians* (Lincoln: University of Nebraska Press, 1984), 98–99, summarizes the construction of the exploring party's Fort Mandan winter quarters. The fullest description is provided in the journal of expedition member Patrick Gass, found in Gary E. Moulton, ed., *The Journals of the Lewis and Clark Expedition*, vol. 10, *The Journal of Patrick Gass, May 14, 1804–September 23, 1806* (Lincoln: University of Nebraska Press, 1996), 61–62. The site, editor Moulton points out, has since been washed away by the Missouri River.

16. Fort Union, which one fur trader described in 1843 as "the principal and handsomest Trading post on the Missouri," was located about six river miles above the mouth of the Yellowstone River. The American Fur Company's headquarters on the upper Missouri, it commanded the trade of the Crows, the Assiniboines, and the Blackfeet. An excellent study of the history of this post is Barton H. Barbour, *Fort Union and the Upper Missouri Fur Trade* (Norman: University of Oklahoma Press, 2001). The construction of the post is described in great architectural detail by Barbour in his first chapter, pages 39–65. See also Thompson's description of Fort Union in "Notes on Men and Things."

17. Larpenteur and Lemon formed a partnership in 1861 to trade with the Hidatsas, Assiniboines, and Crows. The two men spent an uncomfortable, quarrelsome winter together at a temporary trading house they built on the Missouri above the mouth of the Big Muddy River, at the site of Old Fort Stewart. When they met the *Shreveport* in 1862, they were retiring to St. Louis with sparse returns. They soon sold out to the La Barge brothers. Sunder, *Fur Trade on the Upper Missouri*, 218–19; Larpenteur, *Forty Years a Fur Trader*, 2:239–42; Thrapp, *Encyclopedia of Frontier Biography*, 2:815.

18. The *Chippewa*, Captain William Humphries, was an American Fur Company steamship. Heavily loaded and overcrowded, the vessel caught fire on June 23, 1861, while navigating a turn in the river, thereafter called Disaster Bend, a few miles below the mouth of Poplar River. Realizing that a large cargo of gunpowder was stowed close to the site of the fire, the passengers reacted in panic. The chief engineer coolly ran the vessel aground, allowing passengers and crew to escape safely, although one deckhand was badly burned. After drifting downstream a mile, the vessel burned to the

waterline, then exploded and sank. Eyewitness accounts attributed the fire to a drunken deckhand who had taken a candle below decks in order to get another pitcher of alcohol from one of the twenty-two barrels of illicit trade whiskey carried aboard the ship. The episode is described in careful detail in Sunder, *Fur Trade on the Upper Missouri*, 224–29. Among the losses was a full cargo of supplies, purchased for $1,400, sent upstream to the Jesuit missions by Father De Smet, who then made plans for a new European trip to solicit replacement funds—the trip that brought him to St. Louis where he let slip the information about the presence of gold in the streams of the northern Rockies. Carriker, *Father Peter John De Smet*, 168.

19. The so-called "nigger" engine was a steam-driven capstan, with power supplied from the ship's main boiler. Thompson describes the process of using the engine in "Notes on Men and Things."

20. For John Mullan and the construction of the Mullan Road, see 263 n. 17.

CHAPTER TWO

1. Edward H. Mead is the only other member of Thompson's company who can be located through the files of the Missouri Historical Society. The Society preserves a copy of his 1914 newspaper account of the upstream voyage aboard the *Emilie*, based on a diary he kept during the trip. This source, however, which includes both a sketch of Mead in 1862 and a much later photograph, only identifies him as "an influential Missourian." Mead, "In the Footsteps of Lewis and Clark."

2. Darius Hunkins was a frontier businessman who made a substantial fortune in the lead-mining metropolis of Galena, Illinois, during the 1850s. After exploring the upper Missouri mining regions, he remained in Bannack during the winter of 1862–63, then returned downriver by mackinaw boat in late August 1863. Subsequently he became involved in efforts to win from President Lincoln a pardon for two Galena Democratic lawyers who were imprisoned by federal authorities for their outspoken opposition to the administration's conduct of the war. See Kenneth N. Owens, *Galena, Grant, and the Fortunes of War* (DeKalb: Northern Illinois University Press, 1963), 45; M. A. Leeson, *History of Montana, 1739–1885* (Chicago: Warner, Beers and Company, 1885), 467; James Harkness, "Diary of James Harkness of the Firm of LaBarge, Harkness and Company: St. Louis to Fort Benton by the Missouri River and to the Deer Lodge Valley and Return in 1862," *Contributions to the Historical Society of Montana*, 2 (1896), 358–61. He appears prominently in Thompson's narrative of his activities in Bannack around the time of the first territorial legislative session. See chapter six.

3. Thompson here summarizes the common Missouri River recollection of Black Bird, a powerful, ruthless, and grasping leader of the Omaha

people in the late eighteenth century, when the Omaha ruled the lower river. He died in 1800 in a smallpox epidemic that drastically reduced the numbers and influence of his people. His era is sketched in Judith A. Baughter, *Betraying the Omaha Nation, 1790–1916* (Norman: University of Oklahoma Press, 1998), 19–22. A detailed account is Tarric C. Thorne, "Black Bird, 'King of the Mahas': Autocrat, Big Man, Chief," *Ethnohistory*, 40 (Summer 1993), 410–37. A short biographical notice is in Thrapp, *Encyclopedia of Frontier Biography*, 1:123–24.

4. Thompson inserts a note at this point: "Patriotic citizens and the state of Iowa, have recently erected a fine monument to his memory. We found about 2200 Indians at the Yankton Sioux agency." Sergeant Charles Floyd died August 20, 1804, near present Sioux City, Iowa, the only casualty among the members of the Lewis and Clark expedition. The cause of his death was probably a ruptured appendix and peritonitis. This condition was not then recognized by medical science, and it remained essentially untreatable until the late nineteenth century. Gary E. Moulton, ed., *The Journals of the Lewis and Clark Expedition*, vol. 2, *August 30, 1803–August 24, 1804* (Lincoln: University of Nebraska Press, 1986), 495, 496 n. 1.

5. Fort Randall had been founded by Major William S. Harney in 1856 when the army abandoned the original Fort Pierre. This post was intended to protect advancing settlements along the line of the Missouri River, the first in a series of forts extending upriver to Fort Benton. Colonel Philippe Regis de Trobriand, who saw the establishment in 1867, stated that it was more a post than a fort, "for the fortifications do not amount to anything." *Military Life in Dakota: The Journal of Philippe Regis de Trobriand*, trans. and ed. Lucile M. Kane (1951; repr., Lincoln: University of Nebraska Press, 1982), 28.

6. Fort Clark was located on a high bluff above the Missouri about eight miles downstream from the mouth of the Knife River. Constructed in 1831 by trader James Kipp for the American Fur Company, it was originally the center for a thriving trade with the Mandan villages. After the disastrous 1837 smallpox epidemic, the surviving Mandans moved upriver to join their Hidatsa relatives, but Fort Clark continued to operate on a reduced basis to serve a small number of Arikara clients. The company abandoned the post at the end of the 1860 season. Sunder, *Fur Trade on the Upper Missouri*, 37, 76, 83, 135, 214, 225.

7. A particularly virulent strain of smallpox arrived on the upper Missouri aboard the American Fur Company's boat *St. Peter's* in June 1837. The Mandans, living a settled life in their farming villages near Fort Clark, were perhaps the hardest hit among all the upper Missouri native peoples. Francis Chardon, chief trader at the fort, estimated that more than eight hundred Mandans and Arikaras had died by September, seven-eighths of the Mandan community and half of the Arikaras. Left principally were the oldest tribe members, who may have acquired immunity from exposure

during earlier epidemics, and the youngest. Chardon placed the number of
surviving Mandans at only twenty-three men, forty women, and sixty to
seventy children. Compounding the disaster, in January 1839 a marauding
Sioux party burned the old Mandan village while its surviving residents
were absent at their winter camp. The fullest discussion appears in the excellent study by Roy W. Meyer, *The Village Indians of the Upper Missouri:
The Mandans, Hidatsas, and Arikaras* (Lincoln: University of Nebraska Press,
1977), 90–100. Among other upper Missouri peoples who suffered severely
in the 1837 epidemic, the Blackfeet were especially hard hit. This upper
Missouri epidemic was part of a smallpox contagion that spread widely
on the commercial borders of the Euramerican world between 1835 and
1840. It took a huge toll among native peoples, for example, in the Aleutian
Islands and Alaska, in Hawaii, and in Australia as well as in many parts of
the American West.

8. Fort Berthold, an American Fur Company post, had been built by
Frances Chardon and James Kipp at Fishhook Bend on the Missouri River
for the trade with the Mandans and Hidatsas about 1839, after the Mandan
smallpox survivors abandoned their former village site near Fort Clark. In
1865 the Indian Bureau made it the headquarters of an agency for the
Mandans, Hidatsas, Arikaras, and Assiniboines. The federal government
subsequently purchased the fort from the Northwestern Fur Company, a
successor firm to the American Fur Company, and it became the adminis-
trative center for a reservation for the Mandans, Hidatsas, and Arikaras
created by presidential executive order in 1870. Henry W. Reed was in
1862 the federal Indian agent for the Blackfeet. Like Captain La Barge, he
concerned himself with efforts to improve the pitiable condition of the
Fort Berthold tribes. Sunder, *Fur Trade on the Upper Missouri*, 83, 260,
262–63; Meyer, *Village Indians of the Upper Missouri*, 112, 114–16.

9. See Thompson's description of the Milk River in "Notes on Men and
Things."

10. Thompson's account is at variance with the story of this incident
told in Chittenden, *Early Steamboat Navigation*, 289–91. Chittenden states
that it was the *Spread Eagle* that gave way to the *Emilie*. In addition to
Captain La Barge's threat, he relates, some passengers aboard the *Emilie*
also prepared to use their guns against the captain of the *Spread Eagle*.
Chittenden asserts that the *Spread Eagle* then fell to the rear "and was seen
no more on the voyage." When the *Spread Eagle* returned to St. Louis,
Chittenden adds, the captain, Robert E. Baily, was brought up on charges
before the steamboat inspector and his license was canceled. Subsequently,
after admitting his guilt to Captain La Barge, Baily declared that the American
Fur Company's agents had instigated the incident. He appealed to La Barge to
give him a recommendation that would allow his reinstatement "for the
sake of his wife and children." La Barge willingly did so. Baily's claim may
have been strengthened by the fact that Charles Pierre Choteau, in charge of

upper Missouri operations for the American Fur Company, was also aboard the *Spread Eagle* on this voyage. Chittenden's version of this June 6th episode is verified by the brief account of John Delany, a passenger aboard the *Spread Eagle*. Delany tacitly acknowledges that the *Emilie* succeeded in passing the *Spread Eagle*, since he records that on June 19, while the *Spread Eagle* was a still day's voyage downriver from Fort Benton, "the Emilie passed us about noon on her way back to St. Louis." John E. Sunder, ed., "Up the Missouri to the Montana Mines: John O'Fallon Delany's 'Pocket Diary for 1862,' Part 1," *Missouri Historical Society Bulletin*, 19 (October 1962), 12, 16. Delany was a companion of Father De Smet, who was returning to the Jesuit mission field aboard the *Spread Eagle* with a large cargo of goods to reprovision the missions after the 1861 *Chippewa* disaster.

11. Apparently he confused the name "Dubois" with Dauphin, since Thompson inserted his entry on Louis Dauphin at this point in his "Notes on Men and Things." In 1863 Captain La Barge hired Dauphin, an experienced hunter married into the Sioux people, to take charge of Fort Galpin, La Barge's establishment that was located on the Missouri River ten miles upstream from Milk River. Despite Dauphin's long friendly association with the Sioux, in 1865 he and others at the fort were killed by Sioux raiders in the aftermath of the Minnesota Sioux War. La Barge then abandoned the site. See Pfaller, "Charles Larpenteur," 1:309.

12. Forty-nine species of fish are native to the Missouri, among them the sauger, northern pike, sturgeon, walleye, gold-eye, and paddlefish. Most prevalent were catfish, which is most likely what the passengers aboard the *Emilie* were catching. Rick Graetz, *Montana's Upper Missouri River Breaks National Monument: The Wild and Scenic Missouri* (Helena, Mont.: Northern Rockies, 2001), 28.

13. Fort Campbell was a small log post built in 1846 by Alexander Harvey, heading a new opposition trading company, Harvey, Picotte and Company, for trade with the Blackfeet. It was located on the north bank of the Missouri just upstream from the mouth of the Marias River, near the American Fur Company's Fort Benton. Harvey, who married into the Piegan Blackfeet tribe, made this post his headquarters until his death in 1854. After the American Fur Company bought out the opposition firm in 1860, the post was closed to trade but Roman Catholic missionaries continued to use the structure as a temporary mission. By 1862 Malcolm Clark, another prominent opposition trader, had moved into the old building with his Blackfeet wife and family. Sunder, *Fur Trade on the Upper Missouri*, 94–95, 164–65, 182–83, 238; Ray H. Mattison, "Alexander Harvey," in *The Mountain Men and the Fur Trade of the Far West*, ed. Le Roy Hafen, vol. 4 (Glendale, Calif.: Arthur H. Clark, 1966), 119–23; John E. Wickman, "Malcolm Clark," in *The Mountain Men and the Fur Trade of the Far West*, ed. Le Roy Hafen, vol. 8 (Glendale, Calif.: Arthur H. Clark, 1971), 69–72; Thrapp, *Encyclopedia of Frontier Biography*, 1:279–80, 2:624–25.

14. The *St. Louis Missouri Republican* for November 27, 1862, carried an obituary notice for Chancellor Joseph G. Hoyt of Washington University in St. Louis. A native of New Hampshire, born in 1815, he attended Yale College, where he earned prizes in mathematics and English composition and served as an editor of the *Yale Literary Magazine*. In 1841 he became Professor of Mathematics and Natural Philosophy at Phillips Academy in Exeter, New Hampshire, where he remained for eighteen years. In 1859 he accepted appointment as Chancellor and Professor of Greek Language and Literature at Washington University. His summer voyage aboard the *Emilie*, while he was suffering the last stages of tuberculosis, must have been both painful and exhilarating for Hoyt, since his favorite field of study was not Greek but rather the natural sciences.

15. This classical term is an esoteric reference to a servant or slave. Who might have filled this description in Thompson's party is not at all clear.

16. Giles F. Filley was renowned in St. Louis as the founder and head of the Excelsior Stove Company. As Thompson mentions in the following chapter, he and his son also were aboard the *Emilie* for this voyage. Filley's company manufactured the Charter Oak cooking stove, one of the best-known kitchen ranges of that time, and other appliances. A native of Connecticut, he had become prominent in Missouri public affairs as a leading advocate for the Free-Soil Party and subsequently as a champion of the Lincoln administration during the Civil War. A biographical notice described him as "one of the most ardent Unionists in St. Louis, and one of the ablest and most influential supporters of the efforts of the national administration to suppress the secession movement." William Hyde and Howard L. Conard, eds., *Encyclopedia of the History of St. Louis: A Compendium of History and Biography for Ready Reference* (New York: Southern History Company, 1899), 2:743–45.

17. The reference is to two of the best-known sculptors of the time, Hiram Powers and William Wetmore Story. Powers was a foremost exponent of neoclassicism, becoming renowned for his heroic bronzes and marble figures, the most famous of which was a female image titled *The Greek Slave*. Story included a broader element of romantic mythology in his creations. Both men spent a large part of their careers in Europe, but Americans proudly claimed the honor of their accomplishments. Wayne Craven, *Sculpture in America*, rev. ed. (Newark: University of Delaware Press, 1984), 111–23, 274–81.

18. Regarding the geology of the upper Missouri breaks, see Graetz, *Montana's Upper Missouri River Breaks National Monument*, 26–28.

19. In addition to this account, the principal source for the history of Fort La Barge is Harkness, "Diary of James Harkness," 343–61. In 1863 La Barge, Harkness and Company disbanded, selling their trade goods at Fort Benton to the American Fur Company. Fort La Barge was abandoned at that point. Sunder, *Fur Trade on the Upper Missouri*, 252–53. Chittenden

places the blame squarely on Harkness for spending only eleven days in attempting to establish his trade in the region, then virtually making a gift of La Barge's trade goods to a competitor in his hurry to abandon Fort La Barge and return to St. Louis. Chittenden, *Early Steamboat Navigation*, 295–96.

20. For a modern descriptive summary of the romantic school of thought regarding American native peoples in the decades prior to Thompson's voyage, see Robert F. Berkhofer Jr., *The White Man's Indian: Images of the American Indian from Columbus to the Present* (New York: Knopf, 1978), 86–96.

CHAPTER THREE

1. Fort Benton's architectural history is summarized in W. S. Bell, *Old Fort Benton* (Helena, Mont.: author, 1909), 12–15; and in John G. Lepley, *Birthplace of Montana: A History of Fort Benton* (Missoula, Mont.: Pictorial History, 1999), 22–24. Alexander Culbertson supervised the replacement of the structure's original wooden walls with adobe in 1860.

2. Thompson is vague on the details of this fight, which took place on July 28, 1806. The trouble began with an attempt by Piegan visitors in their camp to steal the guns of Lewis's small party. When Lewis and his men foiled that effort, the Piegans then attempted to run off the expedition's horses, getting away with one of them but leaving most of their own animals behind. Lewis's journal entry describing this encounter is in Gary E. Moulton, ed., *The Journals of the Lewis and Clark Expedition*, vol. 8, *June 10–September 26, 1806* (Lincoln: University of Nebraska Press, 1993), 133–35. According to Moulton, it is not clear whether one or two Piegans lost their lives in this encounter. One man stabbed by Reubin Field died, but a second man shot by Lewis may have survived. Ibid., 136 n. 2.

3. Sketches of the careers of William Henry Ashley and Andrew Henry may be found conveniently in Thrapp, *Encyclopedia of Frontier Biography*, 1:39–40, 2:648; and in Lamar, *New Encyclopedia of the American West*, 64–65, 482.

4. The early history of the upper Missouri fur trade first received detailed treatment in Hiram Martin Chittenden, *The American Fur Trade of the Far West: A History of the Pioneer Trading Posts and Early Fur Companies of the Missouri Valley and the Rocky Mountains and of the Overland Commerce with Santa Fe*, 2 vols. (1902; repr., Stanford, Calif.: Academic Reprints, 1954). The most complete modern study is Sunder, *Fur Trade on the Upper Missouri*.

5. Lesley Wischmann, *Frontier Diplomats: The Life and Times of Alexander Culbertson and Natoyist-Siksina'* (Spokane, Wash.: Arthur H. Clark, 2000) provides a highly readable joint biography of Culbertson and his wife, who was a resourceful, diplomatically skilled, exceedingly influential Piegan woman.

6. See Thompson's entry on Cracon du Nez in "Notes on Men and Things."

7. Thompson apparently based his account on James H. Bradley, "Affairs at Fort Benton from 1831 to 1869, From Lieut. Bradley's Journal," *Contributions to the Historical Society of Montana*, 3 (1900), 207–10. Alexander Philip Maximilian, Prince of Wied-Neuwied (1782–1867), the eighth child of King Friedrich Karl, in 1832 began an extensive excursion into western North America, accompanied by his personal servant and the young Swiss artist Karl Bodmer. Pierre Choteau gladly assisted the royal German adventurer in arranging a trip up the Missouri River to the American Fur Company trading posts. After stopping briefly at Fort Pierre and Fort Union, the Prince's small party reached Fort McKenzie in the heart of Blackfeet territory in August. The battle between the Blackfeet and Assiniboines beneath the very walls of the fort, described by Thompson, convinced Prince Maximilian to abandon a plan to travel even farther west. Instead, in September he and his two companions moved downriver to Fort Clark, near the villages of the Mandans and Minitaris, where they settled for the winter in a drafty, cold two-room cabin built for them by the post trader. After a difficult winter, the three travelers returned to St. Louis with a large cargo of ethnological, botanical, and zoological specimens (including two caged bears), as well as Bodmer's crowded sketchbooks, and began a slow trip homeward.

The narrative of Prince Maximilian's western trip first reached the literary and scientific public in 1841 with the appearance in Coblenz of an elegant two-volume work, *Reise in das Innere Nord-America in den Jahren 1832 bis 1834*, accompanied by an atlas of Karl Bodmer's superb engravings. A French edition and an English version, translated by H. Evans Lloyd as *Travels in the Interior of North America*, both appeared by 1843. The Prince was still at work with his collections at the time of his death at Coblenz in 1867. In English, Prince Maximilian's *Travels in the Interior of North America* is conveniently available as volumes 22–24 in Reuben Gold Thwaites, ed., *Early Western Travels, 1748–1846*, 32 vols. (Cleveland: Arthur H. Clark, 1904–1907), an edition that also includes a biographical sketch by the editor. The scientific accomplishments of Prince Maximilian, as well as Karl Bodmer's artistic contributions, receive a sympathetic evaluation in William H. Goetzmann's introduction to *Karl Bodmer's America*, annotated by David C. Hunt and Marsha V. Gallagher (Omaha/Lincoln: Joslyn Art Museum and the University of Nebraska Press, 1984).

8. The story of the Crow peace with Culbertson and the American Fur Company is told in Bradley, "Affairs at Fort Benton," 215–16. The story is retold in Wischmann, *Frontier Diplomats*, 60, though this author also notes the different version that appears in Edwin T. Denig, *Five Indian Tribes of the Upper Missouri: Sioux, Arickaras, Assiniboines, Crees, Crows*, ed. John C. Ewers (Norman: University of Oklahoma Press, 1961), 177–84.

9. An extremely vivid eyewitness account of the 1837 smallpox epidemic among the Blackfeet is Bradley "Affairs at Fort Benton," 221–26. See also John C. Ewers, *The Blackfeet: Raiders on the Northwestern Plains* (Norman: University of Oklahoma Press, 1958), 64–66; and Wischmann, *Frontier Diplomats*, 167–76.

10. This deplorable episode, which occurred February 19, 1844, is summarized in Ewers, *The Blackfeet*, 66–68. As explained by historian Dan Thrapp, responsibility for staging the murder of the unsuspecting Blackfeet rests with Alexander Harvey rather than Francois Chardon, who "presumably was incapacitated by alcohol" at the time. "A vindictive and violent man," Thrapp states, Harvey fired the cannon, killing or wounding mortally at least four Blackfeet and injuring seventeen others, then rushed among the wounded with his axe, splitting their skulls and scalping them. This massacre, Thrapp remarks, "became celebrated in fur trade legend." Thrapp, *Encyclopedia of Frontier Biography*, 1:254–55, 2:624–25. The eyewitness account of George Weippert is in *Contributions to the Historical Society of Montana*, 10 (1940), 247–49.

11. See Thompson's description of Malcolm Clark in "Notes on Men and Things."

12. Senator Thomas Hart Benton's close relationship with the Choteaus and the American Fur Company is discussed in William Nisbet Chambers, *Old Bullion Benton, Senator from the New West: Thomas Hart Benton, 1782–1858* (Boston: Little, Brown, 1956).

13. Andrew Dawson, the American Fur Company's manager at Fort Benton, was a Scot who arrived in St. Louis in 1843 and entered the fur trade as a company employee the following year. After serving at Fort Pierre and Fort Clark, he succeeded Alexander Culbertson as chief trader at Fort Benton. He is credited with naming Fort Benton after his friend the Missouri senator, who had shielded the company from federal prosecution for illegal sales of liquor in Indian country. The Fort Benton journal, published by the Montana Historical Society, was kept most of the time by Dawson. He retired in 1864 with a considerable fortune and lived in Scotland until his death in 1871. Thrapp, *Encyclopedia of Frontier Biography*, 1:383; James Dawson, "Major Andrew Dawson, 1817–1871," *Contributions to the Historical Society of Montana*, 7 (1910), 61–72.

14. For the Blackfoot treaty negotiations conducted by commissioners Stevens and Cumming, see Kent D. Richards, *Isaac I. Stevens: Young Man in a Hurry* (Provo, Utah: Brigham Young University Press, 1979), 230–34. Hazard Stevens, the teenage son of the governor, was also present. He provides an account of his adventures in his admiring biography, *Life of Isaac Ingalls Stevens*, 2 vols. (Boston: Houghton Mifflin, 1900). Also pertinent is the account in Wischmann, *Frontier Diplomats*, 249–59.

15. Alfred Cumming was a Georgian who served with distinction as mayor of Atlanta during that city's 1849 cholera epidemic. He is best known

in western history for his term as territorial governor of Utah, replacing Brigham Young and contributing to the peaceable conclusion of Utah War, a story well told in Eugene E. Campbell, *Establishing Zion: The Mormon Church in the American West, 1847–1869* (Salt Lake City: Signature Books, 1988), 244–50. For General Harney's antipathy to the advocates of an Indian peace policy during this era, see George R. Adams, *General William S. Harney, Prince of Dragoons* (Lincoln: University of Nebraska Press, 2001).

16. Big Gwynn, with no other known identity, is recorded in Leeson's pioneer history as a resident of Bannack during the winter of 1862–63. Leeson mentions his death—an incidental fact also pointed out by Thompson in his "Notes on Men and Things"—at the hands of the Sioux on the Missouri River in 1863 in Leeson, *History of Montana*, 467, 468.

17. Captain John Mullan, a Virginian and a West Point graduate, was a member of the Northern Pacific Railroad Surveying Expedition of Governor Isaac I. Stevens that explored a prospective transcontinental rail route from St. Paul to Puget Sound in 1853. In fall 1853 Stevens assigned Mullan the task of laying out a military wagon road between Fort Benton and Walla Walla on the Columbia River, the route that became known as the Mullan Road. Mullan's work was interrupted in 1855 when he was ordered to Florida to take part in the Third Seminole War. He returned to his road building project in 1858. By 1862 he and his work crews were completing the assignment, described in his *Report on the Construction of a Military Road from Fort Walla Walla to Fort Benton* (Washington, D.C.: Government Printing Office, 1863). After resigning from the U.S. Army in 1863, Mullan unsuccessfully attempted to make a living in the Pacific Northwest as a rancher and mail contractor. He subsequently opened a law practice in San Francisco and later moved to Washington, D.C., where he died in 1909 at age 79. The construction of the Mullan Road was beyond doubt his finest achievement. Biographical sketches are in George F. Weisel, ed., *Men and Trade on the Northwest Frontier as Shown by the Fort Owen Ledger* (Missoula: Montana State University Press, 1955), 66–73; Thrapp, *Encyclopedia of Frontier Biography*, 2:1032; and Allen Johnson and Dumas Malone, eds., *Dictionary of American Biography*, vol. 7 (New York: Scribner, 1931), 319–20. The Mullan Wagon Road project is described most fully in W. Turrentine Jackson, *Wagon Roads West: A Study of Federal Road Surveys and Construction in the Trans-Mississippi West, 1846–1864* (Berkeley: University of California Press, 1952), 257–78.

18. The Indian Bureau's Blackfeet Indian farm at Sun River was established by Indian agent Alfred J. Vaughan in 1857 under the terms of the 1855 Blackfeet treaty. Little Dog, the Piegan head chief, was the only prominent leader who showed interest in this experiment, and even he never totally adopted an agricultural way of life. Henry Reed, Vaughan's successor, dismissed the farm in 1863 as a project with no practical value. This attitude helps explain Reed's virtual abandonment of the Vails during their

difficult year in charge of the farm, even though Reed had been their minister in Iowa. When Thompson met them aboard the *Emilie*, the couple were entering on their new assignment with more optimism than the situation warranted. Good-hearted, honest, and naive in the extreme, they lacked any apparent qualifications for their post except a certain foolish bravery. For his part, Reed fits well historian John Ewers's description of Blackfeet agents during this period as "weak, inept men who had little experience in Indian affairs." See Leeson, *History of Montana*, 501, 515; and Ewers, *The Blackfeet*, 231–32, 236–37.

19. Bird Tail Rock is a prominent natural feature described in Roberta Carkeek Cheney, *Names on the Face of Montana: The Story of Montana's Place Names* (Missoula: Mountain Press, 1983), 24.

20. Ibid., 181–82, describes Medicine Rock Hill as a series of white sandstone buttes, covering about a square mile, towering about eight hundred feet above low sandy hills, and now eroded.

21. On the Mullan Road, Thompson's party crossed the divide for the first time near McDonald Pass and descended along the Little Blackfoot River.

22. Here on the west slope, Thompson had his first experience fishing for the native cutthroat trout of the Rocky Mountain region, then abundant and easily caught by many types of natural bait or artificial lures.

23. Employing rudimentary equipment brought across the Bitterroots from the Salmon River diggings, the Stuart brothers were using sluices to mine the placer deposits they had located on Gold Creek, following techniques they had learned in northern California. See Cheney, *Names on the Face of Montana*, 121.

24. For Johnny Grant's establishment and his career in the Deer Lodge region, see his recollections, skillfully edited by Lyndel Meikle, *Very Close to Trouble: The Johnny Grant Memoir* (Pullman: Washington State University Press, 1990). Coming from Salt Lake City, Ed Purple reached Johnny Grant's establishment a few weeks after Thompson. His description of the little settlement and his warm tribute to Grant appear in Edward Ruthven Purple, *Perilous Passage: A Narrative of the Montana Gold Rush, 1862–1863*, ed. Kenneth N. Owens (Helena: Montana Historical Society Press, 1995), 83–85. Thompson also includes a biographical notice for Grant in his "Notes on Men and Things."

25. See Thompson's explanatory note on Beaverhead country in "Notes on Men and Things."

26. John W. Powell was a Virginian, born in 1834, who had been a member of Governor Isaac I. Stevens's 1853 Northern Pacific Railroad Surveying Expedition from St. Paul to Puget Sound. He remained in the northern Rockies, married a Bannock woman, and made a living of sorts by trading, raising cattle, and prospecting, though less successfully than his friend Johnny Grant. He failed to profit from the discovery of gold on the North Boulder River on this 1862 excursion with Thompson and his

comrades. According to Ed Purple, Powell told him a few weeks after this trip with Thompson that he had exaggerated the extent and richness of the gold diggings they discovered "to get the country prospected." After remaining some years in the Deer Lodge area, Powell moved to Trapper Creek, where the mining town of Glendale later briefly flourished. He died there in a quarrel in 1879. Thrapp, *Encyclopedia of Frontier Biography*, 3:1168–69; Purple, *Perilous Passage*, 101.

27. Although Ed Purple's dating is questionable, he and his companions followed this same route coming in the opposite direction within a week or two after Thompson's party passed through on their way south. Purple provides a fuller description of the hot springs mound, which today is the site of the upscale Fairmont Hot Springs Resort, located just off Interstate 80 between Deer Lodge and the Anaconda exit. Purple, *Perilous Passage*, 82.

28. A native of New York state, William Graham came west to St. Louis in 1845, a year after he was dismissed from West Point. Following various adventures in the upper Mississippi country and in the Santa Fe trade, he joined the California gold rush and remained in northern California as a trader and miner until 1861. He then came to the upper Missouri region in response to the first reports of new placer mining discoveries in the northern Rockies. An experienced frontiersman, he was continuing his prospecting when Thompson met him. Two years later he at last struck it rich, discovering the Deer Lodge lode. He settled in Phillipsburg, served in the territorial council, and died a respected Montana pioneer in 1878. Thrapp, *Encyclopedia of Frontier Biography* 2:578.

29. This animal, indigenous in the northern Rockies though relatively scarce even before the advent of Euramerican fur hunters and fur traders, is referred to today as the mountain buffalo, classified as *Bison athabascae*. It is the same species as the so-called wood buffalo found in the Canadian far north. Mountain and wood buffalo are characteristically larger than the better known American buffalo of the Plains region, *Bison bison*, with hair that is finer, darker, and curlier than the Plains buffalo. Except for a small remnant population in Canada's Wood Buffalo National Park, the species is now extinct, although a hybrid strain apparently survives among the Yellowstone National Park buffalo herd. See David A. Dary, *The Buffalo Book: The Full Saga of the American Animal* (Chicago: Sage Books, 1974), 44–51; and Frank Gilbert Roe, *The North American Buffalo: A Critical Study of the Species in its Wild State*, 2d ed. (Toronto: University of Toronto Press, 1951), 33–68.

30. Helen Fitzgerald Sanders, *A History of Montana* (Chicago: Lewis, 1913), 1:167–69, describes the Powell party's discovery of the "Old Bar" on North Boulder creek, which came almost simultaneously with the first placer strikes on Grasshopper Creek by the John White party and the discovery of the diggings at the head of the North Fork of the Big Hole River

by a party led by Jack Slack. Later mining activity in this area is described in Ruth Staunton and Dorothy Keur, *Jerkline to Jeep: A Brief History of the Upper Boulder* (Harlowton, Mont.: Times and Clarion, 1975), 12–26.

31. The Pike's Peak refugees were foremost in the 1862 rush into Idaho's Salmon River mines, with a large number diverting themselves to the upper Missouri area. Ed Purple estimated that during the week in early July he and his party were delayed at the Snake River ferry near Fort Hall, at least 1,000 to 1,500 men crossed the river headed for the Salmon River mines, "most of whom were from Pike's Peak, Colorado." Purple, *Perilous Passage*, 41. James and Granville Stuart shared some of the responsibility for this rush, since they had written a letter to inform their brother Tom in Colorado about their strike on Gold Creek, news that Tom circulated widely.

32. The 1862 James Fisk expedition from Minnesota to the upper Missouri gold country is described in Helen McCann White, ed., *Ho! For the Gold Fields: Northern Overland Wagon Trains of the 1860s* (St. Paul: Minnesota Historical Society, 1966), 23–72.

33. Thompson mentions his first meeting with Langford in St. Paul while both men were getting started in the banking business in a biographical note on Langford in his "Notes on Men and Things." Although Thompson sometimes refers to him as Governor Langford, the title was honorific. Langford was nominated for the territorial governor post by President Andrew Johnson at the eleventh hour of his administration, but Radical Republicans in the Senate, strengthened by the election of Ulysses Grant to succeed Johnson, refused to confirm his appointment. Langford then returned to Montana, in the words of one friend, "the most terribly disappointed man I ever saw." Clark C. Spence, *Territorial Government and Politics in Montana, 1864–89* (Urbana: University of Illinois Press, 1975), 57–58. Before this episode he did serve as federal collector of internal revenue, 1864–1868, and then became the first superintendent of Yellowstone National Park in 1872, a post he held until 1877. Subsequently he returned to St. Paul, where he died in 1909. A small collection of Langford's papers, SC 215, is located in the Montana Historical Society Archives, but according to a notation at the Minnesota Historical Society, a trunk full of his records was destroyed by his descendants some years after his death. Biographical sketches include Leeson, *History of Montana*, 1229; and Thrapp, *Encyclopedia of Frontier Biography*, 2:811–12.

34. This episode is best documented in the journal of James Stuart, one of the volunteers who hanged Spillman. Stuart, *Forty Years on the Frontier*, 1:218–20.

35. The rocker was a device widely used in the early phase of placer mining, apparently developed in Georgia and popularized further during the California gold rush. In essence, it consisted of an elongated box mounted on a slanted cradle, with a sieve-like plate located at the upper

end of the rocker top and a series of small slats fastened atop the rocker bed. One miner shoveled gravel and sand from a placer location onto the sieve and washed it with a stream of water while a second miner shook the cradle, allowing the finer, heavier, gold-bearing sand to work along the rocker bed and settle behind the slats as the coarser and lighter materials washed out the open lower end of the apparatus. As needed, the miners would stop to collect the gold-bearing sand deposits, which they would then process further to achieve a final separation of gold from the sand, either by panning or commonly through the use of mercury to make an amalgam that could be retorted, leaving the gold behind. The early technological development of placer mining is fully described in Otis E. Young, *Western Mining: An Informal Account of Precious-Metals Prospecting, Placering, Lode Mining, and Milling on the American Frontier from Spanish Times to 1893* (Norman: University of Oklahoma Press, 1970), 109–26.

36. Sources for the gold discovery on Grasshopper Creek by the White party are reviewed in Purple, *Perilous Passage*, 80 n. 49. A biographical sketch of White appears in Thrapp, *Encyclopedia of Frontier Biography*, 3:1552.

37. Development of Mormon freighting and trade between Salt Lake City and the upper Missouri mining country is described in careful detail in Betty M. Madsen and Brigham D. Madsen, *North to Montana! Jehus, Bullwhackers, and Mule Skinners on the Montana Trail* (Logan: Utah State University Press, 1998), 23–69.

38. William T. "Wild Bill" Hamilton was a mountain man who became a respected pioneer settler and lawman in the Bitterroot Valley. His autobiography was published in 1905 as *My Sixty Years on the Plains* (New York: Forest and Stream, 1905). Edited by Donald J. Berthrong, a new edition appeared from the University of Oklahoma Press in 1960. Thrapp, *Encyclopedia of Frontier Biography* 2:610–11, provides a biographical sketch. See also *Contributions to the Historical Society of Montana*, 3 (1900), 33–123.

39. Colonel George Wright's hard-hitting campaign of "pacification" during the Spokane and Palouse War is ably described from the military's viewpoint in Robert M. Utley, *Frontiersmen in Blue: The United States Army and the Indian, 1848–1865* (New York: Macmillan, 1967), 193–210. A radically different perspective informs Clifford F. Trafzer and Richard D. Scheuerman, *Renegade Tribe: The Palouse Indians and the Invasion of the Inland Pacific Northwest* (Pullman: Washington State University Press, 1986).

40. For a biographical sketch of Vaughan see Anne McDonnell, "Alfred J. Vaughan, 1801–1875," *Contributions to the Historical Society of Montana*, 10 (1940), 272–73. His career among the Blackfeet is ably summarized in Ewers, *The Blackfeet*, 228–38, where he is characterized as "an experienced and able agent" who made a conscientious effort to put into operation the federal government's policy to "civilize" the Blackfeet by transforming them into Christian farmers at the Sun River agency site.

41. Little Dog and his son Fringe were foremost among the Piegan Blackfeet in establishing and maintaining peace with the Anglo-Americans and seeking to adjust to the new social order advocated by the representatives of the federal government. In May 1866 the two men became victims of their peacemaking efforts. Leaving Fort Benton after turning over to the acting Indian agent twelve horses that their tribesmen had stolen from whites, they were murdered and mutilated by another party of Piegans. In reporting the incident, the agent declared they had been killed because of their friendship with the whites. Ewers, *The Blackfeet*, 242.

42. For brief notices of Calf Shirt and Father of His Children, leaders of the Bloods (northern Blackfeet), see *Contributions to the Historical Society of Montana*, 10 (1940), 275, 276. The story of Calf Shirt's murder by traders appears in Ewers, *The Blackfeet*, 260.

43. For the Kootenai people and their history, the best source is Olga Wedemeyer Johnson, *Flathead and Kootenay: The Rivers, The Tribes, and the Region's Traders* (Glendale, Calif.: Arthur H. Clark, 1969).

44. The Nez Perce band led by Lawyer (Hallalhotsoot) was resolutely friendly with Anglo-American protestant missionaries, traders, and government officials. The fullest account can be found in the brilliant work by Alvin M. Josephy Jr., *The Nez Perce Indians and the Opening of the Northwest* (New Haven, Conn.: Yale University Press, 1965).

45. A similar encounter by the Lewis and Clark expedition in mid-August 1805 was critical for the success of that enterprise, enabling the explorers to trade for the horses they needed to carry their party and supplies over the mountains. This well-known episode is documented in Gary E. Moulton, ed., *The Journals of the Lewis and Clark Expedition*, vol. 5, *July 28–November 1, 1805* (Lincoln: University of Nebraska Press, 1988), 76–83, 87–92, 109–18.

46. Thompson includes a biographical entry for John Owen in his "Notes on Men and Things." Born in Pennsylvania, Owen established himself as a trader in the Bitterroot Valley in 1850, when he purchased the St. Mary's Mission property from the Jesuits and built Fort Owen. With the active assistance of his Shoshone wife Nancy, he became the dominant trader of the region, his influence reaching from Fort Benton to Fort Dalles and south to Fort Hall. In 1856 he received an appointment as federal agent to the Salish (Flathead) people, a post he held for six years. He lived "like a king," according to one who knew him well, but in the 1870s his health and mental powers began to fail. He retired from the trade and in time moved east to Philadelphia, where he died in 1889. The principal biographical source is Paul C. Phillips's introduction to *The Journals and Letters of Major John Owen, Pioneer of the Northwest, 1850–1871*, 2 vols. (New York: Eberstadt, 1927). Additional details concerning his career in Montana can be found in George F. Weisel's introduction to his volume *Men and Trade on the Northwest Frontier*, xvii–xxxi.

47. The defeat of Colonel Edward Steptoe and his troops by a combined force of Spokanes, Coeur d'Alenes, and Palouses in May 1858 is recounted in Utley, *Frontiersmen in Blue*, 201–3. A fuller telling appears in Robert Ignatius Burns, *The Jesuits and the Indian Wars of the Northwest* (New Haven, Conn.: Yale University Press, 1966), 199–230.

48. Most likely Thompson's catch were bull trout (*Salvelinus confluentis*), a species of char similar to the Dolly Varden (*Salvelinus malmo*) that is native to the waters of the mid-Columbia Basin and adjacent areas. Like Dolly Varden, bull trout have vivid coloration similar to that of brook trout but lack the vermiculation of the back and dorsal fin that distinguishes the brook trout. See Robert H. Smith, *Native Trout of North America* (Portland, Oreg.: Frank Amato Publications, 1984), 101, 138–39; Robert R. Behnke, *Trout and Salmon of North America* (New York: Free Press, 2002), 291–99.

49. Sacred Heart Mission among the Coeur d'Alene people had been founded by the eminent Jesuit pioneer missionary Pierre-Jean De Smet. The most isolated from white contact of all the Jesuit missions in the Oregon country, it was located on the north bank of the Coeur d'Alene River about ten miles upstream from Lake Coeur d'Alene. The mission establishment was remarkable for its church, a wooden structure in a baroque style, ninety feet long and sixty feet tall, built totally without nails by converts under Father Anthony Ravalli's direction. An excellent description is in Burns, *Jesuits and the Indian Wars*, 192–98.

CHAPTER FOUR

1. At this site the town of The Dalles sprang up. For a summary of its early history see Chuck Williams, *Bridge of the Gods, Mountains of Fire: A Return to the Columbia Gorge* (New York and White Salmon, Wash.: Friends of the Earth and Elephant Mountain Art, 1988), 103–4.

2. Now called Beacon Rock, part of the Washington state park system, this monolith is the basaltic core of an ancient volcano eroded by the Columbia River. It measures 848 feet high, second in size only to Gibraltar among the world's giant monoliths.

3. In addition to the Williams volume, *Bridge of the Gods*, the scenic grandeur of the Columbia River Gorge and its landmarks are well described in Jim Atwell, *Columbia River Gorge History*, 2 vols. (Skamania, Oreg.: Tahlkie Books, 1974–75). The steamboat era on the river is the subject of Randall Mills, *Stern-Wheelers Up the Columbia* (Palo Alto, Calif.: Pacific Books, 1947). The Columbia Gorge Scenic Highway—constructed during the 1920s along the south, Oregon side of river—provides auto access to Multnomah Falls, Bridal Veil Falls, and other locations of great natural beauty seen by Thompson, most of which are bypassed by the modern river-level

freeway, Interstate 94. The north side, in Washington state, is rimmed by State Route 40, now known as the Lewis and Clark Highway.

4. Addison C. Gibbs, a pioneer Oregon lawyer and in politics a War Democrat, had been elected Oregon's governor on the Union ticket in 1862. A popular figure, he narrowly failed to win election as U.S. senator when nominated by the Union caucus in 1866. Charles Henry Carey, *A History of Oregon* (Chicago: Pioneer Historical Publishing, 1922), remains the standard account of the state's nineteenth-century political history.

5. Thomas Starr King arrived in San Francisco from Boston in 1860, taking the pulpit of the city's First Unitarian Church, the only Unitarian congregation west of St. Louis. Fiery, young, an ardent Unionist, and a highly inspirational preacher, he was himself inspired by the natural beauty of California and the bright prospects for American civilization on the Pacific Coast. He became an eloquent spokesman for the Unionist cause. His death at age 39 in 1864, caused by diphtheria and pneumonia, brought about a huge outpouring of public grief that helped fix his name in California history. A sparkling account of his brief, brilliant career in California appears in Kevin Starr, *Americans and the California Dream, 1850–1915* (New York: Oxford University Press, 1973), 97–105.

6. Arthur L. Throckmorton, *Oregon Argonauts: Merchant Adventurers on the Western Frontier* (Portland: Oregon Historical Society, 1961), 247–51, expertly discusses the founding of the Oregon Steam Navigation Company to monopolize the Columbia River shipping trade and the company's construction of the two portage railroads: a fifteen-mile railroad from The Dalles to Celilo Falls and a six-mile railroad at the Cascades. This last project, as Thompson remarks, was not yet completed when he traveled upriver in April of 1863.

7. Thompson is describing here Celilo Falls, the most famous of all the native fisheries on the Columbia River, now drowned by the Army Corps of Engineers project ironically named Chief Joseph Dam.

8. Throckmorton, *Oregon Argonauts*, 253–54, summarizes the attempt led by Henry Corbett and Captain A. P. Ankeny to run the *Spray* in opposition to the Oregon Steam Navigation Company steamships. The venture had ended by the time Thompson rode upriver, when the OSN directors purchased the *Spray* and again secured their firm's monopoly of the Columbia River steamship trade.

9. For brief discussion of the possibility that William Clark had a son among the Salish people see John Fahey, *The Flathead Indians* (Norman: University of Oklahoma Press, 1974), 318 n. 21; and Purple, *Perilous Passage*, 115 n. 75. Thompson describes presumably a different person among the Spokanes who was making a similar claim.

10. Steptoe Butte is located two and a half miles northeast of the town of Steptoe and twelve miles north of Colfax in Whitman County, Washington. Steptoe Butte State Park offers a panoramic view of the Palouse country.

11. For a biographical sketch of Antoine Plante, a former employee of the Hudson's Bay Company, see Jerome Peltier, "Antoine Plante," in *The Mountain Men and the Fur Trade of the Far West*, ed. Le Roy Hafen, vol. 5 (Glendale, Calif.: Arthur H. Clark, 1968), 291–96.

12. George Weisel identifies Lachlan McLaurin as a Hudson's Bay Company trader who in 1861 took charge of the company's establishment at Fort Connah on Post Creek, in the Flathead Valley, ninety miles north of Fort Owen. Weisel, *Men and Trade*, xxxiii, 103, 106.

13. Thompson's route led through the site of Sandpoint and eastward on a line paralleled today by State Route 200, the Pend Oreille Scenic Route.

14. This chilling experience took place just east of the modern town of Kootenai, Idaho.

15. Apparently this was at Trestle Creek, which today is paralleled by Forest Road 275.

16. Continuing along the line of modern State Route 200, Thompson followed the north shore of the river he called the Pend Oreille, now known as the Clark Fork of the Columbia. Ten miles upstream from its mouth, the Clark Fork is now dammed by Cabinet Gorge Dam. The Bull River enters the Clark Fork twelve miles farther upstream.

17. The Vermilion River today is paralleled by Forest Road 154. Fourteen miles downstream the Clark Fork has been dammed by the Noxon Rapids Dam, forming Noxon Reservoir.

18. Thompson's "salmon trout" may have been either steelhead (anadromous rainbow trout) or spring run coho (silver salmon). The best known fishery site was at Thompson Falls on the Clark Fork, about ten miles downstream from the mouth of the Thompson River.

19. The Cabinet Mountains were a few days' travel behind Thompson at this point. He likely refers to a rough trail south of Big Hole Peak, with camp being made in the prairie surrounding the present-day town of Plains, at the edge of Lolo National Forest.

20. Camas Prairie Basin is located along the southwestern border of the modern Flathead Indian Reservation, drained by Cottonwood Creek and Camas Creek.

21. Every botanical guide and every volume on native food plants of the Pacific Northwest describes the camas and bitterroot plants. Thompson's accurate description of the food preparation procedures for these plants demonstrates again his natural curiosity and his sure powers of observation.

22. The Jesuits in 1854 relocated St. Ignatius Mission from an original site among the Kalispels two hundred miles to the northwest to this site south of Flathead Lake. At the time of Thompson's visit, the mission superior was Father Adrian Hoecken, Dutch in origin, who supervised four lay brothers and one additional priest, each from a different western European Catholic country. The mission establishment and its operations are described in Burns, *Jesuits and the Indian Wars*, 85–94. The town of Ravalli on the Jocko River,

named after Father Anthony Ravalli, S.J., was the nearest secular settlement to the mission site.

23. The federal Indian agency for the Flatheads was located south of St. Ignatius Mission where the town of Arlee grew up.

24. Thompson and his two companions followed the natural trail route southward, along the line of modern U.S. Route 93.

25. A native of New York state, Frank Worden sought his fortune in gold rush California, Oregon, The Dalles, and Walla Walla before moving near Hellgate, at the Bitterroot River's confluence with the Clark Fork. He and his partner, Christopher Higgins, opened a store at Gold Creek in 1862 and another at La Barge City in 1863, soon after Thompson's visit. The following year he and Higgins moved the Hellgate store upstream to the lower end of the canyon of the Clark Fork, expanded their operations, and established a town first named Wordensville and later Missoula Mills, then Missoula. He enjoyed a long and successful career identified with Missoula, active in civic affairs and highly respected throughout Montana Territory. Biographical accounts include Wilbur F. Sanders, "Francis Lyman Worden," *Contributions to the Historical Society of Montana*, 2 (1896), 362–64; and Thrapp, *Encyclopedia of Frontier Biography*, 3:1596–97.

26. Thills are the shafts between which a horse is hitched to a wagon. Thompson describes what we might recognize as a chariot-like conveyance, pulled by one horse.

27. Frederick H. Burr had been a member of Governor Isaac Stevens's Northern Pacific Railroad Surveying Expedition, then served as second-in-command to John Mullan in constructing the Mullan Road. He remained in the Bitterroot Valley, married a Shoshone woman who was the sister of Granville Stuart's wife, and followed a frontier life of trading, ranching, and occasionally mining. He became the sheriff of Deer Lodge County when it was organized in 1864. Most likely Burr made his home at Deer Lodge. He died some time after 1899. Biographical notices include Weisel, *Men and Trade on the Northwest Frontier*, 80–82; and Thrapp, *Encyclopedia of Frontier Biography*, 1:197.

28. The Alder Gulch placer gold discovery is documented in Henry Edgar, "Journal of Henry Edgar—1863," *Contributions to the Historical Society of Montana*, 3 (1900), 124–42.

29. Sanders, *A History of Montana*, 1:166–82, provides a succinct summary of the early Montana gold discoveries. She describes the sequence of events that brought miners to Prickly Pear Creek on pages 178–79.

30. Mather, *Gold Camp Desperadoes*, 49–53, identifies Doctor Howard as New York–born David Renton, who had left a wife and family to join the California gold rush. Although perhaps falsely accused, Mather states, he was convicted of grand theft in Sacramento and served a short term in San Quentin state prison before Governor Weller pardoned him on the condition that he leave the state. He then headed for the gold camps in

eastern Washington Territory, where he was known as a gambler. James Romaine, "a suave gambler," Mather declares, had also been in northern California but had no previous criminal record. Ibid., 45, 47.

31. Matthew Carroll and George Steell established a trading partnership at Fort Benton, built the first store outside the fort, and in 1863 were just entering the wagon freighting business. Their firm is mentioned in Paul Sharp, "Merchant Princes of the Plains," *Montana The Magazine of Western History*, 5 (Winter 1955), 2–20; and in John E. Parsons, "Steamboats in the 'Idaho' Gold Rush," *Montana The Magazine of Western History*, 10 (Winter 1960), 51–61.

32. The trip to Bannack by the Edgerton and Sanders families, sixteen people with three ox-drawn wagons, is described in Plassman, "Biographical Sketch of Hon. Sidney Edgerton," 330–40; and in the first chapter of James L. Thane Jr., ed., *A Governor's Wife on the Mining Frontier: The Letters of Mary Edgerton from Montana, 1863–1865* (Salt Lake City: University of Utah Library, 1976). Another personal account is Harriet P. Sanders, "Diary of a Journey across the Plains in 1863 and Reminiscences of Early Life in Montana," a manuscript located in Small Collection 1936, Wilbur Fisk and Wilbur Edgerton Sanders Papers, 1886–1904, MHSA. These sources all date the party's arrival as September 18th. See also Thompson's descriptions of Sidney Edgerton and Wilbur Sanders in "Notes on Men and Things."

33. As reported here, Thompson's information was not wholly accurate, but it reflects Plummer's reputation as a killer and desperate character that apparently preceded him into the upper Missouri country. Henry Plummer's background receives detailed examination and analysis in Mather and Boswell, *Hanging the Sheriff*. These two authors deny that he was the leader of a criminal gang in the Bannack and Virginia City region in 1863 until his death in January of 1864. A carefully noncommittal biographical sketch by Richard Maxwell Brown, who simply reports the assertions of Plummer's innocence by Mather and Boswell, appears in Lamar, *New Encyclopedia of the American West*, 893. Thrapp, *Encyclopedia of Frontier Biography*, 3:1151–53, provides a more critical biographical summary that concludes with this statement: "Latter-day suggestions that his outlaw career in Montana was largely unproven and that he seriously intended to go straight following his marriage . . . need not be seriously entertained unless believable evidence is forthcoming." Such additional evidence has not been forthcoming since the appearance of Thrapp's publication.

34. Thompson's account of the death of Jack Cleveland obviously relies on the version in Langford, *Vigilante Days and Ways*, 1:131–33, which differs in some slight particulars from the telling by Dimsdale in *Vigilantes of Montana*, 28–30. Thompson had not yet returned from the Pacific Coast at the time of these events.

35. Langford's book also is the primary source for Thompson's account of the ongoing quarrel between Plummer and Hank Crawford, who,

by the appointment of a miners' court, was serving as the sheriff of the Bannack mining camp until his departure in the spring of 1863.

36. This description is copied from Langford, *Vigilante Days and Ways*, 1:161.

CHAPTER FIVE

1. This dating of Electa Plummer's departure, two days after Thompson's arrival with his disreputable trail companions, raises of course the possibility that Sheriff Plummer had encouraged her to leave because of his anticipation of trouble with Doc Howard and the others in the party from Lewiston.

2. As Thompson makes clear, his telling of this episode rests on the narrative in Langford, *Vigilante Days and Ways*, 1:328–48. In addition to the similar versions by Dimsdale and Langford, we now have two carefully researched modern studies of this well-known crime story: Julia Conway Welch, *The Magruder Murders: Coping with Violence on the Frontier* (Helena, Mont.: Falcon, 1991); and Ladd Hamilton, *This Bloody Deed: The Magruder Incident* (Pullman: Washington State University Press, 1994). All agree substantially on the same set of facts.

3. For details of Plummer's election as sheriff at Bannack, which took place May 24, 1863, see Purple, *Perilous Passage*, 185–86. The election is documented in Small Collection 238, Bannack Mining District Records, 1862–1863, MHSA. His supposed election at Virginia City took place on October 18, 1863, in a balloting arranged surreptitiously by the portly Col. Samuel McLean, a recent arrival from Colorado who—according to Sam Hauser—meant to become the master Democratic politico for the upper Missouri mining region. Hauser's acerbic account of the election is found in a letter to his partner Nathaniel Langford dated October 19, 1863, located in SC 215, MHSA. Hauser regarded the whole affair of Plummer's election, he declared, "as an electioneering scheme, the office entending [to please] P. acquaintances— & being a kind of endorsement to him. They played the trick well."

4. Among the other men who had come independently to believe by November that Plummer was deeply involved in the wave of holdups and murders on the roadways of the region were cattleman Conrad Kohrs and mining entrepreneur Sam Hauser. Kohrs stated his suspicions—which caused him to avoid the convenient, customary stage route that went past Rattlesnake Ranch on his trips between Bannack and Virginia City—in his autobiographical statement, found in Small Collection 222, Conrad Kohrs Papers, 1864–1904, MHSA. This account has been published as Conrad Kohrs, *An Autobiography* (Deer Lodge, Mont.: Platen Press, 1977). Hauser's suspicions were shown by his dealings with Plummer when he traveled from Virginia City to Bannack with fourteen thousand dollars in gold on November 13th, preparing to depart with Langford the following day on a

trip to Salt Lake City, St. Louis, and Washington, D.C. Both Dimsdale and Langford relate this story, which Thompson retells in the following pages. None of these authors, however, give due emphasis to the fact that Hauser's suspicions, like those of Kohrs, were fully aroused at this early date, before Henry Tilden secretly told Judge Edgerton and Wilbur Sanders that he could identify Plummer as one of the men who had threatened him at gun point outside Bannack.

5. Interpretation of this remark is central to historians' appraisal of the relationship between Thompson and Plummer. Were the two men really good friends, as some writers have claimed? My opinion is that they were not, given Thompson's early and persistent sense of suspicion about Plummer's background and his activities in Bannack. The more likely construction of this sentence is that Thompson understood why his young friend could have affection for Plummer, but not that he shared such affection.

6. There is a dating discrepancy in connecting the events related here by Thompson. He and Langford both state that the robbery of the Peabody and Caldwell stage on the way from Virginia City to Bannack took place in the latter part of October. But it was not until November 14th that Hauser and Langford departed from Bannack late in the day to join the Mormon wagon train on the first leg of their trip. By all accounts it was on that same evening, November 14th, that young Tilden had his encounter with the masked road agents, who stopped him after they failed to intercept Langford and Hauser. Thus the meeting between Thompson and Edgerton could not have taken place immediately following the late October stage robbery if Edgerton then related that Tilden had identified Plummer as one of the holdup men he encountered. There is no good explanation for this discrepancy except to recognize that memory can play tricks on even the most attentive eyewitness over a long period of years. We can reasonably conclude, however, that likely not long after November 14th—rather than in late October—Thompson and Edgerton did have a confidential discussion in Thompson's store when the two friends shared their independent conclusion that Plummer was implicated in the wave of crimes on the roadways. Their agreement this early, with Thompson able to confirm circumstantially the suspicions of Edgerton and Sanders, is critical in explaining the sequence of events that subsequently brought Sanders to his prominent role in the vigilante movement while Judge Edgerton looked on with approval.

7. See Thompson's note on Samuel T. Hauser in "Notes on Men and Things."

8. While John Featherstun is otherwise unknown to history, Scottish-born Neil Howie gained renown for his courage in an adventure-filled career. Twenty-nine years old at the time of these events, he had been in Colorado and then came to the Beaverhead country, where Henry Plummer reportedly tried to recruit him for criminal activities. After serving in the vigilantes, he became sheriff of Madison County by the appointment of

Governor Edgerton. Subsequently he was the first deputy U.S. marshal for Montana and in 1867 a colonel in the 1st Montana Volunteer Cavalry, gaining a reputation as one of the best officers in the territorial militia. Subsequently he moved to Colorado, then to Utah, and later he became assistant superintendent for the Remington Company's quartz mining operation on the island of Trinidad. In this position he fought off attacks by revolutionary insurgents, adding to his reputation as "the bravest of the brave." He died on Trinidad, apparently of malaria, in 1874. Thrapp, *Encyclopedia of Frontier Biography*, 2:685.

9. See Thompson's note on the first school in Montana, conducted in Edgerton's house by his niece, Lucia Darling.

10. The reference here is to Joaquin Murieta, the semi-mythical bandit chief who figured largely in the stories about hostilities between Hispanics and Anglos in gold rush California during the early 1850s. Contrasting views about Joaquin's historical identity are reviewed in Lamar, *New Encyclopedia of the American West*, 748; and Thrapp, *Encyclopedia of Frontier Biography*, 2:727–28.

11. After returning to Cedar Rapids, Electa Bryan Plummer later rejoined her sister and brother-in-law, the Vails, after they had moved from Montana to Vermillion, Dakota Territory. She became a school teacher, later remarried, and had two sons. She died in May 1912 and is buried in Wakonda, South Dakota. Clifford Myrtle, "Three Women of Frontier Montana" (master's thesis, Montana State University, 1932).

12. From this point forward Thompson's account follows Langford's narrative closely.

13. Walter B. Dance was another prominent pioneer of the gold rush era in Montana. A native of Delaware, he arrived at Gold Creek in July of 1862, moved to Bannack (where he chaired the April 1863 meeting that elected Plummer as sheriff), then joined the rush to Alder Gulch. Dance was a business partner with James and Granville Stuart at Virginia City and later at Deer Lodge, though his later years were devoted to ranching and the lumber business. Thrapp, *Encyclopedia of Frontier Biography*, 1:373–74.

14. Cornelius C. "Baron" O'Keefe, a native of Cork, Ireland, was an Irish revolutionary in his youth. Captured by the English and transported to Van Dieman's Land, he escaped to the U.S. in 1853. From New York he ventured first to California, then to Washington Territory, where he found employment in a work crew for the Mullan Road project. He settled and began ranching on a spread fifteen miles west of Missoula at the mouth of O'Keefe Canyon. A man of great physical strength and ardent temperament, he was a well-known character in early Montana and was active in public service for Missoula County. Folklore has it that when the vigilantes came to arrest Bob Zachary, O'Keefe insisted first on giving the doomed man a good breakfast, saying "ye can't hang a man on an empty stomach." O'Keefe died in 1883, leaving a large family. Edith Toole Oberly,

"The Baron C. C. O'Keefe: The Legend and the Legacy," *Montana The Magazine of Western History*, 23 (Summer 1973), 18–29; Thrapp, *Encyclopedia of Frontier Biography*, 2:1077.

15. According to both Dimsdale and Langford, Hunter's admission was a tacit one; he said nothing in response to a recitation of his supposed crimes by the vigilantes, but merely turned pale, requested that his friends not be told the manner of his death, asked for a drink of water, and shook hands with each of the vigilante party before being hanged. Dimsdale, *Vigilantes of Montana*, 190; Langford, *Vigilante Days and Ways*, 2:229–30.

CHAPTER SIX

1. No regularly constituted court was organized in the new territory until three weeks prior to the first meeting of the territorial legislature.

2. B. B. Burchett was elected judge of the Bannack district in May of 1863, at the same election that resulted in Henry Plummer becoming sheriff. He was one of the few family men at Bannack during the winter of 1862–63, having brought his wife and two daughters to the mining region. In 1864 he served as foreman of a miners' court jury at Helena for that town's first murder trial. Leeson, *History of Montana*, 266, 302, 467, 468.

3. Thompson quotes Plassman, "Biographical Sketch of Hon. Sidney Edgerton," 334.

4. Langford and Hauser were also prominent among those who advanced Edgerton's candidacy for appointment as territorial governor, while Edgerton in return endorsed Hauser's unsuccessful application to become the first secretary of the new Montana Territory. Nathaniel Langford and Samuel Hauser et al. to President Abraham Lincoln, March 17, 1864, Edgerton Appointment file, Letters of Application and Recommendation, Appointments Division, RG 59, NA; W. H. Wallace to President Abraham Lincoln, March 30, 1864, ibid.; Memo of Applicants for Montana Appointments, [June 1864], in Basler, *Collected Works of Lincoln*, 7:371–72.

5. For sketches of Charles Upson of Coldwater, Michigan, and William B. Washburn of Greenfield, Mass., see *Biographical Directory of the American Congress*, 1742, 1780.

6. Although the Montana men were not fully aware of it, political jockeying in Congress over the boundaries of the prospective Montana Territory reflected, in part, the agenda of Idaho's delegate William H. Wallace and Anson G. Henry, a leader among Washington Territory Republicans, who was serving as territorial surveyor general. Their goal was to divide the Democratic voters of the new interior mining camps and keep their political realm safely under the control of the Republican majority in the Puget Sound counties. This story is told in Merle W. Wells, "Territorial Government in the Inland Empire: The Movement to Create Columbia Territory, 1864–1869,"

Pacific Northwest Quarterly, 44 (April 1953), 80–87. Wallace's career in Washington and Idaho territories is described in Annie Laurie Bird, "William Henson Wallace, Pioneer Politician," *Pacific Northwest Quarterly*, 49 (April 1958), 61–76.

7. The creation of Montana Territory with its western boundary on the Bitterroot Divide and the appointment of Sidney Edgerton as territorial governor were combined in the political maneuvering before the House Territorial Committee that involved the Montana men with Delegate Wallace and Rep. James M. Ashley of Ohio, chair of the Territorial Committee and Radical Republican caucus spokesman. Ashley, who subsequently introduced the impeachment resolution against President Andrew Johnson, later would served a short, divisive term as governor of Montana Territory, highlighted by the efforts of Montana Democrats to discredit him in Washington by a virtual impeachment at the hands of the territorial legislature. See Kenneth N. Owens, "Frontier Governors: A Study of the Territorial Governors in the History of Washington, Idaho, Montana, Wyoming, and Dakota Territories" (Ph.D. diss., University of Minnesota, 1959), 70–72; and more fully, Spence, *Territorial Government and Politics in Montana*, 62–73.

8. The Oliver & Co. stage line was organized in November 1862 by A. J. "Jack" Oliver and three partners. Operating without a contract to carry the U.S. mail, the company ran a weekly trip during the summer to connect Salt Lake City with Bannack and Virginia City and made a monthly trip during the winter. The fare in 1864 was fifty dollars in coin to Bannack and sixty dollars to Virginia City. In 1865 Oliver's firm expanded its service with routes to Deer Lodge, Helena, and Fort Benton. Short on amenities, as Thompson reports, the firm's service was quite profitable until Ben Holladay's Overland Stage Company began a rival operation that forced Oliver & Co. to quit in August of 1866. Madsen and Madsen, *North to Montana!* 95–98, 103–6.

9. See Thompson's note on the price of provisions in "Notes on Men and Things."

10. Two prospective appointees, the Reverend Henry P. Torsey of Maine and John Coburn of Indiana, declined the honor. The position remained unfilled until August 1865 when President Andrew Johnson bestowed the office on the colorful, erratic Irish expatriate and former Union Army general, Thomas Francis Meagher. Spence, *Territorial Politics and Government in Montana*, 18.

11. Governor Doty, a non-Mormon and a firm friend of the national administration, was serving in a difficult role as Utah's territorial chief executive in Salt Lake City, where church president Brigham Young continued to wield the real power as Latter-day Saints dominated the legislature and local courts. On various occasions Governor Doty acted as a political spokesman for the new territories of the northern Rockies. His

career is well described in Alice E. Smith, *James Duane Doty, Frontier Promoter* (Madison: State Historical Society of Wisconsin, 1954).

12. For the amazing career of Meagher see Robert G. Athearn, *Thomas Francis Meagher: An Irish Revolutionary in America* (1949; repr., New York: Arno, 1976). An Irish insurrectionist in the Young Ireland movement during his youth, then caught and transported by the English authorities to the Tasmanian penal colony, Meagher escaped and made his way to New York, where Irish immigrant voters elected him to Congress. He was commander of the Irish Brigade during the Civil War. After being cashiered from the army for drunkenness at the war's end, he came to Montana with ambitions to lead the Fenian movement in an invasion of Canada. While still serving as the territory's acting governor, he died mysteriously at Fort Benton, drowning one dark night in the flooding Missouri River. A heroic bronze equestrian statue of Meagher occupies a place of honor in front of Montana's state capitol, the donation of another ardent Irishman, copper king Marcus Daly.

13. James Tufts was a lawyer from New Hampshire by way of Iowa. He had previously served in the legislatures of both the Nebraska and Idaho territories; later he became Montana's territorial secretary and acting governor. For a brief sketch see Spence, *Territorial Politics and Government in Montana*, 55 n. 93.

14. For a balanced summary of the Iron Clad Oath controversy in the first territorial legislature, see ibid., 24–25.

15. In "Notes on Men and Things," Thompson explains that he later had a small printing press sent to Montana, which he used to produce a short-lived newsletter in Bannack.

16. The term War Democrat referred to members of the Democratic Party who supported the national administration's conduct of the war against the Confederacy. The Union Party in 1864 represented a coalition of War Democrats and Republicans.

17. Thompson's sketch for a territorial seal can be found in Small Collection 839, Francis McGee Thompson Papers, 1865–1915, MHSA (hereafter SC 839).

18. The founding and early years of the Montana Historical Society are described in Brian Shovers, "Saving Montana's Past: The Creation and Evolution of the Montana Historical Society and *Montana The Magazine of Western History*," *Montana The Magazine of Western History*, 52 (Spring 2002), 43–59. According to Shovers, the inception of the Historical Society came from an 1865 meeting at the Dance and Stuart store in Virginia City involving Granville and James Stuart, Wilbur Sanders, territorial chief justice Hezekiah Hosmer, and mapmaker Walter DeLacy, as well as Frank Thompson.

19. The staff members of the Montana Historical Society, to their great regret, now are unable to find any record of these items.

20. The death of Malcolm Clarke and his son in 1868, coming at the hands of young Piegans who included relatives of Clarke's wife, is another

well known story of this era. See the account Thompson includes in his "Notes on Men and Things," apparently based on the James H. Bradley manuscript, "The Blackfoot Indian War against the Whites," subsequently printed in *Contributions to the Historical Society of Montana*, 9 (1923), 252–55. Thompson probably had also seen the vivid eyewitness account by Clarke's daughter: Helen P. Clarke, "Sketch of Malcolm Clarke," *Contributions to the Historical Society of Montana*, 2 (1896), 255–68. A detailed modern retelling of Clarke's death and its circumstances is in Wischmann, *Frontier Diplomats*, 321–24. See also Wickman, "Malcolm Clark," 8:69–72, for a substantial biographical account.

21. Mountain Chief became head chief of the Piegan Blackfeet following the death of Little Dog in 1866. After signing an ill-fated peace treaty in 1868, he found himself at the center of growing anger among both the Piegans and the whites, with a series of fractious incidents culminating when General Alfred Sully ordered the capture of Mountain Chief and other hostile Piegan leaders. Under these orders Major Eugene M. Baker with two squadrons of Second Cavalry in January 1870 attacked the camp headed by the friendly chief Heavy Runner, killing 173 (including as many as 153 women and children according to the Piegans), destroying all the lodges and camp equipment, then turning loose in severe wintry weather 140 homeless, virtually helpless, grieving women and children. First called a military victory, this action became a public relations disaster for the U.S. Army. Immediately labeled the Baker Massacre in the eastern press, it was instrumental in discrediting the so-called Peace Policy of the Grant administration. But in Montana, it also persuaded Mountain Chief and other Piegan leaders to become firm advocates for their own enduring peace policy toward the whites. An excellent examination of this episode is in Wischmann, *Frontier Diplomats*, 327–34.

22. Bostwick is identified by Henry Boller as "a long-haired mountaineer" who accompanied Boller on a trading excursion to the Assiniboines from Fort Atkinson during the late summer of 1858. As indicated by Milo M. Quaife, the editor of Boller's account, he had previously guided the hunting party of Sir George Gore in 1854 and 1855. Bostwick was killed in August 1877 at the Battle of the Big Hole while serving as a scout for Colonel John Gibbons' command in the Nez Perce War. Boller, *Among the Indians*, 127 n. 45.

23. The annihilation of the infant settlement at Ophir, carried out by a war party of two hundred Bloods under the leadership of Calf Shirt, is described in detail in James H. Bradley, "The Blackfoot War," 255–57. See also Wischmann, *Frontier Diplomats*, 309–11; and Ewers, *The Blackfeet*, 239.

24. The Sun Dance ceremony that Thompson witnessed among the Gros Ventres is quite similar to the Mandan ritual that artist George Catlin described and sketched in 1836, recorded in his work *O-kee-pa, A Religious Ceremony, and Other Customs of the Mandans*, ed. John C. Ewers (New Haven, Conn.: Yale University Press, 1967). Central to the spiritual life of the northern Plains peoples, the Sun Dance was targeted for extinction by

Christian ministers and their allies in the U.S. Bureau of Indian Affairs during the latter part of the nineteenth century. In its revived form the Sun Dance ritual among the Shoshones and Utes has received detailed attention from anthropologist Joseph G. Jorgensen in his work *The Sun Dance Religion: Power for the Powerless* (Chicago: University of Chicago Press, 1972).

25. An example of Thompson's promotional efforts is a one-page flyer extolling the richness of Montana Territory and its mining properties, preserved in the SC 839, MHSA.

BEING NOTES ON MEN AND THINGS

1. A biographical sketch of Maillet appears in Thrapp, *Encyclopedia of Frontier Biography*, 2:930–31.

2. This passage from Lewis's journal, dated June 17, 1805, is reproduced in Gary E. Moulton, ed., *The Journals of the Lewis and Clark Expedition*, vol. 4, *April 7–July 27, 1805* (Lincoln: University of Nebraska Press, 1987), 303.

INDEX